The World of Model Ships and Boats

The World of Model Ships and Boats

Guy R. Williams

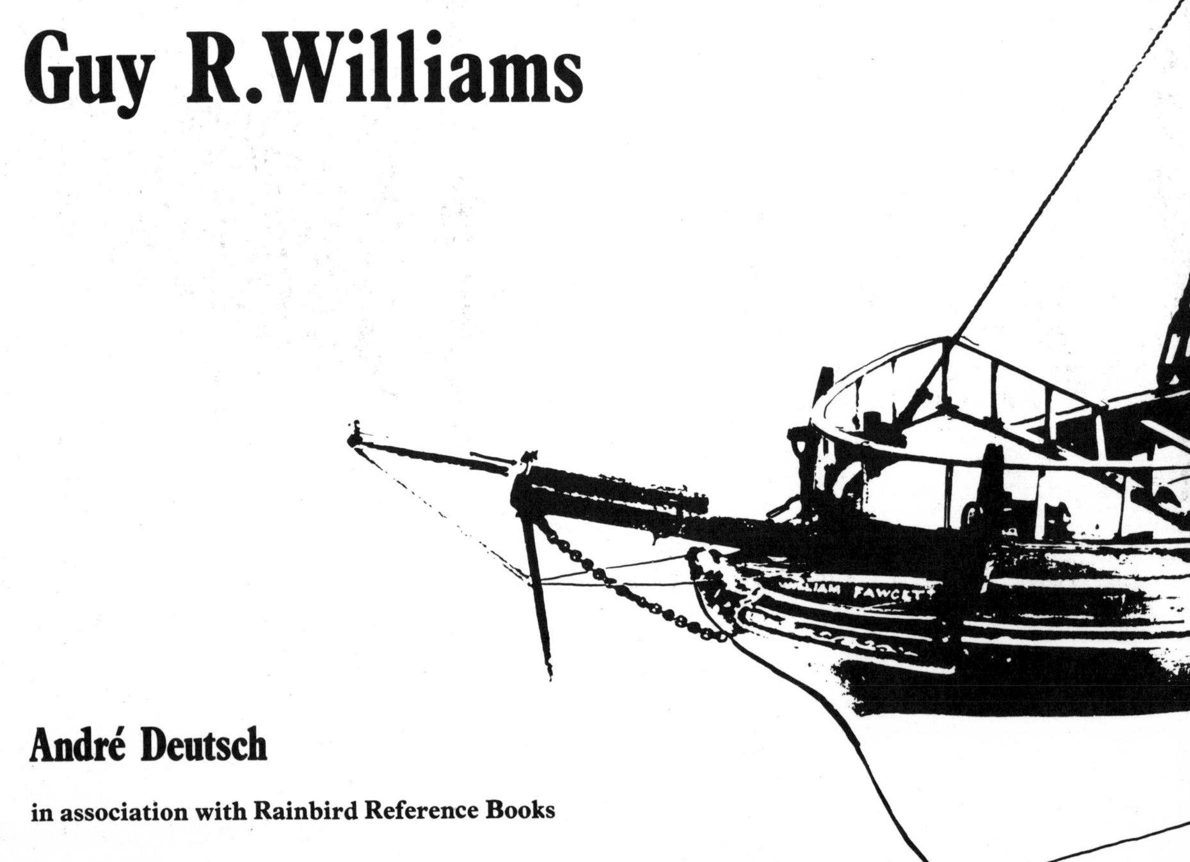

André Deutsch

in association with Rainbird Reference Books

Companion volumes by Guy R. Williams

In preparation

The World of Model Cars

The World of Model Aircraft

Already published

The World of Model Trains

This book was designed and produced by
Rainbird Reference Books Limited,
Marble Arch House, 44 Edgware Road, London, W2,
for André Deutsch Limited
105 Great Russell Street London WC1

House Editor: Peter Coxhead
Designer: Gwyn Lewis

First published 1971

The text was set in Monophoto Imprint 11/13 by
Jolly & Barber Limited, Rugby, England
The book was printed and bound by
Dai Nippon Printing Company Limited,
Tokyo, Japan

ISBN 0 233 96288 3

PRINTED IN JAPAN

Contents

List of Colour Plates

Acknowledgments

No book of this kind, dealing with so wide-ranging a subject, could be compiled without much assistance from the recognised authorities. Among those to whom I am especially grateful are the following people and companies who have contributed significantly to the material contained in the book, or who have most generously given information or advice, or have helped in other ways. Nevertheless, full editorial responsibility for the text and for the captions to the pictures is my own.

Australia

G. Middleton: Honorary Secretary, the Australian Model Yachting Authority.

Denmark

Billing Boats: Lunderskov.

France

Le Vice-Amiral d'Escadre de Bazelaire: La Musée de la Marine, Paris.

Germany (West)

Johannes Graupner: Kirchheim-Teck.
Steingraeber: Ship Model Kits, Kreis Marburg.

Great Britain

John Bartlett: Director, the City and County of Kingston-upon-Hull Museums.
Bassett-Lowke (Northampton) Limited.
Lt. Col. S. N. Beattie: formerly of 'Beatties of London'.
Anthony S. E. Browning: Curator, the Department of Technology, The Glasgow Museums and Art Galleries.
G. A. Colbeck: Honorary General Secretary, the Model Power Boat Association.
A. A. Cumming: City Curator, the City of Plymouth Museum and Art Gallery.
G. R. M. Garratt: Keeper of Department Five, the Science Museum, South Kensington, London.
Stuart M. K. Henderson: Director, the Glasgow Museums and Art Galleries.
David Hinton: Departmental Assistant, the Department of Antiques, The Ashmolean Museum, Oxford.
T. A. Hume: Director, the City of Liverpool Museums.
E. Keil and Company Ltd.: Wickford.
L. E. Kimpton: Curator of Archives, the Peninsular and Oriental Steam Navigation Company.
G. H. Leeds: Honorary Publications Secretary, the Model Yachting Association.
J. Colin Marl: Borough Librarian, the County Borough of South Shields.

Commander G. P. B. Naish: Keeper, the National Maritime Museum, Greenwich.

H. M. Sell: Late Manager, Messrs. Bassett-Lowke's showroom, London.

M. K. Stammers: Assistant Keeper of Shipping, the City of Liverpool Museum.

J. D. Storer: Assistant Keeper, the Royal Scottish Museum (Department of Technology), Edinburgh.

W. J. Walker: General Manager, Western Morning News Company Ltd., Plymouth.

Holland

H. Hazelhoff Roelfzema: Director, the Nederlandsch Historisch Scheepvart Museum, Amsterdam.

B. C. W. Lap: Assistant Keeper, the 'Prins Hendrik' Maritime Museum, Rotterdam.

New Zealand

G. Britt: Honorary Secretary, the New Zealand Authority, The International Model Yacht Racing Union.

Norway

Svein Molaug: Director, Norsk Sjøfartsmuseum, Oslo.

Spain

José Fernandez Gaytán: El C. de N. Subdirector, Museo Naval, Madrid.

Sweden

Göran Sundström: Statens Sjöhistoriska Museum, Stockholm.

United States of America

Philip L. Budlong: Registrar, the Marine Historical Association, Inc., Mystic, Connecticut.

Robert H. Burgess: Curator of Exhibits, the Mariners' Museum, Newport News, Virginia.

Fred Frey: Honorary Secretary, the Model Yacht Racing Association of America.

Captain Dale Mayberry: Director, The Museum, the United States Naval Academy, Annapolis, Maryland.

Philip Chadwick Foster Smith: Curator of Maritime History, the Peabody Museum, Salem, Massachusetts.

1 The World of Model Ships and Boats

'The World of Model Ships and Boats' . . . What is the difference, the observant reader may ask at once, between a model ship and a model boat? Turning to one of the most authoritative dictionaries that has ever been compiled, we find that a ship may be defined as:

A large sea-going vessel . . .

while a boat rates this modest description:

A small open vessel in which to traverse the surface of water . . .

'The word *boat* is also applied to various vessels that differ in some way from a ship', adds the dictionary helpfully, instancing small sailing vessels employed in fishing or in carrying mails and packets, and small steamers. A rough-and-ready classification used by seafaring men suggests that a boat is any vessel that could be used, if necessary, in an ancillary capacity to a ship. There is no doubt at all, in the professionals' judgement, as to which is the more important!

In 1733 a Royal Academy was opened in Portsmouth Dockyard, in the south of England, at which young gentlemen might be educated for the sea service. Nine years later, six of these young gentlemen wrote to the members of the Navy Board, complaining of a model of the 100-gun ship *Victory* that had been provided for their instruction:

> 'The model of the VICTORY is so small, her rigging is so slight, that we cannot learn anything from it, neither do we know anything of rigging or the stowage of anchors or cables, we are quite ignorant of everything that belongeth to sails . . .'

1 A documentary model of the Battle of Trafalgar. This comprises part of the Spanish and English fleets, each ship well modelled in wood with guns, decks, galleries, life-boats and flags, and with paper sails naturalistically peppered with shot. The model was on view in the Banqueting Hall at the Royal United Services Institution, Whitehall, London, for over one hundred years.

They petitioned the use of an old yacht, converted to two masts, to improve them in the art of rigging of ships, and their request was granted.

As long ago as that, models of ships and boats were being made for purely practical purposes in the dockyards of almost every maritime nation. Models of ships and boats were being made – and had been made for several centuries – by sailors wishing to obtain

divine protection. Models of ships and boats were being made for aesthetic reasons. No doubt, small model ships and boats were also being made in all parts of the world as toys for children, though we have few records of these. And, models of ships and boats have gone on being produced ever since then, in ever-increasing profusion.

How can one possibly start to get one's bearings in such a confused and bewildering subject?

It helps, to remember that the vast majority of model ships and boats – other than those made purely as toys, or for amusement – fall into three clearly defined categories.

First, there are the models made by sailors, active or retired, and by those closely connected with the sea.

Journeys made in the great sailing vessels of the past tended to consist of short periods of intense physical and mental activity, punctuated by longer spells of comparative calm. To relieve the

2 Above left – The frigate Norske Løve. *A model ship made in ivory with guns and ropes of silver, 1654, now in the Royal Collection at Rosenborg Castle, Copenhagen.*

3 Above – A model of a Dutch 'botter', or fishing boat, used along the south-western coast of the Zuider Zee.

4 Below – A model of the boat found at Hjortspring, South Jutland in 1921. The boat is more than 2000 years old.

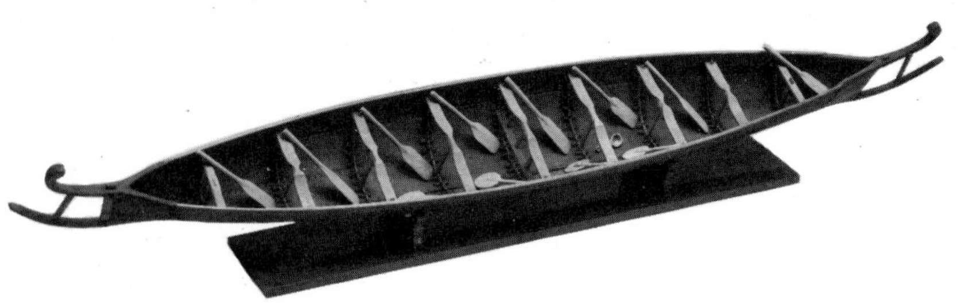

5 Above – This model warship may be the toy given by Phineas Pett to Charles Stuart, later King of England.

6 Above right – A model of the Victory, *100 guns, that was wrecked on the Casquets, near Alderney, in 1744 with the loss of all hands. The model is said to have been made after the tragedy with a view to a possible enquiry into the ship's seaworthiness.*

tedium during their periods of enforced leisure, the sailors of those days developed certain special and extra skills. They became adept at decorating every surface on which they could legally lay their hands – even, their own bodies, which they delighted in tattooing. They practised, most skilfully, every known kind of ornamental ropework. And, one of the most popular of all their recreations was the reproduction, on a small scale, of the vessels they knew so well, and in many cases of which they were so fond. Some exquisite models have been executed on board ship by men working under cramped conditions with little space in which to keep their equipment and materials. In these difficult circumstances, it is surprising that any kind of craftsmanship thrived.

In the best models of this sort, we find a close approximation to the true proportions of the original. Exactitude was dependent in every case on the eye of the model-maker, who in most instances had worked without so much as a drawing to guide him. Understandably it would hardly be fair to expect true proportions. Many freehand models are clumsy, and others may even be comically grotesque in their misproportion. (Age, here, by adding its own glamour and by softening crudities of colour, may lend considerable charm even to the roughest work.) It is safest to say that models of this kind are to be enjoyed by those with imaginative minds, rather than studied too closely by seekers after exact knowledge.

More reliable, as sources of detailed information, are models in the second category: those made as part of the process of ship- and boat-building.

Unlike railway models, which will normally have been made after the prototypes have proved their practical value, and are, therefore, even at their best, merely reproductions of existing man-made machines and objects, a large number of model ships and boats have been created before the full size versions were constructed.

For some centuries, shipwrights and boatwrights have been accustomed to making models as a means of working out their ideas. They have tended to use these models to show to everyone concerned, from the men who would have to pay for the finished vessels to the men who would have to use them, that their ideas would work. If modifications have had to be suggested, the most convenient time for doing so has been at the preliminary submission.

The most splendid of these try-out samples are undoubtedly the official dockyard models made for the responsible naval authorities during the seventeenth and eighteenth centuries. These are among the finest examples of the model-maker's craft in existence, having all details down to the last bolt or treenail in the hull and (in some cases) the last lashing in the rigging executed in meticulous perfection. To examine a fine model thoroughly is an experience very like that of going over the ship herself. The care taken with these models was, of course, a promise of the skill that would be lavished afterwards on the full size vessel if it were actually laid down. These models will be studied at greater length later in this book.

The third extensive category of model ships and boats includes all those that have been made in the commercial world for prestige purposes – even, it would be fair in most cases to say, as advertisements. These models, many of them exact replicas of ships and boats already launched, have been intended for the boardrooms and display windows of the various shipping companies and shipyards, and they have been meant to demonstrate the beauty and high degree of finish typical of the company's products. The majority of these models have been built by highly skilled professional workers to a scale of a quarter of an inch to the foot, or to an even larger scale, as it has been thought important for as many as possible of the smallest details of the prototypes to be shown, executed in model form with superlative craftsmanship. These vessels, too, will be considered more fully in a later chapter.

Having decided that a model may belong, roughly, to one of these main types, according to the purpose for which it was made, the student may then attempt to classify it further, according to the way in which it has been constructed, or its shape. It is not always easy to say positively that a model is of one particular kind, since

7 Above – A fine and rare English dockyard ship model constructed of boxwood and pearwood of a two-decked man-of-war mounting 62 guns, the hull unplanked to the water level.

8 Right – A stern view of the same model.

9 Far right – A fine model made for prestige purposes of the Norwegian America Line's Bergensfjord.

BERGENSFJORD

in certain respects the categories shade into each other. Some terms that are applied to ship and boat models, however, convey their meaning without much possibility of confusion.

Wooden models of ships and boats, for example, may be referred to as block models (that is, their hulls are made from single pieces of wood) or built models (the term itself suggests the difference). The dockyard models of the seventeenth and eighteenth centuries were invariably built. If a sailor's model were made at sea, its hull might be built after a fashion, but if so its timbers and planking would usually be of a very simplified kind that did not imitate those of the ship itself. More often, its construction would be even simpler than this, the whole hull being carved or whittled from a single block.

A half-model shows only one half of a vessel's hull, the whole being split longitudinally from keel to deck along the fore-and-aft centre line. Since each half will normally be the exact counterpart of the other – except, possibly, for some small variations in deck and internal fittings – shipwrights in the past have found scale models of this kind quite adequate for portraying body characteristics and hull lines, and, in many cases, for arriving at them too. Frequently a shipwright would try to improve the lines of a ship by working on the half-model itself – rasping or shaving off a little bit of wood here and leaving an extra fullness there until he was satisfied that the hull would be as nearly perfect as he could possibly make it. Then, he would use his small model as a master from which he would create the full size hull.

There are important collections of shipbuilders' half-models at several museums that are in close proximity to the principal shipbuilding centres of the world. The Art Gallery and Museum at Glasgow, on the River Clyde in Scotland, for instance, has several representative groups – most of them donated by the firms for whom they were made. Not all of these are kept permanently on view, for half-models, being rarely rigged, are not of unlimited interest to the general public. There are also some good groups at the Mariners' Museum at Newport News, Pennsylvania. One of the earliest and finest groups in the Mariners' Museum is that assembled by Henry and George Steers, and made available to the museum by the estate of Henry Steers in 1936. This is composed principally of models of small wooden-hull schooners and yachts that were built during the first half of the nineteenth century. In the group, there is a model of the New York pilot boat *Mary Taylor*, built in 1849, which is believed to have been a prototype of George Steers' famous yacht *America*, built for him by William Brown of New York two years later.

The *America* had a long and eventful history. With a syndicate to support the venture, she was sailed to England, challenging the

10 Top – A block model of the Hampton Court, *70 guns, 1744.*

11 Centre – A half model of the wooden screw sloop Rinaldo, *17 guns, 1860.*

12 Bottom – The builder's half model, now in the Mariners' Museum, Newport News, of the schooner yacht America *designed by George Steers.*

British to a race round the Isle of Wight. The best British yachtsmen took up the challenge, and offered a cup as the trophy. The American yacht won easily. (So easily, in fact, that when Queen Victoria, viewing the race from her royal yacht, asked of an aide 'And who is second?' she was told, with due respect, 'Your Majesty, there *is* no second.') The *America* was sold in England in 1851, renamed *Camilla* in 1853, and rebuilt at Northfleet in 1859. In 1861 she was resold in America, and used by the Confederate forces under the name *Memphis*. After being scuttled, captured and refloated, she was used by the Federal Navy under her original name. Sold in 1873 and again rebuilt at Boston in 1880 she was used for cruising and racing until shortly before the outbreak of the First World War. Since 1921 she has been laid up at Annapolis, Maryland.

Models of the *America* are to be seen in many collections. There is a fine half-model of her at Newport News. This model, made to the scale of one half inch to the foot, is mounted on a maple plaque that also carries two oval silver plates. One plate gives the dimen-

sions of the vessel. The other records that the model was intended for presentation to the British Queen Victoria. Before the gift could be made, George Steers died – at the early age of thirty-seven – and his widow gave the model instead to a friend of the family. This was Daniel B. Martin, who was Engineer-in-Chief of the United States Navy. It remained in the Martin family until 1949, when it found its way to the Mariners' Museum.

A graceful model of the *America* can be made, today, by any moderately skilled person who cares to purchase one of the fine kits marketed by Model Shipways Company, Inc., of Bogota, New Jersey, U.S. Each kit includes a carved pine hull, wood materials for the timbers needed, deck furniture and spars, decking scored so that it seems to have been made with miniature planks, lead castings, brass parts, cordage, plans and instructions. The cost? Less than the cost of a night's stay for two at many a mid-town hotel. Even cheaper is the kit offered by the Marine Model Company, Inc., of Halesite, Long Island, New York, though the model produced by this is not quite as large as the model that results from the Model Shipways outfit.

Waterline models – that is, models which show only the parts of a ship or boat that are above the waterline – are found more often in smaller sizes than in large. Mounted on flat bases or on surfaces that have been carefully modelled and coloured to simulate water, they may seem more convincing, even, than models with complete

13 Above – Two views of the America *made by W. E. Hitchcock from one of Model Shipways Company's kits.*

14 Right, above – A group of waterline ship models of historic significance. Made to exact scale to demonstrate the relative strength of the principal navies of the world, it was displayed in London at the 1913 Imperial Services Exhibition.

15 Right – Some of the waterline models in the Mariners' Museum at Newport News.

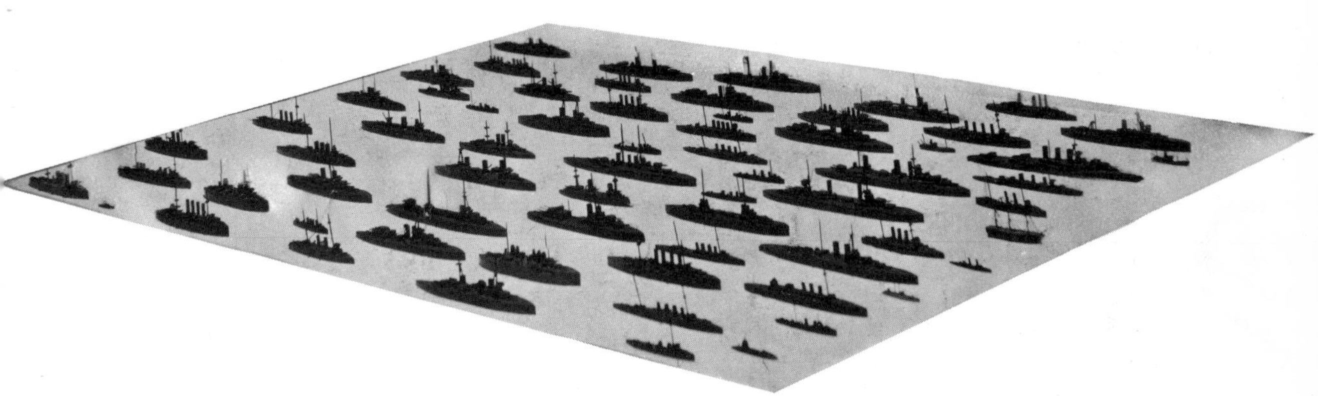

1 2 3 4 5 6
INCHES

hulls – probably, because our eyes are not accustomed to seeing a part of a ship or boat that is normally below the surface of the water.

One of the best displays of waterline models in the whole world is to be seen in another part of the Mariners' Museum at Newport News. (What a place for model lovers that is!) These models – approximately 225 of them – were built for identification purposes for the United States Navy during the Second World War. They were made in two scales – 1:500 and 1:200 – and they show, in the most careful detail, combat ship types and auxiliaries of the United States, British, French, German and Japanese Navies of the period 1941–1945.

If one of the most compulsive urges that may affect certain members of the human race is the desire to make models, another irresistible temptation that is apt to disturb other people is the absolute necessity to collect them.

The infection may be caught almost by accident. One man who describes himself as an average collector has told how he was prowling with his wife through a scruffy little curio shop on the Yorkshire coast, looking for old and beautiful things, when they came across their first model ship. They promptly bought it for £1. That was more than a quarter of a century ago. Now, they own close on thirty model ships, some of which are of considerable saleroom value. Having glass showcases on every available inch of wall and shelf space, these enthusiasts are having to move to a larger house so that they can accommodate any further specimens they may be compelled to acquire.

However they may start, collections of model ships and boats tend to increase in size fairly steadily – changing hands a few times,

16 The scale model of the clipper Enterprise *at Chester.*

possibly, in the process – until at last one of their owners presents them or bequeaths them to some museum or gallery where they can be publicly seen and admired. As a result, there are splendid collections of model ships and boats to be viewed, for free, in many large cities and towns in practically every country in the world that has a maritime history.

In all of these collections there will be, by their very nature, a number of remarkable model ships and boats that only a connoisseur can fully appreciate. But there will be, too, a large quota of models that any ordinary visitor, who has had no special technical training, can enjoy looking at. And even in the smaller museums and galleries there will be at least a few models which – quite apart from their intrinsic value as examples of fine craftsmanship, or as miniature replicas of full-size ships or boats – have some particularly colourful histories or romantic associations that make them specially interesting. In the Grosvenor Museum at Chester, England – to take a fairly typical example – there is a scale model of the Clipper *Enterprise* of that city. This ship, one of the last to use the port of Chester before it finally silted up, used to sail between Chester and Woolwich with military stores, doing the 700-mile journey on one occasion in 72 hours. She was lost with all hands (four men) in 1888. The model was made by a Mr W. Lewis, of Port Erin in the Isle of Man, who had sailed with the *Enterprise* between 1883 and 1887.

The United States is rich in great collections of model ships and boats. Besides the extensive displays at the National Museum (the Smithsonian Institution) in Washington, D.C., the United States Naval Academy at Annapolis, and the Mariners' Museum at

17 The 9-foot model of the Friendship *now in the Peabody Museum at Salem, Mass.*

Newport News already mentioned, there are internationally respected collections at the Headquarters of the Mystic Marine Society at Mystic, Connecticut; at the River Museum, Campus Martius, Marietta, Ohio; at the Boston Marine Museum, Old State House, Boston, Massachusetts; at the San Francisco Maritime Museum, Aquatic Park, San Francisco, California; at the U.S. Merchant Marine Academy, Kings Point, New York; at the Great Lakes Museum, Belle Isle, Detroit, Michigan; at the New Bedford Whaling Museum of the Old Dartmouth Historical Society, New Bedford, Massachusetts; at the Whaling Museum at Nantucket; at the Peabody Museum at Salem, Massachusetts; and at several other centres.

The Peabody Museum was founded by the East India Marine Society in 1799. In the museum, there are approximately 700 rigged and half-hull models of the greatest interest, but of especial significance to the ordinary viewer is the earliest known contemporary model of the United States Frigate *Constitution*, which was given to the society in 1813 by her commander, Captain Isaac Hull. Visitors to the Museum can enjoy seeing, too, the 9 foot model of the ship *Friendship*, built at Salem in 1797. This model was made by the ship's carpenter during a voyage to Sumatra, and was fitted with brass guns ordered from native metal workers on the ship's arrival at that island. The carpenter meant the model to be the best-surprise-ever for the young son of the ship's commander, Captain William Story of Salem. Unfortunately for the good man's intentions, a 9 foot model proved to be much too large for the Captain's house (or, perhaps it should be said, for Mrs Story's house) and it had to be donated discreetly to the Society in 1803.

Great Britain, too, has some splendid collections of model ships and boats on public view. One of the largest and most easily accessible is that at the Science Museum in South Kensington, London; there are also collections well worth visiting at the Imperial War Museum, in South London, and at the local museums at Bristol, Edinburgh, Glasgow, Hull, Liverpool, Portsmouth, Plymouth, South Shields and other centres. None of these, however, can rival the rich and valuable collection for which the British National Maritime Museum at Greenwich is famous.

This museum is situated on the Thames a few miles downstream from the centre of London. The collection is housed in a beautiful setting in, and in buildings close to, Inigo Jones' Queen's House, which was built for James the First's consort, Anne of Denmark. A great number of the models in the Greenwich Museum were transferred there in 1934 from the museum attached to the nearby Royal Naval College, built as a king's palace by Sir Christopher Wren. These models came, in the first place, from three separate sources. One of these was the collection formed by Sir Robert

18 The model of the frigate Seahorse *that may have been made from part of the mainmast of* L'Orient, *a French flagship.*

Seppings, Surveyor of the Royal Navy from 1813 to 1832, and enlarged by his immediate successors. The second was the collection of models given at various times to the Greenwich Hospital – maintained, chiefly, for the upkeep of disabled seamen – among these being a number of important examples presented by William the Fourth in 1830. The third major source was the collection founded by Sir James Caird in 1929 when he bought the entire contents of the museum of the training ship *Mercury*. (He added to them, afterwards, by many judicious purchases in the open market).

With so varied and distinguished a history, it is hardly surprising that the collection at Greenwich contains an unusual number of models that are of peculiar interest to the ordinary member of the general public, as well as to the specialist, and the particularly informed. Let us take only three examples of the models there that have some romantic or sentimental appeal. The visitor to Greenwich can see a model of the frigate *Seahorse*, thirty-eight guns. This model is believed to have been made from part of the mainmast of *L'Orient*, the French flagship at the Battle of the Nile in 1798. He may also see a silver model of the flagship *Britannia*, 120 guns, that was presented by the Royal Navy to Queen Victoria in the occasion of her Jubilee in 1887. Perhaps on a slightly less exalted plane he may examine a model of the steam yacht *Dolphin*, fitted with clockwork engines, that was made in 1822 by a craftsman named Allen Hunt when he was at the advanced age of eighty-one.

Occasionally, a model ship or boat may be found to hold some interesting or amusing secret. There is on view now, at Greenwich, a model of the merchantman *Samuel Enderby*. This modest ship

19 *Above – The model of the* Samuel Enderby *that contained a hidden message.*

20 *Right – A model of the 50-gun* Amarant *in the Statens Sjöhistoriska Museum, Stockholm.*

21 *Right, below – A detail of the great dockyard model displayed in the same museum.*

was built at Cowes, in 1834, for Messrs Enderby of London and was employed partly as a whaler and partly as a general trader. The model was made by Samuel White, son of the builder of the ship. When the model was being overhauled in 1947, a piece of paper was found concealed in it. On the paper was written:

> 'This model built by Sam White, West Cowes, Isle of Wight. Completed Christmas 1835 and presented to Messrs Charles, Henry and George Enderby being the model of a ship called the *Samuel Enderby* (their father) built by my father for the South Sea Whale Fishery in 1834. Sailed 1st voyage to South Seas Oct. 1834 and I am satisfied you who read will say, "Well poor fellow he has been dead years, yes, and I remember your breath is in your nostrils, in a short time you will be numbered with Sam White therefore prepare while you live to die, that your death may be one which shall secure to you a lasting eternity of endless bliss – Goodnight." Sam White born 1815–'

At the age of twenty, as the museum authorities so rightly observe, Samuel White was either a very pious model-maker, or else he possessed a somewhat macabre sense of humour.

The museum at Greenwich gives a remarkably extensive account of the history, over many centuries, of a great maritime nation, but it is not the only one in Europe of the kind. Sweden has a 1,680 mile coastline – equivalent, that is, to the coastal length between Skagen in Denmark and the French-Spanish border at Biscaya. A large proportion of the population draw their livelihood directly from the sea, and that has been the case for several hundred years. The National Historical Maritime Museum (Statens Sjöhistoriska Museum) at Stockholm has been specially designed and stocked so that it will show as graphically as possible the work and adventures of Swedish seamen during that time. One of the exhibits in the museum that attracts particularly close attention – especially from the young – is a model of the big municipal shipyard at Stockholm in about 1780.

In France, the Musée de la Marine has one of the most important collections of ships' models in the world. It includes models as venerable as that of the line-of-battle ship *Le Royal-Louis* of 1692;

22 *A model of one of the ships principally associated with Christopher Columbus – the caravel* Pinta. *Made in 1892 to the designs of Capt. Enrico D'Albertis the model is to be seen in the Museo Navale at Genoa.*

models as remarkable as the *Louis XV*, believed to have been used to instruct that monarch when he was a child; models as magnificent as the *Ville de Dieppe*, offered by the townspeople of Dieppe to Napoleon the First on the occasion of the birth of his son, the King of Rome; and many models that represent ships and boats of a comparatively recent date, such as the helicopter carrier *Jeanne d'Arc*, launched in 1961. The collection is housed now in the Palais de Chaillot, in Paris. There are also excellent, but smaller collections in the public museums at Bordeaux, Brest, Dunkirk, Marseilles, Rochefort and Toulon. A museum made at St Malo to commemorate the activities of the famous privateers that operated from that port was completely destroyed, with many splendid models, during the Second World War.

The principal collections in Denmark are housed at the Naval Museum in the Royal Dockyard at Copenhagen, and at the Museum for Commerce and Shipping in Kronborg Castle, at Elsinore. Opened in 1915, this museum occupies thirty rooms and gives a comprehensive review of Danish maritime trade.

Some of the finest collections of ship and boat models in Germany disappeared (like the collection at St. Malo) during the Second World War. The collection in the Deutsches Museum at Munich, for example, suffered extensive loss and damage; the collections in the Kolonia-und-Übersee Museum and the Focke-Museum at Bremen were completely destroyed. There are still,

23 A model of the 60-gun Wasa *to be seen in the Sjöfartsmuseet, Gothenborg. The* Wasa *was built in 1778 at Karlskrona Navy Yard*

however, excellent displays of models in the museums at Altona, Flensburg (where a contemporary model of the Danish warship *Urania*, of 1690, can be seen), Lübeck, Tönning, and other towns.

Holland's greatest collections of ship and boat models can be seen at Amsterdam, where the Netherlands Museum of Shipping (Netherlandsch Historisch Scheepvart Museum) contains a large number of models of men-of-war, merchantmen, fishing vessels and inland water craft; there are a few models in the historical section of the Rijksmuseum; at Rotterdam, the Maritime Museum (Maritiem Museum 'Prins Hendrik') has among many other fine models the splendid old votive vessel from the church at Mataró that will be described more fully later in this book.

This catalogue of great public collections of ship and boat models could be extended to an unreadable length – there has been no mention, yet, of the Norwegian Maritime Museum (Norsk Sjøfarts-museum) at Oslo, the Maritime Museum at Bergen, the Portuguese Maritime Museum (Museu de Marinha) at Lisbon, the Spanish Ministry of Marine (Museo Naval) at Madrid, or the Historical Naval Museum at Venice, all of which have displays that attract many thousands of visitors in the course of each year. But models from each of these collections – and from others, too – are to be described or shown in illustrations, or both, in the course of this book. We must go on now to make a short chronological survey of the whole world of model ships and boats.

2 Early Vessels and the Models that have been made of them

Ships and boats come, ships and boats go, but the models that are made of them may last – almost – for ever. It is not surprising, then, that the scholar who wishes to study the long development of navigation, or of naval architecture, will turn for his prime sources of information to any contemporary models that may still exist. When an important vessel has been broken up, or has rotted away, any accurate model of it that survives immediately achieves the status of a precious historical document.

Ship models are known to have been made for at least five thousand years, and it is possible that some may yet be discovered – perhaps in Crete, or on one of the Aegean Islands, or in some other part of the eastern Mediterranean region where the earliest civilizations were mostly centred – that will be much older than this.

The rudimentary Bronze Age models with which any survey must start were made with clay. They appear to represent rough, canoe-like boats that were made from single tree trunks and hollowed out with some crude implements, or with fire. (Even today, in underdeveloped parts of the world, primitive people use logs, log rafts, and inflated skins for crossing rivers and narrow inland waterways.) Unfortunately, these early models from the Mediterranean Islands are not sufficiently detailed to be of any great interest, except to experts. For all practical purposes, the history of model ships and boats may be considered to have begun on the banks of the River Nile.

In the earliest dynasties of which any kind of a clear picture has emerged, transport on the Nile was carried on by means of canoe-type vessels made of reeds. These were not so insubstantial as their basic material might suggest. Some of them were quite large, and could carry considerable loads.

Later Nile ships were built of wood, but as the only timber available was that of the acacia or 'sunt', and as this provided only short and irregular lengths, their design was subject to severe limitations. At a later date still, cedar was imported from the Lebanon. After that, Egyptian shipwrights were able to be a little more ambitious in their constructional techniques.

24 The contemporary model from the church at Mataró of a fifteenth century caravel. The model is now in the Maritime Museum 'Prins Hendrik', Rotterdam.

The hulls of most of these early wooden Egyptian ships were

spoon-shaped, and were invariably pointed at both ends. They were built without stems, sternposts, keels or ribs. First the planking was laid along the centre line of the future craft. Then the planking would be laid along the upper longitudinal edges, or gunwales. The planking that was to form the middle curves or bilges would be fitted last, to complete the hull. The planks would be connected together, as they were successively assembled, with rectangular wooden dowels and double triangular wedges.

A reliable impression of an early Egyptian ship can be gained from a small model in the Science Museum at South Kensington, London. This model was made in the museum workshops from information derived from a bas-relief discovered in the pyramid tomb of King Sahure at Abusir, near Cairo. This sculpture, which has been ascribed to the Fifth Dynasty (*c.* 2600 BC), provides the earliest known representation of any sea-going vessel.

An interesting feature of this model is the cable or hogging truss that runs longitudinally from end to end. The cable, in the original vessel, would have been secured at the bow and the stern of the ship, and supported at intervals along the hull by vertical struts or queen-posts. By being tightened, by means of the device known now as a Spanish windlass (in its simplest form, this consists merely of a stick pushed through the cords of a rope, and twisted), the cable would help to prevent 'hogging' or drooping at the extremities, a weakness from which long shallow vessels are particularly liable to suffer.

Nobody will ever know who first thought of using the power of the winds to drive a boat forward, for the origins of sailing are lost in the mists of pre-history. One small representation of a sailing craft has been found in the decorations of a vase that is known to be at least six thousand years old, and may even be older. This primitive vessel, which is shown quite simply in silhouette, has a single mast, placed well forward, with a sail that is roughly rectangular. A rudimentary arrangement of this kind would only have been used for sailing when the wind was directly aft.

By the year 2000 BC, the Egyptians were making and using sailing vessels of a more sophisticated type. Carved reliefs that have survived from that time show sailing craft with bipod masts and high sails. (Oarsmen, as many as two or three dozen, would supply the necessary motive power when the wind was not in a convenient quarter.) More important, from the point of view of this book, are the contemporary models found in the tombs of the Pharoahs and other powerful men that give us additional information about the steering oars, deck cabins, and other notable features of these ships. The Egyptians believed that the human spirit, after death, was capable of travelling where it liked on dry land, but they believed, too, that it required assistance before it could cross the waters of the

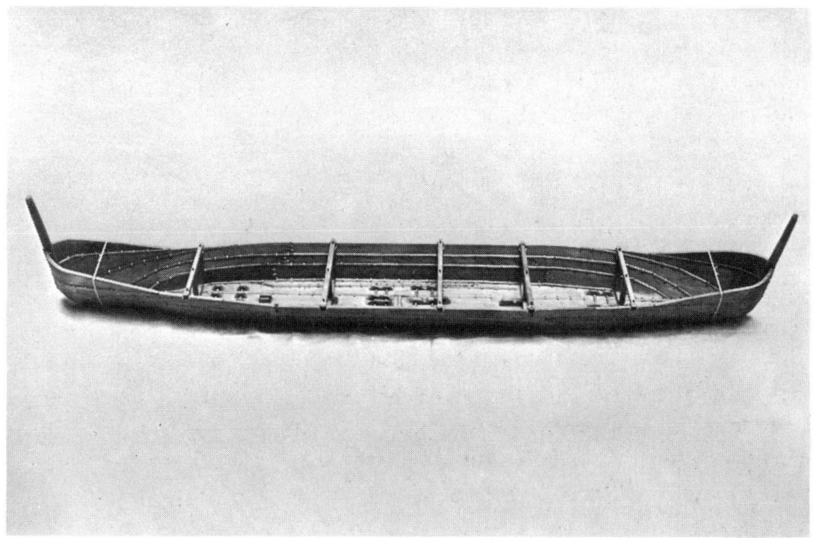

25 Top – Scale models of the remains of Bronze Age boats found at North Ferriby, Yorkshire.

26 Centre – This model shows one of the North Ferriby boats in a reconstructed form.

27 Right – A model of an Egyptian sailing ship. The prototype may have been one of the earliest sea-going vessels.

28 A rigged model of an Egyptian ship of 2000 BC.

Nile. So with their dead they buried the model boats called 'spirit ships' to assist this passage. The tomb of Mehenkvetre, Chancellor and Vizier of the Pharaoh Mentuhotep, for example, was found to be lavishly furnished with models – model houses, model animals, models of household implements, and models of several other kinds. Among these were a number of replicas of boats, of the types made either of papyrus or of a local wood, that would have been used at that time on the Nile.

Another remarkable model, now treasured in the Science Museum, London, came from a Twelfth Dynasty tomb at Beni-Hasan. From this model, when it was originally found, the mast and sails were missing, but modern replacements for them have been made, based on the masts and sails of other models of roughly the same date that were subsequently discovered at Thebes.

All the contemporary boat models of the Eleventh (*c.* 2000 BC) and Twelfth (*c.* 1900 BC) Dynasties that have survived and that we can actually see and inspect, are made 'in block'. In every case, the hull of the model has been extended downwards so that it forms a flat base or foot on which it will stand without support. The same feature, which could give anyone who had not been forewarned a false idea of the prototype, may be found in many present day models from the region of the Ganges.

Not a contemporary model, but one that throws an interesting light on the customs of ancient Egypt is the one-tenth scale representation of a twelfth century funerary boat that is also kept on view at the Science Museum in London. Boats of this kind were used only once – to take the corpse of an important person across the Nile to its last resting place. The model is based on an actual boat that was unearthed in 1893 near the 4000-year old pyramid of Dahshur. The prototype boat is now preserved in the Museum at Cairo.

In general design, the hull of the boat is of crescent form, with its greatest width (or beam) slightly forward of the midship section. The colouring of the original boat has been carefully reproduced in the model, but the general finish of the model is a little less crude than that of the prototype, the rough surface of which had to be given a liberal coating of gypsum before it could be painted.

The Phoenicians and Greeks of the pre-Christian eras were greater seafarers than the Egyptians, but no contemporary models of their more advanced vessels have ever been found. However, a sufficient number of representations of the various parts of their warships and trading vessels has been discovered – in sculptures, on vases (whole, or in fragmentary form) and in wall reliefs – for experts to have been able to make what are believed to be reasonably accurate models of these speedy and elegant craft without having to rely too much on inspired guesswork.

Biremes (the Greek galleys that were propelled by as many as fifty oarsmen, arranged in two banks) are definitely known to have been built with wood, on a structure of ribs. The Corinthian shipwrights were much too sophisticated ever to have been satisfied with the old dugout warships.

Triremes were more ambitious still. A trireme would be pulled by one hundred and sixty-eight oarsmen, arranged in three banks, of which the uppermost would contain thirty oars a side, while the middle and lower banks would each have twenty-seven oars a side. In addition there were two steering oars. Present-day craftsmen who decide to make models of these long-lost craft are helped by an inventory found in the dockyard of the Piraeus, which showed that no oar used in them exceeded 14.2 feet in length. For guidance on the overall dimensions of these ships, model-makers have relied on the slipway still preserved in the harbour of Zea. This ancient structure suggests that a trireme must have been about 150 feet long, with a breadth of hull of about 16 feet. This would have been much too narrow for the sides of the hull to be used as supports for the oars, so strong but light outriggers were added, increasing the overall breadth of the galley to 19 feet.

All the contemporary representations of Grecian galleys that have survived confirm that each bireme or trireme had a single

mast, with a sail carried on a long slender cross-member or yard. This sail was used to provide extra motive power when the vessel was travelling with the wind aft. Some vase-paintings suggest that the masts could be lowered when the ships went into combat, or when they were being rowed into the wind. A yoke or Y-shaped support would be fitted on each galley, on which its lowered mast could rest.

By the end of the second century after Christ, the Romans were all-powerful in southern and western Europe, and the sea routes of the Mediterranean were thronged with ships carrying men and arms, and merchantmen laden with grain and other necessities. The galleys used by the Romans do not appear to have differed to any marked extent from those used earlier by the Greeks, but the other ships developed to meet the demands of this maritime traffic were broad-beamed and round, rather than straight and long. It was scarcely practicable or economic to provide oarsmen for these capacious craft in the necessary numbers. So, the use of oars was rapidly abandoned as the potentialities of sail power were further explored.

We know, from relief carvings found at Ostia and Porto near the mouth of the River Tiber and at Tarsus and Sidon on the Syrian Coast, how these Roman merchant ships were built and rigged, and several attractive models based on these contemporary representations have been constructed – usually, to take an important place in the display cases of one of the great museums or galleries of the world.

Each had a single central mast on which was hoisted a large square sail. Above the yard on which this sail was carried, there would be two, or possibly more, triangular topsails. Over the bow, and raking well forward, there would be a heavy spar called an *artemon* on which would be set a small head-sail or fore-sail. There is little doubt that the primary function of this head-sail was to assist the steering, since a vessel rigged with one would be much more easily kept on a steady course than a vessel without. After the collapse of the Roman Empire, however, no more ships were made with this simple but valuable contrivance until it reappeared in a modified form in the second half of the fifteenth century, after which the spar became known as the bowsprit and the sail associated with it as the spritsail.

With the decline of Roman power, there were few further developments in shipbuilding of any real significance in the Mediterranean area for several centuries. The important changes during this time took place instead in northern Europe. To appreciate the fundamental difference between the southern and northern techniques of planked hull construction, one has to know exactly the difference between carvel- and clinker-building:

29 Above – A model of a Greek galley of the fourth century BC.

30 Left – A model of a Roman merchant ship of the second century AD.

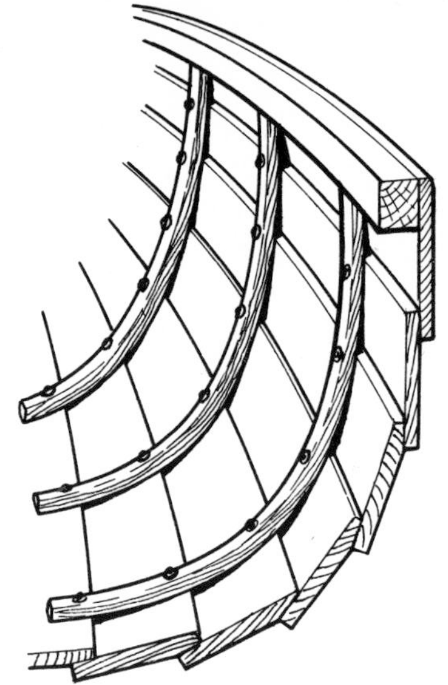

In a *carvel-built* hull, the individual planks are placed edge to edge. Usually, the edges that are to butt together will be chamfered first, so that the surface produced after the joints have been caulked will be perfectly smooth and continuous.

In a *clinker-built* hull, the planks are positioned so that they overlap, and are held in place by being fastened on to underlying ribs and to each other. All clinker-built hulls can be recognized immediately by the ridges or steps that are produced where the exposed narrow sides of the planks meet, squarely, the broader surfaces of the planks that are placed next to them.

The clinker-built hull is definitely associated – at least as far as its development is concerned – with northern rather than southern Europe. Probably, it evolved in stages from the simple dug-out log, the first step having been taken when longitudinal planks were added to each side of a hollowed-out tree trunk to give the little boat some extra width and stability.

The remains of a planked vessel that demonstrate a slightly more advanced stage in the development of the clinker-built hull were discovered in 1921 at a farm at Hjortspring in the Island of Als, in South Jutland. It has been estimated that this craft may date from the period 400–200 BC. It was made from five broad planks sewn together with cord. In every case, the edge of the upper plank projected over the adjoining lower plank, clinker-fashion. On each plank, there were a number of raised lugs or cleats that enabled it to be lashed tightly to the boat's ribs, which were made from hazel branches.

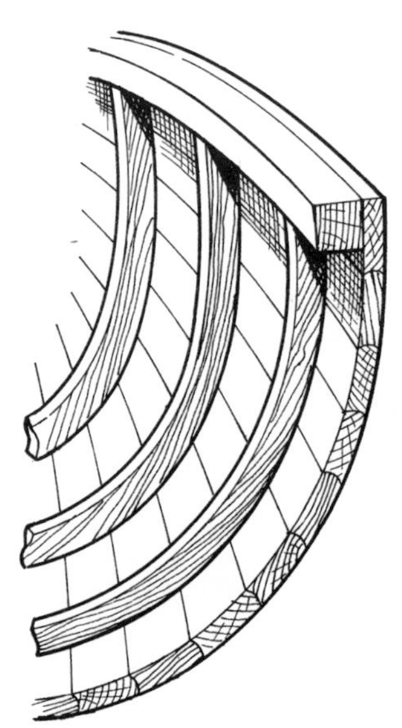

31 Above – A diagram to show the difference between, at the top, clinker-built, and below, carvel-built hulls.

The next stage in the history of clinker-building can be studied in a vessel that dates from about 400 AD and was found in 1863 in a peat-bog in Schleswig. Known as the Nydam Boat, it was double-ended and undecked. Constructed of oak, it had no real keel as we understand that word today. Instead, it had a thick, wide, centre-line plank or bottom board, on each side of which there were five overlapping planks, joined together with iron clench nails. The nineteen ribs were, as in the earlier vessel found at Als, lashed to the planks.

The Kvalsund boat, found in Norway in 1920, has been ascribed to the seventh century after Christ. This boat is of much historical importance, because it has a shaped keel that can be conveniently regarded as the half-way stage between the wide thick centre plank of the Nydam Boat and the true upright keel that gave such wonderful stability to the later boats of the Vikings.

These swift, graceful boats, usually known as longships, which sped over the waters of the northern hemisphere during the tenth and eleventh centuries, are of considerable interest to many present-day model makers. We know more or less exactly what

Right – Three models of Viking ships : above (32) – A model of the ship found at Gokstad ; centre (33) ; – A 12 foot long model made for the Columbia Pictures film 'Longships' ; below (34) – A model at Greenwich.

these extraordinary vessels looked like, because two practically complete examples have been discovered and restored for public exhibition – one, in 1880, in a tumulus at Gokstad, near Sandefjord in Norway, and another, in 1904, at Oseberg in the same country.

The ship found at Oseberg is considered by experts to be the older. Its hull was made entirely of oak, and it was built with twelve planks placed clinker-fashion on each side of a massive keel. There were oar-ports cut in the sides for fifteen pairs of oars, and provision was made for a mast to be raised when the ship was to be sailed. The deck was stepped at the forward and aft ends to form two raised platforms or vantage points. The ends of the hull are notable for their intricately carved decorations.

The Gokstad ship was also made of oak. It was nearly 80 feet long from stem to stern, its breadth at its widest point being approximately 17 feet. Like the Oseberg ship, it had a sturdy keel, with sixteen planks on either side, laid on in clinker fashion.

The ship was propelled both by sail and by thirty-two oarsmen – that is, there were sixteen oars on each side, each oar being approximately 18 feet long. As in the Oseberg ship, there were circular oar-ports cut in the sides, and these were fitted most ingeniously with pivotted shutters that would help to keep the water out when the ship was under sail. The vessel was steered by means of a rudder, shaped like an oar, that pivotted on a conical wooden chuck secured to the starboard (or steer board) side.

When the Gokstad ship was discovered, nearly ten centuries after it was buried, thirty-two coloured shields were found attached to each side. Though this may have been the customary practice only when conditions of weather and water were favourable, nearly all models of Viking ships made since that time do, in fact, show the shields most decoratively in place. (Marine Model Company, Inc., of Halesite, Long Island, New York, market a kit with which a splendid model of a Viking ship can be made by any reasonably handy person. In this kit, a number of boldly ornamented shields are included in the list of wood and metal parts, which total more than one hundred).

After the pioneering work done by the Vikings, the sailing ship developed fairly rapidly in northern Europe during the Middle Ages. We know, approximately, what the ships built in the eleventh and twelfth centuries looked like, because some are shown in the Bayeux Tapestry. They were not unlike the Viking longships, but as less and less use was made of oarsmen, and more and more use was made of sail, ships had to be built with greater beam and greater depth so that they could carry safely the increased area of canvas.

For information about the ships built in northern Europe during the thirteenth and fourteenth centuries, we cannot turn to contemporary models, for none are known to exist. There are few pictures to guide us, for the works of most medieval artists were completed for religious or ideal purposes, and they do not provide much reliable evidence about the shipwright's activities. Treatises on ship design were, of course, unknown.

By a fortunate coincidence, at that time when so many important advances in ship construction were being made, charters were being granted in a generous fashion to the towns that were being developed most rapidly. Many of these charters were given a proper degree of authenticity by the attachment of blobs of wax, into each of which was pressed some appropriate emblem or badge. In the seals designed for sea-coast towns we tend to find naturally enough, representations of ships and boats. Many of these are extremely beautiful, having been produced with metal dies cut by skilful engravers who were naturally good designers. But, not all of these men were thoroughly conversant with the finer points of the shipwright's trade and their work cannot be taken too literally.

In one respect especially, these seaport seals tend to be misleading. As the spaces to be filled by the seal designers were, in almost every instance, round, the ship-images they fitted into them were invariably shorter and deeper than the shapes of the vessels on which they were based.

In spite of these reservations, these seals are important sources of historical information. On them, we find pictorial evidence of the steps by which the ancient quarter rudders attached to the ships' sides were transformed into the more advanced median rudders. One particular seal – that of Elbing, 1242 – shows the earliest known illustration of a rudder slung to a stern-post. Further seals provide precise indications of the various points in history at which windlasses were devised for working anchor cables; bowlines and reef points were introduced into the gear used for controlling sails; and many other only slightly less important innovations were made by ingenious shipwrights.

At some early stage in the history of shipbuilding, a shipwright who was more enterprising than any of his predecessors hit on the idea of adding to one of his vessels a raised platform of some kind that would give warriors or look-out men all the advantages of extra height above water level. This may have been in some pre-Christian era – there are suggestions of elevated structures, amidships, in carved representations from the Nubian Desert of river craft which may be as much as 6000 years old. (Were these structures altars? Or cabins? Or awnings intended to protect the most distinguished passengers or the more vulnerable items of the cargo from the blazing sun? Nobody now knows for certain.) We do know surely, though, that many Roman warships had, in the foreparts, amidships or in the stern, some kind of armour-clad tower or poop that would have had a military significance. We know, too, that the

35 Three charter seals : above – The seal of Hythe, Kent, late twelfth or early thirteenth century ; centre – The seal of Sandwich, late thirteenth or early fourteenth century ; and, below – The seal of Dover, 1305.

36 A model of a ship of the Cinque Ports of the thirteenth century.

longships of the Viking period had elevated platforms of a rudimentary kind in their forepeaks. These are shown in the pictures and carved stones that have survived from that era, as well as being present in the actual ships that have been disinterred.

By the thirteenth century the seals of the principal port towns of northern Europe were illustrating ships that had, raised on pillars, platforms of a more formidable kind. With their crenellated walls, these platforms were obviously inspired by the almost impregnable turrets and towers that were important features of the stone-built, land-based fortresses of the period. Later again, they were to be developed into the massive, fortified, fore-, top-, and after-castles that made the fighting ships of the principal maritime nations in the sixteenth and seventeenth centuries such formidable instruments of war.

Although they were intended originally for the same purpose, the fore- and after-castles were soon put to different uses. The forecastle kept its primary function as a raised fortress, but on most ships the after-castle (or, as it was often called, the summer castle) was set aside as a fine vantage point for the most important people on board. During the second half of the fifteenth century, which was to be a momentous period in the history of shipbuilding, successful attempts were made to incorporate the after-castle into the ship's hull so that it would become an integral part of the whole instead of being, very clearly, an appendage. At the same time, the stern of the ship was seen as the obviously appropriate place for superior cabin accomodation.

There is in the Museum 'Prins Hendrik' at Rotterdam a model of a ship that is probably unique – it is, as far as we know, the only ship model still in existence that was actually made during the middle decades of the fifteenth century – that is, while the men who were to sail on the first recorded voyages from Europe to the New World were learning how to handle ships of a similar type. It has been called 'The most interesting of all ships' models.' The model has a romantic history. For hundreds of years, it hung under the roof-beams of a little chapel in a small seaside town called Mataró on the coast of Catalonia. In Spain, as in other countries, it was a very ancient custom to hang ship models in churches *ex voto* – that is, in fulfilment of some vow. Usually these models, made by rough seamen and presented on their safe return from especially dangerous journeys, were relatively crude and unreliable as sources of detailed information, but the Mataró model is most carefully constructed. There may be a good reason for this.

Votive offerings are not the only ships' models to be found in churches in Spain and Portugal. In some churches, small silver models are used on the altars, to hold incense, which is taken out with a silver spoon; and it is quite easy to find images of saints,

The alabaster boat found in the annex to Tutankhamen's tomb. The prow and stern represent the head of a Syrian ibex.

Overleaf, a model of an Egyptian ship, c. 1300 BC.

1937·249

particularly those of St Elmo, that have a ship's hull in their arms. Undoubtedly there is a ritual significance in this emphasis on sea-going vessels, and a large painting called *La Promesa* (The Promise), now in Madrid, helps to explain this. The picture shows fishermen and their wives carrying various items of a ship's equipment – an oar, a rudder, a yard, the part evidently meant to represent the whole – to a crucifix standing on a hill near the coast, to receive a blessing. The model from Mataró may well have been specially built to be carried in such processions. If it was, the care taken with its construction can be easily understood.

The stages by which the Mataró model travelled from Spain to its present resting place in the Netherlands have never been fully explained. It has been alleged that at one time it passed into the possession of an important Spanish family. What is known for certain is that in the early nineteen thirties it turned up in New York – in the Reinhardt Galleries, at the corner of 5th Avenue and 57th Street.

The importance of the model as a source of historical information was immediately recognized. Experts who saw it reported that they were amazed that a model of such antiquity should be so little impaired by the ravages of time. The wood of the model was worm-eaten – that of the rails having suffered particularly – and, as might have been expected, nearly all the original rigging was gone, the little that was left being in such confusion that it seemed as if some-one wholly ignorant of the uses of the various appliances had tied up the cords in a haphazard way. The paint had almost entirely disappeared. There were left only some traces of a red colour, and a partly obliterated zig-zag design around the guard-rail of the main top. In most other respects, the model appeared to be in a remarkably good state of preservation.

Since it was acquired by Mr D. G. van Beuningen of Rotterdam and lent by him to the Maritime Museum 'Prins Hendrik', the Mataró model has been submitted to some prolonged and searching surveys. The most surprising fact that has emerged from these examinations concerns the number of the ship's masts. When found in New York, the model had three masts – but experts have decided that when it was first constructed the little vessel had only one large and tall mast, centrally located. The fore and mizzen masts, they say, are both later additions.

Their theories are supported by the outward appearance of the existing masts. None of the three masts is cut specially from a solid piece of wood. Instead, all three are crooked and unevenly surfaced, being merely slim branches that have had the bark removed. It seemed to the experts hardly likely that a craftsman skilful enough to have fabricated the hull – it is a built model, not block carved – and to have shaped so successfully the main top and the yards would

A rigged model of a Flemish carrack, c. 1480. The hull is carvel built.

37 Above – A model of a carrack.

38 Left – A votive model of a galleon of 1540.

39 A bronze gilt clock made at Augsburg in the sixteenth century.

have been so slovenly in the provision of masts. Ergo, the masts are by another hand.

The development of the three-masted ship was one of the most significant innovations in the whole history of sailing vessels. It happened, like so many other important changes, during the second half of the fifteenth century. The experts' verdict suggests that the Mataró model, in its original unaltered form, may have been in existence in 1450, or even a little earlier. The man who tampered with it was merely bringing it up to date.

A good idea of the appearance of a fairly typical early three-master from northern waters can be gained from the model in the Science Museum at South Kensington, London, of a large clinker-built English ship of the period. (This type was usually known as a 'Cog'.) The sources of information from which this model was made in the museum workshops are unusually well-authenticated – there is a manuscript in the British Museum, produced between the years 1485 and 1490, and called *The Pageant of Richard Beauchamp, Earl of Warwick*, which describes, with a number of beautifully detailed illustrations, the pilgrimage of the great English nobleman to Palestine, early in the fifteenth century. The ships shown in these views had not yet been built when the Earl of Warwick made his famous expedition, but they are the ones that would be well known by the artists commissioned to record his exploits, half a century later.

With the gradual perfection of the three-masted vessel in the second half of the fifteenth century and the early years of the sixteenth century it became possible for some remarkable trans-oceanic voyages of discovery to be made. There were, for instance, the several expeditions sent out by successive Kings of Portugal in their determined attempts to find a sea route to India. In 1488, Bartholomew Diaz, commander of one of these expeditions, managed to double the Cape of Good Hope before he turned, again, for home. Vasco da Gama, nine years later, not only rounded the Cape, but he also managed to land – on Christmas Day, 1497 – in what is still known as Natal, before successfully completing the voyage to India.

More significant in their effect on the history of the world, even than the journeys of either of these men, were the journeys of Christopher Columbus. The great Spanish explorer made his first landfall in the New World on 12 October 1492, when he discovered the island he was to call La Espanola, or Little Spain. He reached Cuba a little over a fortnight later, believing it to be part of the western mainland of India. Further voyaging took him to Puerto Rico in 1493, Jamaica in 1494, and Nicaragua and the coast of Colombia in 1502.

As we have seen, quite a lot of useful information is available

40 A conjectural model of the Santa Maria *made in 1892 to the designs of Capt. Enrico D'Albertis.*

about the ships that Christopher Columbus would probably have seen around him as he sailed from his home waters. But no one, anywhere, knows exactly what his flagship *Santa Maria* looked like. That has not stopped model-makers all over the world making their own personal versions of the *Santa Maria* – hundreds of them, thousands of them, they are in constant production. Many of these models are attractive, some of them are admirably detailed. There is only one thing that is incontrovertibly wrong with all of them – they are based, without a single exception, on guesswork. The *Santa Maria* was an undistinguished merchantman which was requisitioned to fulfil her historic task, and she was never brought back to Europe to be measured for the records, so that was that.

Even the models of the *Santa Maria* that have been made under more or less official auspices can hardly be guaranteed. There was a model made (for instance) in 1892 under the personal supervision of the Director of the Museo Naval in Madrid, who should have known all there was to be known about the *Santa Maria* if anyone did. Unfortunately for his personal prestige, that model had (and still has) a square transom stern. Scholars working later than 1892 have established that sterns of that kind were not introduced until the beginning of the sixteenth century. The ship that set sail from

A rigged model of the Great Harry *(1540). Left (41) – a close-up of the bows, and right (42) – a broadside view.*

the harbour at Palos on 3 August 1492 almost certainly had a round stern. In later models sponsored by the Spanish authorities, this error has been corrected.

Craftsmen wishing to make models of the *Henri Grace à Dieu* (colloquially referred to as the *Great Harry*), which was one of the most famous warships of the sixteenth century have had little more on which to base their work than an artist's impression contained in Anthony Anthony's *Roll of the Navy*, compiled in 1546 and now preserved in the Pepysian Library at Magdalene College, Cambridge, and the few facts that have been recorded about her tonnage, her crews, and her armament (21 heavy brass guns, 130 iron guns and 100 hand guns, after she was re-built in 1536-9). The colourful model made for the Science Museum at South Kensington, London, can be taken as a representation of the vessel that is as close as possible under the circumstances.

Even less is known about the *Great Michael*, built at Newhaven, Midlothian, in Scotland, at approximately the same time. There is a conjectural model, in the Royal Scottish Museum at Edinburgh, of this great ship, whose building 'wasted all the woods of Fife'. The model is largely based on a stirring account of her given by Robert Lindsay of Pitscottie in his *Historie and Chronicles of Scotland*, where he tells how 'all the wrights of Scotland and many strangers were, by the King's command, at her device one year and a day ere she was complete.' Then, she 'cumbered all Scotland to put her to sea'.

Most people who have little real knowledge of the history of sailing ships refer to all models of sixteenth- and early seventeenth-century men-of-war as model galleons. It is a convenient term to use, as it conveys a certain mental image even when it is applied to a vessel that is not, strictly speaking, a galleon at all. Though the word 'galleon' is thought to have been derived from 'galley' – a warship remarkably like the bireme of classical times, which was operated principally by oarsmen, pulling as many as seven to the oar – it seems likely that even the earliest galleons were entirely sail-propelled. Contemporary models of galleons do, in fact, exist – there is one which dates from 1540 in the Museo Naval at Madrid that shows no trace of oars.

There is a later model galleon, in the same museum, that was given to Philip the Second in 1593 by his loyal Flemish subjects. This model is beautifully carved, gilded and painted – the open-work between the two tiers of guns and along the long round-ended gallery being especially fine – but it may not be to scale. The streamers show the Pillars of Hercules, the ragged staff cross of Burgundy, and other heraldic emblems of Spanish rule in the Netherlands.

Of all the modern reconstructions of galleons, it would be hard to find a more authentic example than the model made in the workshops of the Science Museum at South Kensington, London, since so much research was done, before the construction of the model was started, to make sure that it would be as complete and accurate as possible. Much of the necessary information was obtained from a manuscript entitled *Fragments of Ancient English Shipwrightry* that was compiled about 1586 by the master shipwright, Matthew Baker. This manuscript, which contains the earliest scale plans of ships known in England, is treasured, like Anthony Anthony's *Roll*, at Magdalene College, Cambridge.

Two ships that made historic voyages during the late sixteenth and seventeenth centuries have attracted the attention of model-makers almost as compulsively as Columbus's *Santa Maria*.

The earlier of these is Sir Francis Drake's famous ship the *Golden Hind*. When he started out from Plymouth in 1577 with the 100-ton *Pelican* and five smaller ships to cross the Atlantic, Drake was to be the first Englishman to go round the world, but by the time he emerged into the Pacific all his squadron had either turned back or had been destroyed. Only the *Pelican* remained, and Drake then changed her name to the *Golden Hind*. Long since given up for lost by those at home, the gallant little ship reached England after her circumnavigation of the globe at the end of September 1580. No contemporary models or drawings of the *Golden Hind* exist, but the model made for the City of Plymouth and now exhibited at Drake's home Buckland Abbey is believed to be the most reliable reproduction to be seen.

43 Above – The model of a Flemish galleon given to Phillip the Second in 1593.

44 Right – A model of an Elizabethan galleon made in the workshops of the Science Museum, London.

45 A waterline model made in 1965 of a Portuguese caravel (c. 1500).

The second of these frequently-modelled ships is the *Mayflower*, in which the Pilgrim Fathers sailed from Plymouth to America in 1620. The *Mayflower* is another model-maker's headache. Little is known of her, other than that she was an ordinary small merchant ship of that period of about 180 tons burden, and that she was by no means a new ship when the Pilgrim Fathers set sail to the West.

One version of the *Mayflower* has proved popular with hobbyists who enjoy assembling their models from commercially produced kits. This has been marketed by Revell Inc., of Venice, California, U.S. Revell researchers, craftsmen and engineers worked closely with the folk of Plimoth Plantation in the preparation of this model. The aim was, to make it an exact replica of William Baker's famous reconstruction job the *Mayflower II*. It is generally agreed that Revell succeeded magnificently.

A one-off-only model of the *Mayflower* that has attracted a good deal of attention is now owned by the proprietors of the *Western Morning News*, a newspaper based principally on Plymouth, England. The model was made by a Plymouth bomb disposal expert – Captain John Sharland, of the 24th Infantry Brigade of

46 The model of the Mayflower *owned by the New York Historical Society.*

the British army. Captain Sharland began making model ships in 1957, purely as a form of relaxation for his off-duty hours. Having no workshop, Captain Sharland spreads his materials and equipment out in his dining-room when he is making models, having trained the members of his family, including his young son Mark, to walk round the bits and not to step on them.

Normally, the captain works from photo copies of original plans that he obtains from the National Maritime Museum at Greenwich. Finding no suitable plans in his own country for his model of the *Mayflower*, the captain was forced to base his work on a German kit plan, which he amended slightly after doing further research. The six sails on the model were made by Mrs Sharland, who had to finish them by hand because she could not find a sewing machine with a small enough stitch. (Each sail took about one week's spare time work to complete.) The eighty-odd 'dead-eyes' in the rigging were carefully hand-made from dowelling and finding that a wood drill split the tiny blocks, John Sharland was compelled to pierce the necessary holes in them with a red-hot needle.

3 Official Ship Models in the 17th and 18th Centuries

Contemporary ship models, made for official purposes, give us, where they are still in existence, a continuous and authentic record of the development of naval architecture. The first models of this kind are known to have been produced early in the seventeenth century. Almost certainly they came into being as a result of the industry and enterprise of the great English shipwright Phineas Pett.

Pett came from a family that had been engaged in ship-building for many generations. He was a more highly educated man than one might expect to have hailed from such a practical background, as he entered Emmanuel College, Cambridge, in 1586 and graduated as a Master of Arts. He had, too, a technical training that was exceptionally advanced for his times, as well as some sea-going experience. In his autobiography, preserved now in the Harleian MSS in the British Museum, he records that he began a small model in December 1599, rigged it, and presented it to John Trevor. This is certainly the oldest known date of an English ship model.

In March 1601, Pett was appointed as assistant to the master shipwright at Chatham Dockyard. He attracted much attention, some two years after this, for his good service in fitting out the fleet in only six weeks, and shortly after the accession of James the First to the combined thrones of England and Scotland he was ordered by Lord Howard, the Lord Admiral, to make a miniature ship – a model, it seems likely, of the flagship *Ark Royal* – for the king's elder son, Prince Henry. The model was finished in March 1604, and Pett took it round to the Thames, where, on the 22nd, the Prince went on board. The Lord Admiral presented Pett to the Prince. On the following day, Pett was sworn as the Prince's servant, and was appointed captain of the little vessel.

In 1607, Pett is known to have made another model – this time, a model of a ship he was actively designing: the *Prince Royal*, of nearly 1200 tons. The *Prince Royal* was, we know, a fine looking ship with admirable bow and stern lines. As might have been expected, for Pett was a great innovator, it had many new features that shocked the older, more orthodox shipwrights of the time,

47 This contemporary dockyard-built model of H.M.S. Prince *is one of the finest models still in existence of English seventeenth century line-of-battle ships.*

48 The Sovereign of the Seas *as shown in the portrait of Peter Pett in the National Maritime Museum, Greenwich.*

and it has been described as the 'parent of all future men-of-war.' With its extensive carving and gilding, the accounts for which are still in existence, it was also one of the most elaborately decorated vessels seen to that date.

Unfortunately, the model of the *Prince Royal* that Pett made with his own hands has long since disappeared, but it seems likely that the sight of it enchanted the king's second son, Prince Charles, who was then aged four. A little later, Pett is known to have made a model as a toy for the younger boy – a ship mounted 'on a carriage, with wheels, resembling the sea'.

Our childhood playthings, we know, may have an important formative influence on us, and it is tempting to think that this particular model may have had a profound psychological effect on the impressionable recipient. On 26 June 1634, Charles, who, as Henry had died, had succeeded as Charles the First to the English throne, went to the shipyards at Woolwich, near London, to look over the ship *Leopard* that was then being built under Pett's supervision. Before he left, later on the same day, the King gave the shipwright an order to build the largest ship that had ever been seen on any sea. Modern psychologists who know so much about compensation might suggest that he sought by this means to emphasize his own dignity (physically, he was an abnormally small

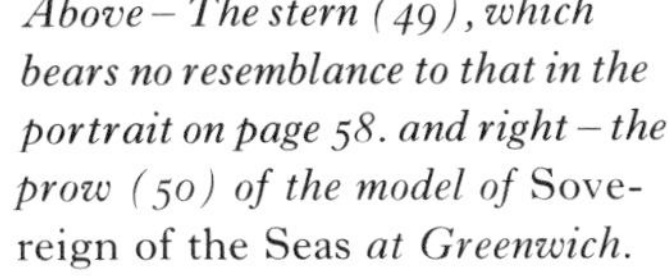

Above – The stern (49), which bears no resemblance to that in the portrait on page 58. and right – the prow (50) of the model of Sovereign of the Seas *at Greenwich.*

man) and to increase his personal authority. Ironically, the tax named Ship Money that he levied to pay for his extravagance was a prime cause of his losing his head.

The royal commission brought the strongest protests from the naval authorities, who held that such a vast vessel would be unwarrantably expensive and virtually unmanageable in the shallow waters that surround the British coasts. In spite of all opposition, the King pressed stubbornly ahead with his plans. Pett had a model of the proposed vessel – to be called, appropriately, the *Sovereign of the Seas* – made before the prototype was started. Sadly, Pett's model of this ship, which, according to contemporary accounts, was of exquisite workmanship, is, like that of the *Prince Royal*, no longer in existence.

If the model of the *Sovereign of the Seas* was anything like the finished, full-size ship, it must have been one of the most magnificent models of any kind that has ever been made. (The model made in 1827 as an addition to the series of models that had been recently established by Sir Robert Seppings, Surveyor of the Navy, is splendid enough, but its elaborate stern decorations bear no resemblance to those of the 1637 ship as described in a contemporary pamphlet.) The great artist Sir Anthony Van Dyck was commissioned to design the decorations and enrichments of the prototype, and they were executed principally by the king's master carver, Gerard Christmas, with his sons and assistants, and gilded so resplendently that the ship was given the nickname *The Golden Devil* by the Dutch mariners who sailed against her in several engagements. At the figurehead, the Saxon King Edgar was shown, riding rough-shod over seven of his fallen adversaries. (We may see here another symptom of Charles's need for re-assurance.) Elsewhere on the ship's sides and galleries there were gleaming gods, goddesses and satyrs; high relief representations of the signs of the zodiac; imaginary portraits of the emperors of ancient Rome; and a rich variety of heraldic devices. On the stern by the ship's rudder glowed this inscription:

> *Qui mare, qui fluctus, ventos, navesque gubernat,*
> *Sospitet hanc arcem, Carole magne, tuum.*

Or:

> May He who governs the tides and the winds and the ships guard this vessel, Oh great Charles!

When, finally, in spite of this and other appeals for divine protection, the great king's power was conclusively eclipsed, orders were given by his conquerors that all the royal ships should be stripped of their enrichments and painted 'sad colour'. But the people of Britain had come to love the exotic embellishments of the *Sovereign of the Seas*, to the payments for which they had previously so strongly objected, and they refused to allow them to be destroyed. The glories of the ship were only dimmed by mis-chance, in a stupendous blaze that lit up the River Medway in 1696. The *Sovereign* had been sent there to be re-built – a fairly common proceeding, in the days of hit-or-miss naval architecture – when a candle was overturned, through the negligence of the ship's temporary keepers, and Pett's masterpiece was consumed as suddenly and completely as if it had been dry tinder.

The Commonwealth Government that ruled England after the overthrow of Charles was headed by a soldier, Oliver Cromwell, and many of his closest associates were military men. There is no doubt that these land-based officials would find extremely con-fusing the line drawings that had to be prepared, discussed, amended and finally approved before a ship's hull could be con-structed. Almost certainly, they would have seen the beautiful little models that Phineas Pett had made of his ships, and they would have realised how very much easier it is for a novice with little marine experience to approve a projected vessel if it has been constructed, first, in a small-scale, three-dimensional form.

So in 1649, the first year of the Commonwealth, the Lords of the

Admiralty, who, in the absence of a King, were responsible for the maritime policy of the nation, sent a letter to the Commissioners of the Navy, who were responsible for advising them on such matters as ship-building, victualling and stores, and for putting into effect their decisions. The letter referred to the building of five new ships of war. In it their Lordships required the members of the Navy Board to invite the master shipwrights concerned to submit their designs, specifying – as far as we know, for the very first time – that as a preliminary measure small scale models of the proposed vessels should be made and sent to the Admiralty.

At least seven of the twelve members of the Navy Board had to be, by the terms of its constitution, professional naval experts. These men realised at once that the new method of commissioning ships was made necessary by their new masters' inability to understand marine drawings and plans. However critical they may have felt of the men they had been appointed to guide, they were obliged

51 Rigged model of an English 56-gun ship of 1652 (period of Oliver Cromwell). This is a restoration of the original Admiralty model.

52 Left – The model of the Naseby *made by Mr Robert Spence, now in the National Maritime Museum, Greenwich.*

53 Below – A model of an English three-decker in the National Historical Maritime Museum, Stockholm, which provided information for Mr Spence's model of the Naseby.

to concur with the instructions they had received, and the dockyard models ordered then and during the next century and a half are among the most splendid examples of fine craftsmanship ever to be produced.

Unfortunately, time has not dealt kindly with the very first models prepared to meet the new Board's requirements. The beautiful rigged model of an unidentified 56-gun ship of 1652 now shown in the Museum of the United States Naval Academy at Annapolis was largely carried out by the skilful hands of the late Henry B. Culver. The original Admiralty Board model was so worm-eaten that it was no longer suitable for display. But most of the gilded carvings on this original model were in a very good state of preservation, so Mr Culver felt free to remove them so that he could incorporate them in his new, meticulously executed 'restoration'.

One of the most illustrious ships to be commissioned in England in the Commonwealth Period was the *Naseby* – best known, to many students of marine history not from a contemporary model, but from the model made by Mr Robert Spence that is on exhibition now in the National Maritime Museum at Greenwich. Mr Spence obtained from contemporary drawings of the ship, and from records of her dimensions, the information he needed for making this model, and he studied, too, the lines of a model of an English three-decker of the same period that is now in the National Historical Marine Museum in Stockholm. The latter model is believed to have been made by Francis Sheldon, an English shipwright who entered Swedish service in 1658. Sheldon would, therefore, have been thoroughly conversant with the methods practised in English shipyards immediately prior to that year.

The *Naseby* was built at Woolwich, on the Thames. In April 1655, the great diarist John Evelyn wrote of her:

> 'I went to see the great ship newly built by the usurper, Oliver, carrying ninety-six brass guns, and 1000 tons burthen. In the prow was Oliver on horseback, trampling six nations underfoot, a Scot, Irishman, Dutchman, Frenchman, Spaniard and English, as was easily made out by their several habits. A Fame held a laurel over his insulting head; the word, God with us.'

In 1659, the *Naseby* was the flagship of the English Commander Edward Montagu in Danish waters, and in 1660 she led the Restoration Fleet that went to fetch Charles the Second home from Holland. On that memorable journey, Montagu had a young kinsman in his service – Samuel Pepys, who was to be, later, Secretary of the Admiralty Board, and, in that capacity, was to be

54 *Another view of Mr Spence's model of the* Naseby.

responsible for commissioning some of the finest dockyard models that survive to this day. After she had carried the exiled king back to his own country, the *Naseby* was renamed the *Royal Charles,* partly in honour of the joyful mission she had just accomplished, but principally because her original name, commemorating one of the most tragic battles of the English Civil War, had particularly unhappy associations for the new Sovereign and his friends. But the *Royal Charles* was not to enjoy her new splendour for long, for, in 1667, the Dutch fleet under Admiral de Ruyter removed her by force from her moorings at Chatham, on the River Medway, and carried her off to Holland. She was broken up there in 1673. The English royal arms with which her stern was decorated are still preserved as a trophy in the Rijksmuseum at Amsterdam.

To show what a meeting of the Admiralty Board would have been like, during the reign of Charles the Second, the authorities of the Science Museum, South Kensington, London have had a special model made in the museum workshops, with figures by Miss B. M. Campbell. This model, which has been designed with a scale ratio of 1:6, shows a typical meeting of the board in the year 1677. The king, his uncle Prince Rupert, the Duke of Ormonde, and the Secretary of State are discussing, with the help of a scale

55 A meeting of Charles the Second and his Admiralty Board as shown in the model in the Science Museum, London.

model, the first establishment of standard dimensions for warships to be built for the English Royal Navy. (Properly, this little vessel could be called a model within a model.) Two members of the Navy Board – Sir Anthony Deane and Sir John Tippetts, both master shipwrights – are present to advise on questions of construction. Samuel Pepys, in his capacity as Secretary to the Admiralty Board, is busily taking notes.

During most of his active career, Pepys is known to have been a keen connoisseur of ship models. There are many passages in his diaries in which he refers to them, a typical entry being dated 30 July, 1662:

> 'Up early and to my office where Cooper came to see me and began his lecture upon the body of a ship which my having a model in the office is of great use to me and very pleasant and useful it is'.

The earliest models for the English Admiralty Board tend to look to the uninformed observer as though they are a little unfinished, as their hulls are left unplanked, and all the framing is open to inspection. In the models for the board after the year 1670, and during the whole of the next half century, the sides were planked above the lower wales, only those parts of the hulls that would normally be under water being left 'in frame'.

Apart from that, the early models made for submission to commissioning boards were, normally, exact representations of the ships that the designers intended should materialize eventually from their plans. In two other significant respects only were these models less than complete – they were rarely rigged, and their framing was not made in the same way as the framing of the real, full-size vessel would have been made. Instead, it was set up according to a conventional formula evolved by the model-makers.

There was another less easily distinguishable difference. In all sizeable real-life vessels at that time, the frames had to be fabricated from a number of different pieces of wood, joined or 'scarfed' together, since there were not available sufficient pieces of timber, large enough to be used alone, to satisfy the demand. When a model was being made, this problem did not arise – for any fairly typical model ship of the period, it would have been possible to shape an entire frame from a piece of wood the size of a chair seat. So, most model-makers were content to compromise. They did not make their frames from a single piece of wood, but they did build them up by uniting just a few separate pieces – representing, usually, the top-timbers, the futtocks and the floors.

The urge to collect models of ships and boats seems to have been felt quite strongly by certain connoisseurs in the second half of the seventeenth century. John Evelyn records being shown, in 1663, the models of another distinguished member of the Pett family – a later Phineas, who was Comptroller of the Stores and Resident Commissioner at Chatham Dockyard. When four years later the Dutch raided the English moorings on the Medway, this Pett seems to have considered himself justified in sacrificing everything else to ensure the safety of his models, a fact that shows how much these models were then valued and cared for. Samuel Pepys, we known, managed during his time with the Admiralty Board to amass a considerable collection, which he bequeathed in his will to his friend William Hewer, once Treasurer of Tangier, with the expressed hope that his ships, united with Hewer's own collection might be 'preserved for publick benefit'.

Among the models Hewer received from Pepys' executors, there may well have been a model of the 66-gun ship *Rupert*, referred to in Pepys' Diary on 19 May, 1666:

> '. . . Mr. Deane and I did discourse about his ship 'Rupert', built by him there, which succeeds so well as he hath got great honour by it, and I some by recommending him; the King, Duke and everybody, saying it is the best ship that was ever built . . .'

56 Above – A rigged Admiralty model of the Grafton, *an English 70-gun ship built at Woolwich in 1679. She took part in the evacuation of Tangier in 1683–4.*

57 Right – The stern of the model of the Grafton, *now in the United States Naval Academy Museum.*

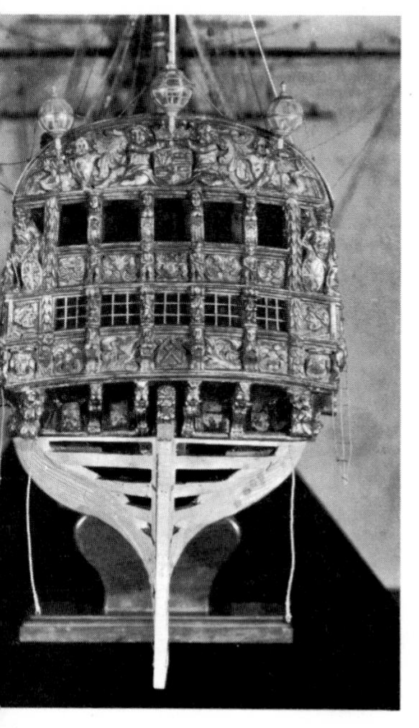

Probably, too, Hewer would have received the splendid boxwood model of the 70-gun ship *Grafton*, now in the Museum of the United States Naval Academy at Annapolis. The *Grafton* was Admiral Lord Dartmouth's flagship in the expedition of seventeen vessels sent to dismantle the pier and evacuate Tangier in 1683–84. Pepys went on this expedition having been requested to do so by Charles the Second, in order that he might act as a 'wise counselor'.

Before they had had much chance to be of any real 'publick benefit', Pepys', Hewer's and Pett's collections appear to have been dispersed. Only the magnificent collection stored for nearly two centuries in the great mansion at Cuckfield Park, in the south of England, seems to have survived in a reasonably intact, though intermittently neglected state. Fifteen of the finest and most famous of the Admiralty Board scale ship models from this collection were purchased from the owners by Colonel Henry Huddleston Rogers (1879–1935), the prominent American capitalist and railroad executive shortly after the end of the First World War, and transported to his estate, Port of Missing Men, at Southampton, Long Island, New York. On his death, they passed

58 Above left – The model of the English 96-gun ship St George *which is one of the treasures of the Henry Huddlestone Rogers Collection. This is the only model in the collection, the complete rigging of which is contemporary.*

The unrigged Admiralty model of the English 100-gun ship Britannia. *59 Left – Broadside view ; (60) Above, right – The fine carvings on the stern ; (61) Right – A view of the prow with the figure head of a gilded equestrian trampling over prone figures.*

by his wish to the Museum of the United States Naval Academy at Annapolis, where they are now among that establishment's most dearly cherished possessions.

The models in the Cuckfield Park collection have been traditionally associated with the name of Samuel Pepys, but although they are all of the greatest interest and value there is little doubt that they are mostly of a later date than Pepys' connection with the Admiralty. There is not much direct evidence that has helped anyone to establish the past history of these models, but scholars, noticing their position in the Cuckfield mansion – that is, in close association with a library of handsome volumes, housed in the original bookcases – ascribed their arrival there to the end of the seventeenth and the beginning of the eighteenth centuries. At that time a Charles Sergison (to whom Cuckfield belonged) was Clerk of the Acts. Sergison succeeded James Sotherne, who was appointed Secretary of the Admiralty in 1690, and he continued to hold this office until 1719. Sergison and Pepys would naturally have been at least acquaintances, and, more probably, friends – both holding, as they did, the same important office at different times. When the younger man started to collect model ships – probably, like Pepys, regarding the chance to acquire them as one of the nicer perquisites of his office – what could have been more likely than that Pepys would have helped him, with fatherly advice? Remembering Pepys' particular interest in the subject, and his own treasured models, we can be reasonably sure that this happened.

'Intermittently neglected', we have said of the Sergison models. A Commander Robinson, who visited Cuckfield Park in 1910, found some of the models relegated to a lumber room. Among these was a model of a barge with its crew – evidently, a barge such as Samuel Pepys would have used, in his capacity as Secretary to the Admiralty Board. The crew of the barge were dressed like the watermen in Francis Sandford's illustrated account of the funeral of the Duke of Albemarle in 1670, except that they were not wearing their doublets, but were in their shirts. The coxswain, who was 'much dilapidated', had on a jacket with a full skirt. 'But the figures appear to have been repainted', wrote Commander Robinson rather tartly afterwards, 'a little soap and water might reveal further distinctive marks'.

The early years of this century saw a revival of interest in the Admiralty Board models that had been (except for those at Cuckfield Park) so widely dispersed. When some of the models that had been acquired over a period of years by Captain Hoare, founder of the Training Ship *Mercury*, were shown at the Naval Exhibition at Earl's Court, in London, in 1905, this interest increased, and gradually there started to drift back into various museums an assortment of nameless hulls, many of which were thought – usually, without much concrete evidence – to have been, originally, in one of the great disbanded collections. After the death of Captain Hoare, even the origins of the 'Mercury' models were found to be largely mysterious. 'Unfortunately', wrote 'G.R.' in the *Mariners' Mirror*, the journal of the Society for Nautical Research, 'nothing is known of the history of the models, but an attempt is being made to find Mr. Baker, an elderly naval man, who in the late Mr. Hoare's time had the models under his immediate care, and it is hoped he will be able to give some information'.

The task of identifying a model ship of which neither the name nor the past history is known can be extremely difficult. There are so many possible alternatives. (Sutherland, writing in 1711, recommended the making of a model of every ship before building, and in 1716 there was a definite Admiralty order that models should be made of all ships, whether entirely new or re-built. Sometimes, to confuse matters even further, a model may represent a proposal that was never put into effect.) But experts do often manage to establish a model's provenance, simply by the light of the evidence that the model itself affords.

The rigging, if it is present, can never be properly relied on. Even when a great part of the original rigging has been preserved, restoration will probably have been attempted at some time or another on a greater or lesser scale, and anachronisms will, almost inevitably, have crept in. The splendid pearwood Admiralty Board model of the 96-gun ship *St. George* is the only one of the Cuckfield Park ships now at Annapolis that still has a completely contemporary rigging. The rigging of all the others has been restored, to a more or less marked degree, at some stage in their history.

The distribution of a ship's gun ports is not much more reliable as a source of information. In the seventeenth and eighteenth centuries, ships' armaments were often changed from time to time, and ports were frequently added merely for ornament or convenience. So this factor can be used only as a very approximate guide to the size of the ship represented, or as a rough check on an identification established by one of the other, less disputable, methods.

Of these, a reference to the measurements, where known, of the probable prototype is undoubtedly the safest. Manuscript lists of ships have existed from early times, but the first systematic publication of lists of the ships in the English navy appears to have begun in the stormy years that preceded the Commonwealth, when the possession of the fleet was becoming all-important to the King's opponents.

By the reign of William and Mary at the end of the seventeenth century, the composition of the fleet was being documented in some detail. The first full list appeared as a small pamphlet of fourteen pages, measuring 7½ inches by 5½ inches, and entitled 'Gloria

62 Top – A contemporary model of the Mordaunt. *The ship was built at Deptford in 1681.*

63 Centre – A profusely carved model of an English 96-gun ship dating from about 1703.

64 Left – Part of a model of a 60-gun ship. The style of the decoration shows the fashionable Chinese influence. The roundhouses, or men's latrines are visible. The officers' privies were inside the bows. The chaplain of the ship was made to use the men's accommodation and a mournful poem 'The Chaplain's Lament' tells how he wished to be classed as an officer in this respect.

Britannica, or the Boast of the British Seas, containing a true and full account of the Royal Navy of England, showing where each ship was built, by whom and when, its length, breadth, depth, draught of water, tuns, the number of men and guns both in peace and war at home and abroad; together with every man's pay from a Captain to a Cabin boy . . . Carefully collected and digested by a True Lover of the Seamen and of long experience in the practices of the Navy and Admiralty. London 1698'. Its price was one shilling. After 1698, Navy Lists are comprehensive and fairly accessible.

Where the identity of a model is not known at all, so that the comparison of its dimensions with those of the many vessels in the published lists is likely to be an unprofitable exercise, a close study of its decorations is called for.

These may provide some fairly obvious clues at a glance. To take a relatively straightforward example, the exceptional richness of the carvings on the unrigged pearwood model of the 100-gun ship *Britannia*, now in the Museum of the United States Naval Academy at Annapolis indicates a lavish commissioning. The stern transoms are crowded with high-relief figures of warriors, fighting on horseback. Prone figures being trampled under the feet of their steeds represent, as a bit of wishful thinking, Britain's unfortunate enemies. Other parts of the hull are just as fancifully encrusted. Such profusion would suggest at once, to the trained eye, that the model is of a ship built before the Order of 1703 which imposed severe limitations on such embellishments. (There is, in this instance, a carved riband at the break of the poop that does bear the ship's name – *BRITANIA* – spelt there with only one *N*, perhaps for reasons of symmetry. This confirms that the model is of the ship built at Chatham, England, in or about the year 1700. This inscription could just as easily not have been there, however.)

Sometimes the information yielded by a ship's decorations may be as specific as that provided by the name on the riband, only, it may need a little more careful interpretation. For instance, the character of the Royal Arms or monograms may help considerably. Also in the Museum of the United States Naval Academy at Annapolis, there is an unrigged Admiralty Board model, made of boxwood, that shows an English third-rate 80-gun ship. Which ship it is, has never been positively decided, but it has been possible to date this model very closely, entirely by means of its decorations. Carved on the taffrail, there is a full-length figure of William the Third of England, surrounded by cupidons and stacks of arms. There is also on this model the royal cipher RWMR – standing, approximately, for William Rex and Mary Regina. The reign of William and Mary began in 1689, and Mary's death occured in 1694. The ship, therefore, is likely to have been built between these two dates.

Sometimes, a heraldic device other than the royal arms or a cipher on a model ship may simplify the task of identification. To take an example, the model of the 46/48-gun ship *Mordaunt*, once in Captain Hoare's *Mercury* collection, and now in the British National Maritime Museum at Greenwich, could be identified with some certainty by means of the coat-of-arms at the break of the poop – 'a chevron between three estoiles' (stars with wavy rays) – which is that of the Mordaunt family. This identification could be confirmed by reference to the known dimensions of the ship, and it showed that the model was of a vessel with a particularly romantic history.

The *Mordaunt* was built by Castle, of Deptford near London, in 1681, for a syndicate in which Lord Mordaunt was the principal shareholder. On the failure of his associates to fulfil their obligations, Lord Mordaunt became the sole owner. Unfortunately for him, people in high places began to suspect that so powerful a ship could hardly be intended merely for trading purposes, and the Spanish Ambassador to the Court of St James complained that he had reason to believe that she was to have a commission from the Elector of Brandenburg, who was then employing his new fleet in an attempt to collect a disputed debt from Spain by forcible means.

So, on 30 June 1681, a warrant was issued for the arrest of the ship, and in July of that year Lord Mordaunt came up for examination. In his defence, his lordship stated that the vessel was merely intended to be 'independent of convoy by man-of-war', and he offered to fix her armament and crew at any figure agreeable to the court. He was, however, obliged in the end to give a substantial bail for her good behaviour.

This was not the only legal difficulty associated with the ship. Two years later, she was arrested, on account of the non-payment by Lord Mordaunt of the crew's wages. At the same time, a warrant was issued for the receipt of the ship into the Royal Navy. She remained in the king's service until she was lost with all hands, off Cuba, on 21 November 1693.

From Stuart days, the ships of the British fleet were divided into rates according to the number of guns they carried. In the original assessment, a first-rate ship had over 90 guns, a second-rate ship over 80, and a third-rate ship over 50. Ships in these three rates were considered to be fast and powerful enough to fight in a line in a naval engagement, and were, therefore, called 'ships of the line.' Smaller and less powerfully armed ships were alloted to the fourth, fifth and sixth rates.

The dimensions of the ships, and the pay of the officers and men who were to serve on them were fixed periodically, according to their rates, by a series of 'establishments'. Dockyard models that represent ships from each of these establishments can be studied

65 *Above – The* Royal William *(100 guns) shown in a contemporary model in the National Maritime Museum, Greenwich.*

66 *Right – Another contemporary model of the* Royal William *in the same museum.*

in the comprehensive displays in the National Maritime Museum at Greenwich. Among the dockyard models of exceptional interest on view there is a model of a ship of 96 guns of about 1703. On the quarter-deck of this model, there is a windlass with ropes running to the tiller, much as those from a steering-wheel would do. The authorities of the museums have suggested that this may well have been an experimental fitting that led, soon afterwards, to the first introduction – in English ships at least – of the wheel. Other novel features on the same model are the two circular enclosures, decorated with carved and gilded pilasters, on the beakhead bulkheads. These are latrines, or 'round-houses', commemorated so lustily in the old sea shanty question:

What shall we do with the drunken sailor?

with the unforgettable and entirely practical answer found in one bawdy version:

'Put him in the round-house till he's sober . . . .

The museum authorities believe that the appearance of this accommodation on this model and on another model of approximately the same date may provide reliable contemporary evidence of yet another small advance in naval architecture.

In the reign of Louis the Thirteenth, the French monarchy became, under the influence of Cardinal Richelieu, more powerful than it had ever been before. One of the most memorable ships to be commissioned in France during this period – *La Couronne* – was built in 1638, the year after Charles the First's *Sovereign of the Seas*, and was intended as an answer to the English king's vainglory. Unfortunately, no contemporary model of *La Couronne* exists. There is only a very splendid modern reconstruction, made in the workshops of the Musée de la Marine at Paris.

After the rise to power of Jean-Baptiste Colbert, who became Secretary of State for the French Navy in 1668, it became customary for exact ship models to be made, for preservation in the French dockyards. In his attempts to revive the power of France at sea, Colbert formed two formidable fighting fleets – an Atlantic fleet, composed mainly of sailing ships, and a Mediterranean fleet, which was made up chiefly of galleys. As Colbert wanted the French ships of the line to have a handsome appearance, in order to impose all foreigners, he engaged prominent artists, such as Pierre Puget, to decorate them. He had no scruples about compelling people to row in the galleys – under his relentless direction, criminals, political offenders, Protestants and slaves seized from Africa and Canada were chained indiscriminately to the benches and lashed.

The richly carved and gilded stern of a contemporary dockyard model of the Prince, *1670.*

Overleaf, a reproduction of the painting 'A New Whip for the Dutch' by J. Seymour Lucas.

LE
LOVIS
QVINZE

It is sometimes possible to assess, by counting the number of official models of it that still survive, the importance attached, during its period of service, to some particular ship that has long since vanished. For instance, there are at least six known dockyard models of the English *Royal William* in existence today, which would indicate that it was a ship of some significance, even if its history had not been fully and accurately chronicled. As it is, we know enough of the story of the *Royal William* to be able to understand the comparative profusion of contemporary scale models of it.

The ship, of 100 guns, was launched at Portsmouth in 1719. It was the third in a line of notable ships, having been rebuilt from an older vessel of the same name. (Rebuilding, the measure referred to earlier, was an economical process that consisted of pulling an out-moded or not wholly successful ship to pieces, the shipwrights then building into a new vessel as much of the old vessel as could possibly be used.) The original *Royal William*, in its turn, had been rebuilt in 1692 from a ship named the *Prince* that had been launched in 1670.

The hull of the *Royal William* was built, principally, of winter-felled timber, the timbers being prepared by being charred with fire. It was remarkable for its sound condition, sustained for nearly a hundred years after the 1719 rebuilding. In the first volume of *The Naval Chronicle*, published in 1799, we read:

> 'This venerable ship should have been broken up long since, but for the particular request of the King. Its timbers are so hard, as almost to resist the impression of any tools. It has long been known among the sailors by the term THE OLD BILLY.'

During its long period of active service, the *Royal William* carried General Wolfe's body back to Britain after the General was killed at the siege of Quebec in 1759, took part in the relief of Gibraltar in 1782, and attended the attempts to raise the hull of the 100-gun ship *Royal George*, which capsized unexpectedly, with a loss of some nine hundred lives, including that of Rear Admiral Kempenfelt, at Spithead in the same year. After that, the *Royal William* became the guardship at Portsmouth. After some years there, the old ship was popularly supposed to be in danger of grounding on the great mass of beef bones that had been thrown overboard. The *Royal William* was not finally broken up until 1813.

There is a splendid dockyard model of the *Royal George* made of pearwood, with a natural finish, in the Henry Huddleston Rogers collection at the Museum of the United States Naval Academy at Annapolis. The stern decoration of this model, showing a bust of George the Second flanked by reclining female figures, is particularly admired. The model was originally owned by either the

The stern of a model in the Musée de la Marine, Paris, of the Louis Quinze *(1692), the magnificent flagship of Louis XV's navy.*

67 Left – The richly-carved figure head on one of the models of the Royal William *at Greenwich.*

second or the third Earl of Sandwich, passing at a later date into the collection of J. Seymour Lucas, the English artist who made model ships – and, especially, the finer Admiralty Board models – the principal subjects of so many of his paintings. Seymour Lucas loved that model so dearly that he refused to part with it during his lifetime. Colonel Henry Huddleston Rogers loved it dearly too, and he was willing to pay dearly for his love. But Henry Huddleston Rogers, greatest collector of model ships in the whole world as he was, had to *wait*.

68 Right – More rich carving. The stern of a rigged model of a British 90-gun ship similar to the Royal George *of 1715.*

69 Below – Part of a model at Greenwich of the Royal George. *One side of this model has been left unplanked to show details of the construction.*

4 The Great Days of Sail

The sailing ship, it has been said, is the most beautiful thing man has made. If that is so, models of the finest sailing ships must compress into a very small compass some of the most splendid design and workmanship there has ever been.

Impressive as many of the men-of-war described in Chapter 3 were, none of them attained the supreme elegance of the fast trading vessels and some of the finest ships built for pleasure during the great days of sail. That is understandable – they were built for power, rather than manoeuvrability, and for strength, rather than speed. In this chapter, then, models of ships built for naval purposes will be matched with models of swifter sailing craft and models that show the sail-propelled merchantman in a few of the stages through which it passed as it developed from the sturdy old carrack of the late fifteenth century into the competitive tea clipper of the nineteenth century – the most admired sea-going craft, possibly, in the history of the world.

We know, more or less, what carracks looked like, because they are shown in several paintings by Carpaccio, and in various drawings, engravings and woodcuts made by other artists when trading vessels of the type were to be seen round most of the coasts of western Europe. The rigged model carrack made in the workshops of the Science Museum at South Kensington, London, was based on a detailed contemporary print, labelled 'kraeck', by the Flemish master 'W.A.' It has a carvel-built hull strengthened and protected by four 'wales', or longitudinal reinforcing members, on each side. The lofty, over-hanging forecastle has two decks, and is covered by an awning. On the round stern, there is a small open gallery with, at either side, a little box-like convenience. At the end of the bowsprit there is a four-fold fishhook-like device known as a 'grapnel'. The carrack, though a merchantman, had, owing to the perilous nature of those times (the late fifteenth century), to be suitably armed. The grapnel was dropped on to any hostile ship that needed to be closely engaged.

70 A fine model of the royal schooner Amphion *designed for Gustav the Third of Sweden by Fredrik Henrik af Chapman.*

During the seventeenth century, several great trading enterprises were formed to send fast merchantmen from Europe to the most distant territories. These vessels – given such designations, usually,

74 Above – A model of the schooner yacht America *(1851), now in the National Maritime Museum, Greenwich.*

as East Indiamen, West Indiamen, Levanters and Guineamen – were designed and constructed more carefully and at much greater expense than most of the craft that were not intended to travel so far. Of them all, the East Indiamen – commissioned by the British, Dutch, French and Swedish East India Companies – were generally acknowledged to be in a class by themselves.

Before they took their final form as small, broad, roomy ships, the East Indiamen intended for trade were constructed in a variety of shapes and sizes. It is said that the size of the majority of them was settled eventually at 499 tons, and that this can be explained by the regulations which laid down that ships of 500 tons and over were bound to carry a chaplain – an obligation that the directors of the companies concerned regarded as an unnecessary expense.

The East Indiamen, like the carracks before them, were armed. They had highly trained crews who were able to fight fiercely for the protection of the ships' valuable cargoes, and were often compelled to. The *D'Bataviase Eeuw*, launched in 1719, was intended to commemorate the centenary of the founding of the Dutch East India Company's eastern capital, Batavia. A superb contemporary model of this ship is one of the most valued possessions of the Royal Scottish Museum at Edinburgh. It is interesting to compare this model with the model now in the Maritime Museum at Gothenburg of a rival vessel of a different – and, some would claim, an even more satisfactory – type: a Swedish East Indiaman, launched in 1750.

A schooner is usually defined as being a two-masted ship, with predominantly fore-and-aft sail, and having the after-mast no shorter than the fore-mast. Small pleasure craft that conformed to this description were seen on Dutch inland waters during the seventeenth century, and a few examples of vessels rigged in this way were recorded in England at the beginning of the eighteenth century.

The first proper schooner is, however, popularly supposed to have been built in Gloucester, Massachusetts, in 1713. (The traditional story tells of the shipbuilder named Andrew Robinson of that town. When he was launching the first vessel of the type, a woman, admiring her progress, said 'Look how she schoons!' meaning, 'Look how she skims over the water!' Robinson, overhearing, retorted, 'A schooner let her be!' A picturesque tale, even if it cannot be guaranteed to be authentic.) The fore- and aft-rig proved to be particularly suitable for coastal work in varying wind conditions, and by the middle of the century schooners were operating along every part of the eastern seaboard of North America, from the Gulf of St. Lawrence to the West Indies.

By the end of the century, schooners were being built, in various

71 Above, left – An interesting view of a model of a fifteenth century Flemish carrack showing the deck plan.

72 Far left – A model, now in the Maritiem Museum 'Prins Hendrik' at Rotterdam, of the warship Veenlust, *c. 1750.*

73 Left – A model of a Dutch East Indiaman (c. 1740) now in the Nederlandsch Historisch Sheepvaart Museum.

75 A model of a 28-gun frigate, c. 1785. The model may represent one of the last ships of this class – the Ariel, *built at Dover.*

forms, in practically every maritime country, and some were adapted for naval use. Some of the earlier schooners were rigged with square topsails and running sails, in addition to their fore-and-aft sails, in which case they were usually referred to as 'brigantines'.

In his great work *Architectura Navalis Mercatoria*, the Swedish master shipwright, Frederik Henrik af Chapman described the sea-going merchantmen that were encountered most frequently at that time in the waters of northern Europe. One of the principal groups he classified as 'frigates' – a word that had been applied to very small, swift, lightly armed craft as early as the beginning of the seventeenth century. In Chapman's time the name was also applied to the small warships that were designed especially for scouting and convoy duties, and for sudden attacks on enemy traders. Between 1777 and 1785 some thirty 28-gun frigates were built for the British Navy. There is a model in the Science Museum at South Kensing-

76 Life on board a fighting ship is graphically represented by this model which shows two gun crews on board the frigate Josephine.

ton, London, that is thought to represent the *Ariel*, built at Dover in 1785, and, therefore, one of the latest of the class.

In the last years of the eighteenth century, three frigates were laid down in the United States that were by a fairly comfortable margin the largest ever built, and, in the opinion of many, the finest. Needless to say, countless models have been made of all three of them. The *United States* and the *Constitution* were launched in 1797. The *President* (which, later, was to be captured by the English) was launched in 1800. The *Constitution* – known irreverently, sometimes, as 'Old Ironsides' – fought a notable engagement with the British ship *Guerriere* in 1812. After that, she served for a considerable time on the Barbary Coast, playing a distinguished part in the suppression of piracy in that part of the world. She can still be seen today – she has been preserved and given a home in the naval dockyards at Boston, Massachusetts. With her graceful hull lines and elegant rigging she makes a beautiful model. The Marine

77 *A model of the frigate* Constitution *now in the Peabody Museum, Salem, Mass.*

Model Company Inc., of Halesite, Long Island, New York offer a complete custom set, with more than nine hundred metal and wooden parts, that enables the home modeller to make a splendid replica of this splendid ship which still lies quietly afloat, the ensign flying proudly from her peak.

Some of the most delightful models of sailing ships that have ever been made are the best of those produced by the Frenchmen – and men of other nationalities – captured by the British and held as prisoners-of-war during the long struggle against Napoleon Bonaparte. Many of these models are still in private hands and fetch large sums when they appear in the salerooms.

At first the prisoners were confined in hulks moored in Portsmouth and other harbours. These floating prisons had originally been large ships-of-the-line. Each vessel, after it had been cleared between decks, held approximately 900 men, this total including both the prisoners and the men given the duty of guarding them.

Then, as the British forces became increasingly victorious, both on the continent of Europe and on the high seas, the number of prisoners that needed to be accommodated increased until there was no longer sufficient space to hold them, even though the hulks were packed with men unmercifully. A report in the *Bristol Mirror* of 13 July, 1805, stated that Mr. (later, Sir Thomas) Tyrwhitt, Lord Warden of the Stannaries, had 'suggested to the Government the propriety of erecting a building . . . . for the deposit of such prisoners of war as may be brought to Plymouth, who can without difficulty be conveyed up the River Tamar and landed within a few miles from the spot. It is said that this plan will be acted upon forthwith, and the barracks built for the reception of a proportionate number of troops'. The Lord Warden's suggestion was favourably received, and the depot was opened to receive prisoners in 1809, the first batch of 2,500 arriving on 24 May. The following month, a further 2,500 arrived. Other prisons were opened ashore, the largest and best known being the establishment at Porchester Castle at the head of Portsmouth harbour.

As they settled in, the French prisoners divided themselves

78 A half model of the United States 44-gun frigate President *(1800).*

noticeably into self-contained groups. Although all had been fighting together under the banner 'Liberty, Equality and Fraternity', the richer and better educated quickly segregated themselves, and were happy to be known as 'les Lords'. Other groups a little lower in the social scale were known as 'Les Laborieux', 'Les Indifferents', and 'Les Minables.' Rejected utterly by their worthier fellows, 'Les Kaiserlies' and 'Les Romans' led an abandoned and degenerate existence, gambling incessantly and parting even with their meagre food and clothing to satisfy their craving for this excitement.

Fortunately for those people who like ship models, the prisoners were allowed to sell anything they could manage to produce in their confined quarters, and were encouraged to augment their sparse rations with any money they were able to earn by their enterprise. As might have been expected, the tradesmen in the neighbouring districts, sensing competition, objected strongly when the prisoners – principally 'Les Laborieux', who consisted in the main of mechanics, carpenters, carvers and jewellers – started to make and sell useful objects that were also manufactured locally, such as shoes and straw hats. So, the prisoners had to fall back on the manufacture of toys and models, specializing in those that relied largely for their effect on intricate workmanship, and finding the production of model ships to be, in every respect, the most rewarding way of getting through their enforced leisure.

Best known of all the ship models made by the French prisoners-of-war are those of bone – the raw material for these, it has been alleged, came from the beef bones left on the prisoners' platters. Other models, many of them more minutely detailed than the little bone vessels, were made from ivory, whalebone, and boxwood and copper. Some very small models were even made from wood chips and shavings.

The standards of craftsmanship attained by the prisoners ranged from masterly to barely adequate. Some of the bone models were relatively crude, with clumsily drawn planking, and details that were wildly out of scale. The best models were usually given a large amount of the most exquisite carving, and a great deal of rigging, both standing and running, and many of the models were provided with sails. There was a steady demand for model warships of all

79 Below – A fine French prisoner-of-war model made of wood.

Two fine bone models made by French prisoners-of-war: Above, right (80) – a model from the United States Naval Academy Museum, and below, right (81) – a model from the National Maritime Museum, Greenwich.

classes, the three-deckers being particularly easily sold. When the little industry started to thrive, the prisoners began to work together in teams so that they could speed up, and increase, the production of their wares.

Exquisite as many of the prisoner-of-war models are, they can never be safely regarded as completely accurate representations of particular, identifiable ships. One factor alone shows that they were not intended to fulfil such a purpose – invariably, they are predominantly French in appearance, though they carry English flags, and have been given the names of English ships, or, in a few cases, the names of prizes captured from the French. The prisoners' patriotism, it is clear, yielded to the demands of the market.

With the end of the Napoleonic Wars, the demand increased for large, swift merchantmen. Both Britain and the United States were free to increase their trade, and with the ending of the East India Company's monopoly in 1833, the sea routes to the East were thrown open, for commercial purposes, to private firms. Fortunes were to be made by the fastest movers.

82 Left – A waterline model made in 1955 of the American clipper ship Flying Cloud *(1851). Much information used in the construction of this model was provided by Mr T. Fitzpatrick Jr.*

83 Below, left – A rigged model of the seven-masted schooner Thomas W. Lawson.

84 Below – A fine model of the clipper ship Cutty Sark *now in the Science Museum, London.*

The exact origins of the famous clipper ships that were produced to satisfy this demand have been debated at great length, without any clear conclusions being reached. Most authorities believe that they evolved gradually from the brigs and schooners built at Baltimore, Maryland, during the eighteenth century, which had long been famous for their speed. Some say that the little *Ann McKim*, built in Baltimore in 1832, has the distinction of being the

first true clipper ship. Others would nominate the schooner *Scottish Maid*, built in 1839 to sail between London and Aberdeen. But the first ship that can really be called a clipper without any possibility of argument was the *Rainbow*, built by John W. Griffiths, and launched at New York in 1845.

The speeds attained by the clipper ships were remarkable. Among the fastest of all were the American *Flying Cloud* (launched in 1851) which travelled from New York to San Francisco, via Cape Horn, in 89 days; and the *Lightning*, launched in 1854. The *Lightning* was the first of four large clipper ships built by Donald McKay of Boston, Massachusetts, for James Baines of Liverpool, her sisters being the *Sovereign of the Seas*, the *James Baines*, and the *Donald McKay*. On her passage to Liverpool, she did a day's run of 436 miles, which was a record never beaten by a sailing ship; she also set up an unbroken record of 64 days for her first return voyage from Melbourne to Liverpool. Unfortunately she was destroyed by fire in the harbour at Geelong, near Melbourne, in 1869.

The clipper ship that has exercised more influence on model-makers than any others in recent years is undoubtedly the *Cutty Sark*, for the simple reason that this ship still exists today – it is preserved in a dry dock at Greenwich – and there it can be studied and measured. The firms that built most of the other clippers have disappeared, and their drawings and records have been destroyed.

The *Cutty Sark* came into being in romantic circumstances. In Britain in 1869 shipbuilding was not yet confined to large public companies and nationalized undertakings. There were many individuals who owned and managed their own ships and took a great pride in their vessels' achievements. The greatest ambition of many of these men was to win the annual 'tea race'. (In the China tea trade competition was keen and the first shipments of the new season's tea crop to reach London fetched greatly enhanced prices and brought much personal prestige to the shipper.) One of these men, John Willis, was a bachelor and very rich. He commissioned a young designer called Hercules Linton to make him a ship that would have embodied in it the cream of all clipper ship experience and would therefore outsail all its contemporaries. But, before the *Cutty Sark* had had a chance to establish its supremacy, the Suez Canal was opened, steam ships started to take over the China trade, and the 'tea race' rapidly became a thing of the past. The *Cutty Sark* was soon transferred to the Australian wool trade, where she served for some years as one of the fastest sailing ships in the world, outstripping, on occasion, some of the swift steamships that were intended to make her obsolete.

With such a record, it is hardly surprising that the *Cutty Sark* should have been chosen by the world-renowned Marine Model Company, Inc, of Halesite, Long Island, New York, as the subject

Above left, a model of an important early Scottish ship, the Great Michael, *1511.*

Above right, a contemporary model of the Dutch East Indiaman D'Bataviase Eeuw.

Below, a model in the Musée de la Marine, Paris, of L'Ocean, *an 118-gun ship of 1786 constructed to the plans of Sané.*

Overleaf, a model, specially built for Lord Montagu, of Buckler's Hard, Hampshire as it would have appeared in June 1803. H.M.S. Euryalus *is shown awaiting her launching.*

of one of its exquisitely worked out home-construction sets. (Each *Cutty Sark* set comprises a carved pine hull, tapered masts and spars, a set of fittings, rigging, and a mahogany baseboard with brass mounting pegs – over 840 metal and wood parts in all). Built to a scale of 3/32 inch to the foot, a model assembled from one of these kits occupies a space 27 inches long and 20½ inches high.

Another firm that features the *Cutty Sark* in its lists is Revell Inc, of Venice, California, U.S. A model of the *Cutty Sark* made from one of Revell's kits purchased for $12 by an Atlanta model builder was later bought from him by a bank in Jacksonville, U.S. The bank had adopted a clipper ship as its trade mark, and wanted an outstanding model for permanent lobby display. The price agreed was $2,000, which may well be a record for a plastic model.

While the clipper ships were racing over the world's oceans, schooners of widely differing types were being built to carry on the less urgent forms of trade. The largest of these, the *Thomas W. Lawson*, was the only seven-masted schooner ever built. Except, however, for the number of her masts and her great size, she was quite typical of the large schooners that had been employed for so long in the coastal trade of the Atlantic seaboard of North America.

The *Thomas W. Lawson* was built by the Fore River Shipbuilding Company at Quincy, Massachusetts, in 1902. The hull was of steel – it was 385 feet long and 50 feet wide – and the ship was fitted with three steel decks throughout her length. Each of the seven masts (known, respectively, as the fore, main, mizzen, spanker, jigger, driver and pusher) consisted of a steel lower mast, 135 feet long, above which was stepped a 58 feet pine top mast.

As in other large American schooners of that era, all the work of hoisting and trimming sail on the *Thomas W. Lawson* was done by means of steam power. Two large winches were fitted, and to these were led the halyards, topping lifts and sheets of the forward and after sails respectively. The lighter work, such as hoisting topsails, was dealt with by four smaller winches, placed amidships, which also served to hoist the ship's cargo. Owing to this very complete mechanical equipment, the *Thomas W. Lawson*, large as she was, required a crew of only sixteen men.

After a number of successful voyages between Texas and Philadelphia, the *Thomas W. Lawson* was chartered in 1907 for a voyage across the Atlantic. On the way, she encountered bad weather, and, finding herself in a dangerous position near the Scilly Islands, anchored in an attempt to ride out the storm. During the night of 13 December, however, she turned turtle. Only one member of her crew survived.

A model of Nelson's flagship Victory, *1765. Its rudder is made from a piece of oak from the actual ship.*

The first English royal yacht has a special significance in the history of shipping. She was built at Amsterdam for the Dutch East India Company, and was then bought by the Dutch Admiralty

Two models of royal yachts: left (85) – the Mary *(1660) and above (86) – a beautiful late Stuart example.*

for presentation to Charles the Second on his restoration to the English throne in 1660. She was named the *Mary* (the anglicized name of his mother, Henrietta Maria). When she arrived in England, this handsome vessel would have been classified by the Dutch term *jacht*, which had nothing to do with pleasure sailing, but meant a swift craft or hunter. Charles, however, coined the English word 'yacht' by changing the Dutch 'j' to a 'y'. By sailing the *Mary* up and down the Thames, and by introducing racing at Cowes, he may be said to have originated the sport that is popular now all over the world. There is a model of the *Mary* in the National Maritime Museum at Greenwich. It was made by F. C. P. Naish from two contemporary drawings of the *Mary*, and from the plans of a similar vessel given in Witens' book on Dutch shipbuilding which was completed in 1671.

The special skills developed by the men who operated the sailing vessels described in this chapter have not disappeared completely from the world of model ships and boats. In several countries, there are model yachting associations that co-ordinate the work of numerous smaller bodies. In Britain, for instance, the Model Yachting Association, established in 1911, has between forty and fifty clubs affiliated to it. Fourteen different countries – Australia, Belgium, Denmark, England, France, Germany, Holland, Italy, New Zealand, Northern Ireland, Norway, Scotland, South Africa, and the United States – are affiliated to the International Model Yacht Racing Union, which allows its various members to compete in the championships held by the other countries.

Model yachts intended for racing under official auspices have to be rated carefully in distinct classes that are recognized by the International Model Yacht Racing Union. The oldest of all these

87 Above – A model of the ocean-going yacht Optimist, *and (88) above right – a model of the sailing yacht* Gracia. *Both models can be radio controlled.*

classes is the 10-rater. Increasing steadily in popularity is the Marblehead class, which originated in the United States. Model yachts designed to conform to this rating must not exceed 50 inches in length, or have a sail area that exceeds 800 square inches. The class used principally in international events is known, usually, as the International A. Models in this category are built according to rigid rules. To qualify, they have to conform to this formula:

$$\frac{L+\sqrt{S}}{4}+\frac{L\times\sqrt{S}}{12\times\sqrt[3]{D}}=39{\cdot}37$$

L being the length of the yacht, S the sail area (in square inches), and D the displacement (in pounds). Boats are normally measured by a specially appointed club official and the full particulars are entered in a central register. New Certificates of Registration have to be obtained every two years – or more frequently than that, if any structural alterations are made to the yacht.

Competitive model yacht sailing of the official kind is regulated by certain clearly defined rules. In a typical meeting, the competitors will be attempting to gain as many points as possible – three points being awarded for success in a beat to windward, two points for a downwind run, and two points each way for a reach (that is, a run with the wind sideways on). Competitors usually sail off in pairs in each direction, and then change opponents, so that each boat, eventually, will have sailed against every other. The principal international awards include the Yachting Monthly Cup, given to the yacht with the highest score at an annual contest; the Wing and Wing Cup, given to the yacht that does the fastest run downwind; and the Johnny Johnson Cup, given to the boat that wins the most beats to windward.

5 Steamship Models

'The transition from sailing ships to power-driven ships was the most profound in thousands of years in maritime history', wrote the Duke of Edinburgh recently. 'Nothing like that revolution will ever be seen again.'

The basic thinking that made the great revolution possible was done over many centuries. As early as 264 BC, Appius Claudius Caudex was transporting his troops over the Straits of Messina in boats propelled by paddle wheels which were revolved by oxen yoked to capstans. Then, during the Rennaissance, the idea was revived, notably by William Bourne, an Englishman who published a theory for making 'a Boate to goe without oares or Sayle, by the placing of certaine wheels on the outside of the Boate'. The first person to suggest that the power needed to turn such wheels should be obtained by means of steam is believed to have been Denis Papin, a French engineer who actually built a rudimentary example in 1707. He is said to have navigated his ship on the River Fulda in Hanover. When he reached Munden, the local watermen were so incensed that they smashed the frightening new contraption to pieces and Papin had to flee for his life.

More experimental steam-propelled boats followed – there was for example, a little boat called the *Pyroscaphe* built by the Marquis Claude de Jouffoy d'Abbans in 1781, which successfully made a quarter of an hour's journey on the River Sâone near Lyons two years later – but none of these are likely to be of more than passing interest to many model-makers. The earliest steam-driven vessel to be of any real practical use – Lord Dundas' little *Charlotte Dundas* – has, however, been reproduced on a miniature scale many times, usually for educational purposes, and has strong claim to be the first vessel to be shown pictorially, in model form, in this chapter.

Lord Dundas had his steamship built in 1801 at Grangemouth, in Stirlingshire, Scotland. He intended her, with a similar boat, to pull barges along the Forth and Clyde Canal, replacing the horses that had been previously doing the work. The ship had a single paddle wheel, placed – not at the sides of the hull, as in many later vessels – but at the stern. This wheel was driven by the first hori-

89 A model, in the Musée de la Marine, Paris, of the 10,600 ton Hoche *(1880) with anti-torpedo nets.*

zontal direct-acting steam engine to be made in Britain. The engine was designed and constructed by William Symington, who had seen, first of anyone, how the piston engines developed by Thomas Newcomen and James Watt could be most practically adapted for ship propulsion. Symington's work could hardly have been more successful, for, in March 1802, the *Charlotte Dundas* towed two loaded vessels, each of 70 tons, for 19½ miles along the canal. The journey, made against a strong wind, took six hours. It caused much excitement, but it also alarmed the owners of the canal, who decided that the use of such vessels, with all their turbulence, would cause too much damage to their precious banks. So, the historic little *Charlotte Dundas* was laid up in a creek and allowed to rot away her remains being finally dismantled in 1861. Poor Symington was entrusted with no more work of any consequence, and died in penurious circumstances.

The honour of being the first man to operate a steamboat in a commercially successful way belongs, then, not to Lord Dundas, but to the energetic American, Robert Fulton.

Fulton was a brilliant and imaginative business-man, whose particular talents found their fullest expression when he was appraising the experimental work of other men and seeing how their ideas could be converted to practicable and profitable use. He is known to have been a friend of Robert Fitch, who had made a journey on the Delaware River in 1786 in a boat propelled by steam-driven vertical oars. Fulton is believed, too, to have been present at the trials of the *Charlotte Dundas*. He had his own first steamboat built at Paris, but when a storm broke as it lay ready for its trials this vessel went, with its hull broken, to the bottom of the Seine. Fulton had the boat salvaged, and he then had a new and stronger hull constructed, into which he fitted the machinery from the prototype that had sunk. Encouraged by the new boat's dramatically successful trials, Fulton returned to work in his native land.

It was Fulton's *Clermont* that really removed all doubts about the great future that lay ahead for the steamship. The *Clermont* was built in 1807. She was 133 feet long, with 18 feet beam, and had an engine built from parts supplied principally by Messrs. Boulton and Watt of Great Britain. When she steamed up the Hudson River from New York to Albany – a distance of 150 miles – in 32 hours she was starting a service that was to be imitated soon and for many years after that by other proprietors, with other vessels, on all the large navigable rivers of North America. The *Phoenix*, constructed in the following year for service on the Delaware River, qualified by the journey it had to make, first, from New York to Philadelphia for the distinction of being the first steamship to go to sea.

90 Above – A model of the stern wheel paddle steamer Charlotte Dundas.

91 Right – A model of the Comet, *the first steamboat to be commercially operated in Europe.*

The first passenger-carrying steamship to be operated in Europe was the *Comet*, built at Port Glasgow, on the River Clyde in Scotland, in the years 1811–1812. The ship was built for Henry Bell, a plain, uneducated but enterprising hotel owner, who had been a friend of Symington and Fulton. Bell put his little ship into regular service between Glasgow, Greenock and Helensburgh in August 1812 – thirteen years, that is, before any public steam railway service had been inaugurated anywhere in the world.

The *Comet* was driven by an inverted beam engine which developed 4 horse power, her best speed being 6·7 knots, which was two knots faster than the best speed achieved by the *Clermont*. Her steam was generated from a boiler set in brickwork. She had both a fore-castle and after cabin, the engine room taking up the space between them. She had, at first, two radial paddles on each side, but for these, at a later date, one pair of wheels was substituted. She was mastless – and this really was an innovation – though her strikingly high smoke stack was used, also, as an upright support from which sails could be set, enabling her to be advertised as being ready 'to sail by the power of air, wind and steam'. She was wrecked, in 1820, when she was on a journey between the Western Highlands and Glasgow. The excellent model of her in the Science Museum, South Kensington, London was made by a Mr T. Rennies from the drawings of the original vessel, which still exist.

The name was chosen to commemorate a comet that had recently blazed in the heavens. Her own career though brief was meteoric, and the influence she exerted on the development of the world's shipping was enormous. By 1818, a steamship service was in operation between Greenock (in Scotland) and Belfast (in Ireland); by 1820, the *Rob Roy* was operating regularly between Dover and Calais; in 1821 the first steamship corporation ever to be formed – the General Steam Navigation Company – began its activities with the steamship *City of Edinburgh*.

The *Charlotte Dundas*, the *Clermont* and the *Comet* were built of wood. The first steam vessel to be constructed of iron was the *Aaron Manby*, built in Staffordshire, Great Britain, in 1822 for service on the River Seine. Once made, the *Aaron Manby* was transported to London in sections and assembled at the Surrey Docks, Rotherhithe. From there, she crossed the Channel to Le Havre and remained in service on the rivers Seine and Loire until 1842.

The honour of being the first steamship to cross the Atlantic – or, indeed, any ocean – belongs to the *Savannah*. This was a vessel with a wooden, carvel-built hull that was laid down at Corlears Hook, New York, by Francis Fickett, and launched on 22 August, 1818. She had a raked curved stem and a plain square transom stern fitted with a narrow square-heeled rudder, and she carried three tall masts with a bowsprit that was steeved well upward. The accommodation on her was divided into two main saloons, and the state rooms were fitted with thirty-two berths. The intention was that as a fully-rigged ship she could join the sail packet service to Le Havre, France.

But this was not to be. Before she had been properly completed, she was purchased by the newly constituted Savannah Steam Ship Company, who proceeded to adapt her for auxiliary steam propulsion, installing an engine of 90 indicated horse power that had been constructed by Stephen Vail at the Speedwell Iron Works, near Morristown, New Jersey. The pipe that carried the smoke from this engine was fitted, at the top, with an elbow which could be turned, when necessary, to divert the sparks from the sails.

92 The American Savannah *became, in 1819, the first steamship to cross the Atlantic. The model shown is in the Science Museum, London.*

The paddle wheels driven by the engine were 15 feet 3 inches in diameter. Each wheel had ten radial arms that were held in position by a pair of chains near the outer ends, but these were made to be collapsible so that the wheels could be folded up like fans and

taken on deck when they were not needed. Ready for work, the wheels were capable of rotating at sixteen revolutions per minute, and would have propelled the vessel, if it had had to rely on steam power alone, at a speed of about four knots.

The *Savannah* underwent her trials during the month of March, 1819. Unfortunately for the enterprising owners, it was a time of acute trade depression, and they were virtually forced to send her to Europe for sale. So, the vessel left her home port on 24 May 1819, reaching Liverpool twenty-seven days and eleven hours later, having achieved a mean speed of approximately six knots. On this momentous journey, the *Savannah*'s paddle-wheels are said to have been used for a total of about eighty-five hours.

From Liverpool, the *Savannah* proceeded to St Petersburg (as Leningrad was called at that time), but she failed to find a buyer there. So, she was taken back to her home port under sail. In 1820 she was sold ingloriously at auction. Her engine was taken out and she was reduced to the status of a mere coastal packet, plying between Savannah and New York. Sadly she ran ashore at Long Island on 5 November 1821, and became a total wreck. Her historic achievement has been commemorated in various ways. For instance, a model of her was presented by the Newcomen Society in North America to the Science Museum in London, and is kept permanently on view there. And, the quarter inch scale model of the *Savannah* now in the Mariners' Museum at Newport News was used as the basis for the United States Post Office Department's commemorative three cent stamp first issued on National Maritime Day, 22 May, 1944.

The first vessel to cross the Atlantic Ocean under continuous steam power was the packet ship *Sirius*. Ironically, this little cross-channel steamer was never intended for the Atlantic service. She was merely built of wood, in 1837, by Messrs Robert Menzies and Son of Leith, in Scotland, for the service between London and Cork operated by the St George Steam Packet Company – known in later years, as the City of Cork Steam Packet Company.

The *Sirius* was a two-masted vessel. She carried three square sails on the fore-mast, her main-mast being rigged fore-and-aft. The figurehead was made in the shape of a dog that held, between its front paws, a representation of the Dog Star, after which the vessel was named. The crew consisted of thirty-five officers and men.

The vessel was propelled by side-lever engines of 320 nominal horse power that had been constructed by Messrs Thomas Wingate and Company, of Whiteinch, near Glasgow. She was one of the first steamers to be fitted with the surface condensers that had been patented by Samuel Hall in 1834. These enabled her boilers to be fed with fresh water.

93 A model of the packet ship Sirius, *which made the first crossing of the Atlantic under continuous steam power.*

The little cross-channel steamer gained her chance of a larger fame almost by accident, when, early in 1838, she was chartered for the Atlantic service by the newly-formed British and American Steam Navigation Company, whose own vessel, the packet ship *British Queen*, had not been completed in time. Under the command of Lieutenant R. Roberts, R.N., the *Sirius* left London for Cork Harbour, where she took on coal. She then left Cork – on 4 April 1838 – with forty passengers, bound for New York. When she encountered strong head winds, a number of the members of the crew protested, declaring that it would be madness to venture further in so small a vessel. Thanks, however, to the determination and competence of her commander, the *Sirius* arrived safely off New York on 22 April, after an Atlantic crossing of eighteen days ten hours at a mean speed of 6.7 knots. Her arrival was treated as an event of great importance. This is an account given in one of the local newspapers:

> 'Nothing is talked of in New York but about this *Sirius*. She is the first steam vessel that has arrived here from England, and a glorious boat she is. Every merchant in New York went on board her yesterday. Lt. Roberts, R.N., is the first man that ever navigated a steamship from Europe to America'.

The *Sirius* left New York for her return crossing on the first day of May. Thousands of people gathered on the wharves to witness her departure, and the Battery fired a salute of seventeen guns, which was a mark of respect that had been seldom or never paid to any merchant vessel before. She reached Falmouth on 18 May, and went on to London later in the same day. She completed a second double crossing of the Atlantic in July 1838, but after this she was used only for home and continental services. On one of these journeys, when she was travelling between Glasgow and Cork in 1847, she ran on to a reef of rocks in Ballycotton Bay and became a total wreck.

By one of the strange quirks of fate that make the chronicles of human endeavour so eternally interesting, the *Sirius*, on her first historic Atlantic crossing, managed to reach New York only a few hours ahead of the packet ship *Great Western*, which was the first steamer to be constructed specially for the Atlantic ferry service. The *Great Western* was to have sailed from Bristol on 7 April 1838 – only three days later, that is, than the date of the departure of the *Sirius* from Cork. But the weather was unfavourable, and it was not until the eighth that she left the mouth of the river Avon. She took fifteen days and five hours to make the journey to New York, at a mean speed of 8.8 knots, arriving, as we have seen, to find that all her thunder had been stolen by the *Sirius*.

Although she was built of wood at Bristol by a Mr William Patterson to the plans of the great engineer Isambard Kingdom Brunel, the *Great Western* was specially strengthened to enable her to withstand the hardest buffetings she could be expected to receive on an Atlantic crossing. She was closely trussed with iron and wooden diagonals and shelf pieces, and she had four staggered rows of iron bolts, each 1½ inches in diameter and 24 feet long, which ran longitudinally through her bottom frames. To make her virtually impregnable, her hull was sheathed with copper below the water line. Three hundred persons could, at a pinch, be accommodated on the vessel.

The *Great Western* left New York for her return trip to Europe on 7 May, and arrived at Bristol on 22 May. She continued to ply between these ports for the next eight years, crossing the North Atlantic sixty-four times in all. In 1847 she was purchased by the British and North American Mail Steam Packet Company, later to become the Cunard Steamship Company, to provide a regular service between Southampton and the West Indies. She was broken up, ultimately, at Vauxhall in 1857.

By a narrow margin, the paddle steamer *Britannia* qualifies for the distinction of being the first steamer built specially to carry the mails between Europe and America. She was constructed of wood by Messrs Robert Duncan and Company, at Greenock in Scotland, for the Royal Mail Steam Packet Company, and launched on 5 February 1840. Her three sister-ships, the *Acadia*, the *Caledonia*, and the *Columbia* were also built on the River Clyde about the same time. These four vessels were intended to establish a monthly trans-Atlantic mail steamship service from Liverpool to Halifax and Boston that was to be subsidised by the British Government.

As will be seen from the model of the *Britannia* displayed in the Science Museum, London, she was a three-masted barque, with two decks, a square stern, and a clipper bow. Her total crew consisted of eighty-nine officers and men. Provision was made for the officers' quarters on the upper deck. The passenger accommodation consisted of a dining saloon and cabins for 115 persons on the main deck, below. There was also accommodation for a number of cows, carried to ensure a constant supply of fresh milk.

The *Britannia* was described by her sponsors as being luxurious, but Charles Dickens, who crossed the Atlantic in her in 1842, thought otherwise. This is the depressing description he included in his *American Notes*:

Two views of a model of the Brunel-designed Great Western; *above (94) – the bow, and left (95) – a broadside view.*

'Before descending into the bowels of the ship, we had passed from the deck into a long and narrow apartment, not unlike a gigantic hearse with windows in the sides; having at the upper end a melancholy stove, at which three or four chilly stewards were warming their hands; while on either side, extending down its whole dreary length, was a long, long table; over which a rack, fixed to the low roof, and stuck full of drinking-glasses and cruet-stands, hinted dismally at rolling seas and heavy weather.'

The *Britannia*, which had paddle-wheels 28 feet in diameter, and could steam comfortably at about 8.5 knots, successfully completed forty crossings of the Atlantic. In the winter of 1844, when the harbour at Boston was frozen over, and the ship was imprisoned in ice, it is recorded that the citizens at their own expense cut a passage 7 miles long and 100 feet wide to enable the vessel to reach clear water. In 1849 she was sold to the German Government who intended to turn her into a warship. Later though, her engines were removed, and she existed for some years as a hulk. She is believed to have been finally broken up at Port Glasgow by the son of her builder.

Still in existence, today, is the hull of one of Isambard Kingdom Brunel's historic vessels, the *Great Britain*. It was planned in 1838 by the directors of the Great Western Steamship Company to be twice the size of their *Great Western* and thus to be the largest ship that had ever been built.

It was not only the projected size of the *Great Britain* that aroused much public excitement. Soon, it was announced that Brunel had decided that it would be impossible to construct so large a vessel from wood, and that the ship would be in consequence the first ocean-going craft to be built mainly of iron. Then the news was given out that she was to be the first ocean-going ship to be propeller-driven. (The 240-ton steamer *Archimedes* built in 1838 and fitted with a screw propeller, had cruised successfully round

The Britannia *(1840) was rigged as a three-masted barque. Left (96) – a model in the Science Museum, London, and right (97) – a close view of the deck.*

the British Isles, convincing even the ultra-conservative Lords of the Admiralty that the paddle-wheel might be on the way out.) No contractor could be found who would be willing to undertake the formidable task of constructing her, so the directors of the company were forced to set up the necessary plant themselves at Wapping Wharf, Bristol, with a special dry dock which is still in use today.

The evolution of the ship, carried out under Brunel's personal supervision, was slow, for, it was said, 'she would combine a greater number of untried principles than ever before united in one enterprise'. (For instance she was the first ship to be given watertight bulkheads.) Immense crowds gathered to see her launched, at last, by Prince Albert on 19 July 1843. She continued in the Atlantic service until 1846 when she went ashore in Dundrum Bay, County Down, Ireland. She lay there for eleven months, but Brunel had a breakwater constructed to protect her until she could be refloated and taken in to Liverpool. The fact that she survived this ordeal at all was taken as proof that the use of iron, for shipbuilding, was a practical innovation.

The *Great Britain* was for some years the largest vessel afloat, but she was made to look relatively small by Brunel's later, gargantuan brain-child, the ship that was to be called by its owners at its launch the *Leviathan*, but which is better known by the name it was given almost immediately afterwards – the *Great Eastern*. The ship was to be five or six times as large as any other vessel then in use. She would be so long, said Brunel, that she would not be affected by even the largest storm waves, and seasickness would be virtually unknown on board. She would be the wonder of the seas.

The first plates of the mammoth vessel were laid at Millwall, near London on 1 May 1854. She could not be built in dry dock, because there was no dry dock in existence that would be large enough. She could not even be raised in the normal way – that is, with her great length at right angles to the river – because the Thames, at Millwall, is not much more than 1000 feet wide. Instead, the intention was that she should be launched sideways when, after the eventful years that would be necessary for her construction, she would be ready to enter the water.

And eventful those years certainly were. Two thousand workers sweated through all the hours of daylight over the 30,000 iron plates, each weighing on average a third of a ton, that were to make up the almost unsinkable hull. Two hundred gangs of rivet-drivers drove into their predestined positions more than 3,000,000 inch-thick rivets, while craftsmen fell to their deaths from scaffolding, apprentices were crushed and impaled, and a basher and his boy assistant 'went missing', never to be seen alive again. (Their bodies were found when the ship was broken up, sealed in the three-feet wide space between the outer and inner skins of the hull.)

A model of the Bristol privateer Mars, *1779.*

Overleaf, a model of one of the last tea-clippers, Thermopylae, *1868, made from contemporary plans and other evidence. The ship was eventually sunk in 1907 as unserviceable.*

F4(10)

As the colossal vessel took shape, a chorus of admiration and criticism rose from all parts of the civilized world. In Massachusetts, Henry Wadsworth Longfellow sang the praises of the Milwall wonder:

> . . . Sublime in its enormous bulk,
> Loomed aloft the shadowy hulk. . . .

while Herman Melville, author of the maritime classics *Moby Dick* and *Billy Budd*, sailing up the Thames after a journey to Holland, wrote in his diary of what he had seen:

'Vast toy. No substance. Durable materials but perishable structure. Can't exist a hundred years hence . . .'

Long before the last plates were rivetted in place, technically minded observers were asking how the ship was, in fact, to be launched. She had been raised more than 100 feet from the high water mark, on ground that sloped towards the river at a gradient of one in twelve. To move her – and she was by far the heaviest object that man had ever attempted to shift – Brunel assembled hydraulic rams to push her from the landward side, and steam tugs to pull her from the water. There was an impressive auxiliary array of winches and windlasses, with several miles of strong chain cable – most of it borrowed from the Admiralty.

In spite of all these preparations, the launching ceremony was a fiasco. Before a deliriously excited crowd – estimated, by one observer, to contain upwards of 100,000 people – Brunel and his assistants struggled unavailingly to get the inert monster to move towards the Thames. Rain was falling heavily and the crowd was shouting with derision, when, after hours spent pushing and pulling in vain, the great engineer was forced to acknowledge that, at least for the time being, his endeavour had failed.

The next attempt to launch the giant vessel took place at the following spring tide, a month later, and on this occasion all unauthorized observers were excluded. Brunel had borrowed more rams and more chains, but even with all this extra equipment his renewed efforts were only marginally more successful. So, he continued to toil desperately after that through two more dark cold wet months, moving the unwieldly hulk sideways, foot by foot and inch by inch until at last, on 31 January 1858, virtually unnoticed by the members of the general public, who were by that time thoroughly bored by the whole affair, he managed to get her afloat.

For many years, in the middle of the nineteenth century, neither the shipowners could be persuaded to trust their property, nor the passengers their lives, to the steam-engine alone. So sea-going vessels continued to be built that had masts and sails as well as the

Above, a model of the beautiful hull of the schooner yacht America, *1851.*

Below, a model of an English ship, c. 1485, with highly decorated main sail.

98 A model of the steamship Great Britain, *the first screw-propelled iron-built vessel to cross the Atlantic.*

newer means of propulsion. A model of particular interest in the City Museum and Art Gallery at Plymouth shows a three-masted barque-rigged screw steamer of this kind – the *Alabama*.

The *Alabama* was built at Messrs Laird's yard at Birkenhead during the war between the northern and southern states of America. She was ordered by the South. As Britain was officially neutral, the northern or federal States regarded this as an infringement of neutrality and demanded an enquiry into the status of the vessel. Before the investigation could take place, the ship – known then only as *Number 290* – sailed out of the Mersey on the pretext of making a trial trip.

Instead of returning, the ship made for the Azores. There she was taken over by an American crew under the command of Captain Raphael Semmes of the Confederate States Navy and named *Alabama*. At the same time she was supplied with guns, ammunition and stores. After that she had a highly successful career as an armed commerce raider, roaming the high seas sinking or burning all the vessels she came up with that belonged to the Federal navy or were known to be supplying them.

In two years the *Alabama* accounted for some seventy vessels. Then she put into Cherbourg, for the purpose of docking and fitting, but she was surprised there by the Federal States frigate *Kearsage*, under the command of Captain John Winslow, who had been seeking her for some time. The *Kearsage* was a similar type of vessel – a barque-rigged screw steamer – though with a slightly heavier armament. The French ordered the *Kearsage* to leave, and on 19 June 1864, she sailed and awaited her opponent some eight

99 The Great Eastern *(1858), a model of which is shown here was unique in having both paddle wheels and a screw propeller.*

miles off the port. After an engagement lasting about an hour, during which the *Alabama* suffered a good deal of damage, the Confederate vessel began to sink. A private steam yacht, the *Deerhound* belonging to a Mr. John Lancaster, of Wigan, who was on a holiday cruise with his wife and family, had taken up a position to witness the fight. Mr Lancaster sent his boats to pick up the survivors from the *Alabama* and he took them back to Southampton.

Discussions regarding the Federal States' claims dragged on until 1871, when it was agreed that Britain should pay an indemnity of over £3,000,000.

The great advances that were made in the design of passenger ships and merchantmen during the period of transition from sail to steam were bound to be noticed eventually by the authorities in charge of the principal navies of the world, though these gentlemen, many of them elderly, proved noticeably reluctant to change their ideas. The large paddle-wheels with which the earlier steamships were fitted were, they said, dangerously vulnerable targets for enemy fire – and, besides, who wanted to have large quantities of inflammable fuel and potentially explosive boilers on board? Ship models of the time show how the new-fangled ideas were slowly but inevitably forced on these die-hards. They give an interesting picture of the various stages in a period of revolutionary change.

As late as 1858 warships that relied principally on sail were still being produced. In the Museum of the United States Naval Academy at Annapolis, there is a model of the U.S.S. *Hartford* – the steam frigate, built in that year, that was to be Admiral Farragut's flagship at the battle of New Orleans. This model shows a splendid example of the American sailing ship at its best – when the clipper had made its indelible mark on the naval architecture of the world, but before the instrusion of steam had forced naval designers to make any really drastic alterations.

With old and new ideas being so tentatively combined, it is hardly surprising that in naval planning circles there were indecision and confusion. This situation proved highly wasteful and expensive. Line-of-battle ships and frigates would be laid down, pushed on with rapidly for a time, and then finally left to rot or be broken up. The model of the U.S.S. *Antietam,* a 23-gun sloop of war, now in the Museum of the United States Naval Academy, is one of the largest ship models in the world. When the *Antietam* was laid down in 1862 she was regarded as the very last word in naval construction. Then came the inevitable wave of doubt and hesitation, and she was written down as obsolete while she was still on the stocks. She was eventually launched in 1876, but even after that she was used only as a store ship.

100 *A fine model of the United States steam frigate* Hartford *(1858).*

The last British wooden three-decker – the 121-gun *Howe* – was launched in March 1860. and she was another remarkable example of the same kind of muddled thinking. In her general form, she was still a 'wooden wall' capital ship of Nelson's time, with square ports, and the stern galleries that had hardly been changed since the seventeenth century. True, she had been given a couple of funnels and a propeller to bring her a little nearer in line with the times. But this token gesture was, itself, a waste. The *Howe* was really out of date before she sailed. Her fate was to be converted into a boys' training ship – under the new and ironically misleading name, the *Impregnable*.

As early as 1825, the distinguished French officer Colonel Paixhans had suggested that warships should be given a 'cuirass' of seven or eight inches of iron. Experiments were made, but the armoured vessels proved difficult to manoeuvre, and were relegated to other duties. It was the battle of Sinope, fought in 1853, at which the Russian navy virtually destroyed the Turkish navy,

101 A model of the Confederate raider Alabama.

102 Above, left – One of the largest ship models in the world is of the U.S.S. Antietam, *shown here in the United States Naval Academy Museum.*

103 Below, left – A model of the last British wooden three-decker, the Howe.

104 Above – It is interesting to compare this model of the Warrior *with the* Howe *because the prototypes were both launched in 1860.*

that unmistakably demonstrated that unprotected wooden ships could not endure the effects of shell fire. The great French naval architect Dupuy de Lôme got to work on the problem. He took a two-decker wooden ship and converted it, by adding a shield of armour plating almost five inches thick, into the first ironclad, the *Gloire*.

At that, the British Admiralty was stirred into action. As soon as the British authorities could, they countered with the elegant iron-built screw frigate *Warrior*, of which there are splendid models in the British National Maritime Museum at Greenwich, the Science Museum at South Kensington, London, and elsewhere. The use of iron made it possible for warships to be built that were much longer than ever before – and so could carry more guns on a single deck. The *Warrior* and her sister ship the *Black Prince* were more than 100 feet longer than their wooden contemporary the *Howe*.

With a ship like the *Warrior* afloat, wooden-hull warships were seen to be obsolete by every nation in the world that had a navy. The point was driven home by the confrontation that took place at the roadstead of Hampton Roads, Virginia, on 9 March 1862, between the Confederate ironclad Ram *Virginia* and the United States Navy ironclad *Monitor*.

The *Virginia* was fashioned in the face of almost insurmountable difficulties from the charred remains of an earlier ship the *Merrimack* by which name it is generally known. This vessel had been launched as a loftily-sparred 275 foot single-screw frigate at the

105 The hull of the U.S. steam frigate Merrimack, *a model of which is shown here, was used in the construction of the Confederate ironclad* Virginia, *pictured opposite.*

Boston Navy Yard on 14 June 1855. Her upper works were burned off when she was set on fire and abandoned by the Federal forces when they evacuated the Gosport Navy Yard during the initial stages of the war between the states. Her hull and machinery were still sound, however, and after she had been raised the Confederate naval constructors were able to sheath her main deck with iron plating and to build a sloping casemated shield on a framework of oak beams and railroad rails above it. Protected in this way, the *Virginia* was reckoned to be well-armoured enough to withstand any Federal fire.

When the Federal authorities became conscious of the reputedly invincible vessel that was to be used against them, they invited the Swedish engineer John Ericsson to build them a ship that would be strong enough and sufficiently well armed to be able to annihilate the re-furbished *Merrimack*. Ericsson, adapting a scheme he happened to have submitted earlier to the Emperor Napoleon III, set to work early in 1862 at Greenpoint, Long Island, and produced the extraordinary vessel the *Monitor*, which was soon given the

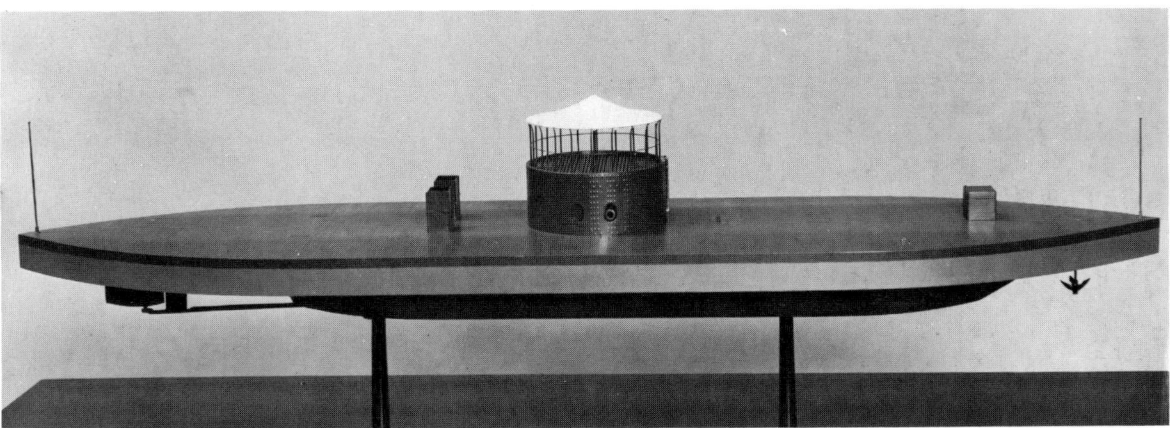

106 Top – A model of the ironclad Virginia *and below it (107) a model of the Union ironclad* Monitor. *In 1862 the two ships fought the first ironclad battle in history.*

nickname 'Cheese Box on a Raft'. In spite of her limited seaworthiness – she nearly sank on her first operational trip from taking in water through the holes in her armour plating – the *Monitor* proved to be just too good for her redoubtable rival. Models of the victorious *Monitor* and of the *Merrimack* in both her original state and as she was when she was resuscitated as the *Virginia* have been specially made in a workshop that was at one time attached to the Mariners' Museum at Newport News, Virginia, for display in that collection.

There were many other extraordinary and experimental vessels built during the later decades of the nineteenth century that we can only fully appreciate now if we study the models of them that survive. One of these was the brainchild of one man – Cowper Phipps Coles, captain in the British Royal Navy. While in command of the *Stromboli*, a paddle-steamer in the Black Sea, Coles devised and constructed a buoyant gun-raft capable of carrying a heavy gun protected by an iron shield four inches thick. He was promptly ordered home to superintend the construction of a number of

similar rafts. While he was doing this he started to plan a warship that should have one or more revolving turrets carrying heavy guns. (Though similar ideas were being developed at the same time in America by John Ericsson, the two men appear to have been working independently of each other.)

The building of a new turret battleship according to drawings submitted by Coles and Messrs Laird was authorised by the British Admiralty on 23 July 1866, in spite of strong opposition from the Controller of the Navy, who considered that she might not be seaworthy. When she was built, the new ship – named the *Captain* – was duly commissioned, though the Lords of the Admiralty took the unusual step of laying the joint responsibility on Coles and the Lairds. After an experimental cruise, the *Captain* joined the Channel Fleet early in 1870, and accompanied it to Gibraltar amid much public rejoicing, being reported a 'most efficient vessel both under sail and steam, as well as easy and comfortable'.

On the sixth day of September of that year, when the fleet, on its return voyage, was off Cape Finisterre, the *Captain* was visited by Sir Alexander Milne, the commander-in-chief. Milne was much struck by the extreme lowness of the ship in the water, so that in a pleasant breeze, 'the water was washing over the lee side of the deck fore and aft, and striking the after turret to a depth of about eighteen inches to two feet'. Accordingly, he remarked to Captain Coles, who, as the designer of the ship, was travelling on her in a private capacity: 'I cannot reconcile myself to this state of things so very unusual in all my experience.'

Later that day, the weather changed for the worse, and shortly after midnight a fresh squall struck the ships. In any other circumstance, this gale would not have been particularly memorable, but it proved fatal to the *Captain*. As soon as the squall struck her she heeled over, proved to have no power of recovery, turned over completely so that she was bottom upwards, and sank. Only a few of those on board were saved, Coles himself going down with the ship.

In spite of this tragedy, the warship's traditional rig became virtually obsolete soon after the *Captain* affair. As the century ended, strongly armoured battleships, carrying large breech-loading guns mounted according to the principles propounded by Ericsson and Coles, were being built by a number of nations. A new age had dawned. The sail-propelled naval vessel had become a thing of the past – to be studied by model-makers and model collectors with fascination tinged with nostalgia.

108 Top – The revolving gun turrets of the ill-fated Captain *are clearly shown in this view of a fine model at Greenwich.*

109 Centre – A model of the cruiser Terrible *(1895). Change in the design of warships at this stage was rapid.*

110 Left – This model is of the twin-screw steamship Campania. *When launched in 1892 this ship was the largest afloat.*

LIVERPOOL

6 Model Ships and Boats in the Twentieth Century

The twentieth century has seen many radical changes made in the design of real, full-size ships and boats. Professional model-makers have had a bewildering variety of prototypes to copy in miniature: the amateur model-maker of the present day tends to take as his source of inspiration the latest nuclear-powered guided missile destroyer as happily as, in earlier days, his predecessors turned to the galleon or frigate.

During the greater part of the century – until, that is, travel by air became a universally accepted convenience – competition between the great steamship lines of the world was fierce. Every company of any consequence had accurate scale models made of all its potentially profitable vessels, and firms such as Messrs Bassett-Lowke of Northampton, England, and Messrs Severn Lamb of Stratford-on-Avon were kept busy satisfying the demand. Of all the thousands of these prestige and advertisement models to be seen in shipping offices and other places, the ones of the most general interest are probably those that show the mammoth liners and those that show the liners which have, for some part of their existence, held the Blue Riband – the legendary award made for the fastest crossing of the Atlantic Ocean.

Models of the screw turbine steamer *Mauretania* engage the attention on both these counts. This famous ship was built by Messrs Swan, Hunter and Wigham Richardson at Wallsend-on-Tyne in the north of England for the Cunard Steamship Company's service between Liverpool and New York, and launched in 1906. On her trials in 1907, the *Mauretania* covered 300 miles at a mean speed of 27.4 knots. She soon wrested the Blue Riband from the steam ship *Kaiser Wilhelm II* (launched in 1903) and she held it until 1929, when the German turbine ship *Bremen*, launched in the previous year, took it from her. After a distinguished career, in the course of which she served at different times as an armed cruiser and as a hospital ship, she was broken up at Rosyth in 1935.

France was to play a significant part in the competition for the transatlantic passenger trade with the giant liner *Normandie*, launched in 1932. The *Normandie* was the first ship to be longer than 1000 feet (if placed on end, she would, in fact, have fallen

111 A stern view of a model of the liner Mauretania.

S.S. NORMANDIE

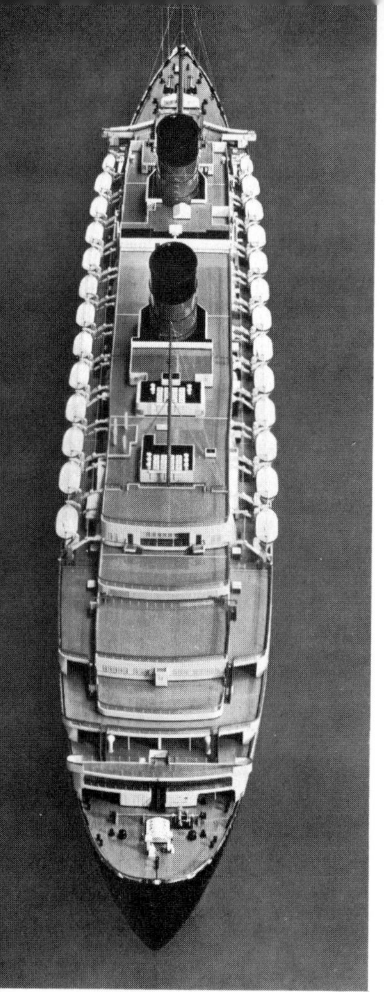

Models of Atlantic greyhounds, on the left from top to bottom : 112, Mauretania; *113,* Normandie; *114,* Queen Mary; *115,* Queen Elizabeth *and above (116) a bird's eye view of a model of the same ship.*

short of the 1046 feet Chrysler Building in New York by only seventeen feet). She had eleven decks, and could carry more than 2000 passengers in conditions of great comfort. With an engine rated at 160000 horse power, she managed to set up a new record with an average speed of 31.3 knots.

Not to be outdone, the Cunard Steamship Company produced, next, the two famous Queens of that era – the Royal Mail Steamer *Queen Mary* and the Royal Mail Steamer *Queen Elizabeth.* These two ships were intended to work in partnership, to provide a weekly Atlantic service – a feat which had never before been achieved by a pair of vessels.

During the preliminary investigations made before the *Queen Mary* was built, the designers carried out in their experimental tank at Clydebank thorough researches on the hull form required for the ship. In this tank, it was possible to reproduce in miniature all foreseeable Atlantic weather conditions, including waves of varying combinations of height and length. Over 7,000 experiments were carried out on numerous models before the best form for the hull was finally determined. During these tests, the models travelled a total distance of more than 1000 miles in their journeyings up and down the tank.

The keel of the *Queen Mary* was actually laid on Clydebank in December 1930, but owing to the serious world financial crisis all work on her had to be suspended a year later, and it was not until April 1934 that her construction could be resumed. Launched in September of that year (the ceremony being carried out by the British sovereign who gave her name to the great vessel), the *Queen Mary* made her maiden voyage from Southampton via Cherbourg to New York in 1936. During the Second World War she served as a troop transport – carrying, in the period March 1940 to September 1946, 810,730 passengers and steaming, to do so, 661,771 miles. In the course of these wartime journeys, she visited Aden, Bombay, Boston, Capetown, Freetown, Fremantle, Hobart, Massawa, New York, Rio de Janeiro, Singapore, Suez, Sydney, Trincomalee and Trinidad. Model-makers who are normally conscious of scale may be interested to note that the *Queen Mary* was nearly five times the length of the first Cunard liner *Britannia* of 1840. Her great size is further illustrated by the fact that her gross tonnage of 81,237 exceeded the combined tonnage of the entire Cunard Atlantic and Mediterranean fleets of 1876. These consisted of 36 ships, and totalled 81,126 gross tons!

The keel of the *Queen Elizabeth* was laid in December 1936, and she was launched, by the lady whose title and name she was to bear, on 27 September 1938. During the ceremony, the Queen referred to the ship as the 'greatest of the ships that ply to and fro across the Atlantic, like shuttles in a mighty loom, weaving a fabric of friendship and understanding between the people of Britain and the people of the United States'.

But, in spite of these optimistic sentiments, the *Queen Elizabeth* was not to do much of this fabric-weaving for quite a time. In November 1939, two months after the hostilities of the Second World War had commenced, the great ship was still lying at Clydebank uncompleted – a sitting target for a possible enemy air attack. By February 1940, the Lords of the British Admiralty were pressing the Cunard Company to move her from the Clyde at the earliest possible date. The problem was, where could she be sent? The number of ports outside the British Isles which could receive the world's largest liner was limited. Obviously, a neutral port was indicated, and none seemed better than New York, which was already acting as host to the sister ship *Queen Mary*. To reach New York meant a 3000 mile voyage across the Atlantic in winter, without the benefit of the extended trials that normally precede the commissioning of a new ship. These trials were now obviously precluded by the dangers of submarine or air attack.

Theoretically, the *Queen Elizabeth* had sufficient reserve of speed to take any evasive action. But, she had never been to sea, and her builders and owners could not be certain of her performance. The risk, however, formidable as it was, had to be taken. It was decided that she should go to New York. The Admiralty were advised, and approval was given to the project. There remained, then, the problem of getting the ship away with the greatest possible amount of security. News of the movements of ships with their landfalls and departures was, of course, rigidly censored at that time. But it would have been impossible to move the *Queen Elizabeth* from her fitting-out basin and down the narrow reaches of the Clyde without attracting a considerable amount of attention. So, it was decided that as a 'blind' arrangements should be made for the *Queen Elizabeth* to proceed from the Clyde to Southampton for drydocking. To give extra authenticity to this plan, quantities of her fittings were sent to Southampton, the graving dock there was prepared for her reception, a crew of some 500 men was signed on for the coastal voyage, and – to complete the illusion – the Southampton pilot was brought to the ship.

At 12.30 pm, then, on Monday, 26 February 1940, the *Queen Elizabeth*, escorted by six tugs, left her fitting-out basin, arriving at the tail of the bank without incident five hours later. Short trials followed, in which the steering gear was tested and the compasses were adjusted, and on the following day, 27 February, the Cunard Company formally took delivery of the ship from the builders. At this stage, the crew were advised of the ship's real destination. With few exceptions, they volunteered for the longer voyage.

Three days later, the *Queen Elizabeth* slipped away down the

117 Top – A model of the Cunard liner Queen Elizabeth 2 *with tug.*

118 Above – This model of the gunboat Peder Skram *(1908) is one of the exhibits at the Danish Naval Museum.*

Clyde on a voyage unique in the annals of the sea. Her sailing was one of the best-kept secrets of the war. The confidence of her owners and builders was completely justified, and five days later an astonished world heard of her arrival in New York. Queen Elizabeth herself expressed her personal interest by sending a gracious message:

> 'I send you my heartfelt congratulations on the safe arrival of the *Queen Elizabeth* in New York. Ever since I launched her in those fateful days of 1938, I have watched her progress with interest and admiration. Please convey to Captain Townley my compliments on the safe conclusion of her hazardous maiden voyage.
>
> ELIZABETH R.'

The great shipping companies of the United States did not build any vessel large enough and powerful enough to be able to take part in the struggle for the Blue Riband of the Atlantic until after the Second World War. Then, in February 1950, the keel of the *United States* was laid – a ship that was to win the coveted honour on her maiden voyage in the summer of 1952 with an average speed of 34.48 knots. One remarkable innovation was made in the construction of the *United States* – for the first time, the superstructure was built almost entirely of aluminium.

Today, anyone who wishes to cross the Atlantic (or any other ocean) quickly will normally elect to travel by air, and passenger liners are no longer designed to outstrip all possible competitors. Instead, they may be thought of as resort hotels – designed, possibly, like the Cunard Steamship Company's *Queen Elizabeth 2* to follow the sun, and to be able to visit, on their journeys, many attractive and hospitable ports that their deep-draughted predecessors were incapable of entering. The *Queen Elizabeth 2*, launched in 1967, is equipped with a computer, for performing such functions as data logging, alarm scanning, machinery control, weather routing, the prediction of fresh water requirements, and the control of food stocks on board; a theatre; a hairdressing saloon staffed by thirteen highly trained stylists; a versatile range of shops; 1300 telephones; facilities for the production of the *Daily Telegraph* on board; and many other amenities of civilized life.

The mammoth warships built during the first half of the twenthieth century, with their congested and heavily armoured upperworks, have now only a limited appeal for the non-professional model-maker. There were a few outstanding vessels during this period, however, that have been reproduced in model form a sufficient number of times to justify inclusion in any survey.

The *Dreadnought*, launched in 1906, was the first large warship to be fitted with turbine engines, and with them she became the

119 Top – A model of one of the German pocket battleships, the Admiral Scheer.

120 Above – Although launched two decades earlier than the Admiral Scheer *the* Barham, *a model of which is shown, was still in commission in 1939.*

fastest battleship in the Royal Navy. She had ten 12-inch guns mounted in five turrets, twenty-seven smaller guns, and a number of torpedo tubes from which these lethal missiles could be discharged under the surface of the water. The design of the *Dreadnought* was so successful that all earlier kinds of battleship immediately became obsolete, and the navies of all competing nations had to be rapidly equipped with vessels of the newer type. Models can be seen, in museums and elsewhere, of the German warships *Nassau* and *Westfalen* (laid down in the year in which the *Dreadnought* was launched); the French battleship *Danton* (launched in 1909); and the United States Navy's *New York* and *Texas*, launched in 1912. All these ships were able to fight at a range of several miles – a qualification made necessary by the rapid development of the torpedo.

At the outbreak of the First World War a number of outstanding battleships were awaiting completion in the shipyards of the combatant countries. Among these vessels were the *Queen Elizabeth* (launched eventually, in 1915) and her sister ships the *Barham*, the *Malaya*, the *Valiant* and the *Warspite*. All were fitted with 15-inch guns that fired shells capable of penetrating the thickest armour plating known at that time; all had boilers fired with oil, and engines that enabled them to travel at speeds of up to 24 knots; and all survived the war successfully and were, in fact, still in commission in 1939. There are models of these ships in the principal maritime and war museums.

During most of the twenty-one years she was in commission, the battle cruiser *Hood* was the largest, heaviest and fastest armoured

121 Top – A model of the German battle-cruiser Scharnhorst. *The prototype was launched in 1936 in defiance of international treaties.*

122 Above – A model of the British battleship Vanguard *(1944) which had a displacement of 42,500 tons.*

ship in the world. She was laid down during the First World War when it became known to the British naval authorities that the Germans had started to build a battle cruiser with 15-inch guns, but she was not completed until after the Armistice. However, she was to play an important part in the Second World War. On 23 May, 1941, the *Hood*, in company with the *Prince of Wales*, spotted the vast German battleship *Bismarck*, then generally regarded as the most powerful warship in the world, with her cruiser escort. As soon as these were brought within range, the *Hood* opened fire. This was returned, and when a shell or shells from the *Bismarck* fell on the *Hood's* fore-deck, a great blaze broke out. Still the *Hood* continued to race towards her formidable adversary. Suddenly, there was a tremendous explosion, and the British warship was reduced in a moment to a mass of burning and smouldering wreckage. The *Bismarck*, forced by the damage she had suffered to reduce speed, was caught and destroyed two days later. Many splendid models of the *Hood* have been made. One of the best is that constructed by Mr Norman Ough, which is now in the Harmsworth Collection of Ship Models in the City Art Gallery and Museum at Plymouth.

After the First World War, the German navy suffered from the severe limitations placed on it by the Treaty of Versailles – no German battleship, this treaty said, was to be larger than 10,000 tons. In an effort to counter these restrictions imposed by the victorious nations, the Germans built three pocket battleships – the *Deutschland*, which was fast enough to show a clean pair of heels to any Allied battleship then in existence; the *Admiral Scheer*; and, just before Adolf Hitler decided to ignore any treaties that might

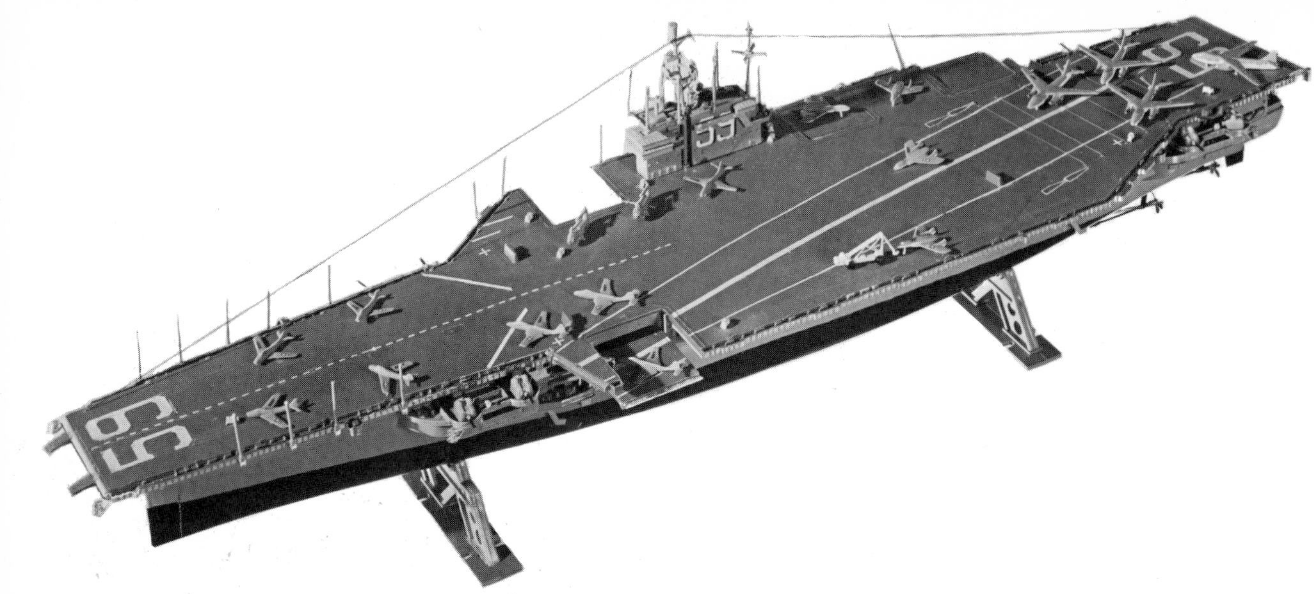

123 *Top – A Revell kit model of the U.S.S.* Forrestal. *This American aircraft carrier was the first to be specially designed for jet aircraft.*

124 *Above – A display model of the aircraft carrier H.M.S.* Eagle *with a busy flight deck.*

be inconvenient to him, the *Admiral Graf Spee*. The *Gneisenau*, *Scharnhorst*, *Bismarck* and *Tirpitz* were built without any concessions being made to the prevailing pressures of international opinion. Models of all these ships have to those who saw the prototypes in operation or who actually served in them, a certain nostalgic fascination.

Even before the end of the Second World War, it had been generally recognized that the battleship, as a fighting unit, was obsolete. It was just a cumbersome and extremely expensive target which stood no chance of survival under the onslaught of the sophisticated weapons that had been developed, in six years of feverish activity, by the leading scientists of the world. As suddenly as the battleship went out, the aircraft carrier, its logical successor, came in.

Most of the earliest vessels used to carry aircraft were limited to the transport of seaplanes. These were lifted out of the ships' holds and lowered to the water's surface by means of cranes. Then came

125 Top – A model of one of the British Royal Navy's guided missile destroyers. The ship's main propulsion system is backed up by gas turbines.

126 Above – A neat model of an escort destroyer of the U.S. Navy.

the *Campania* – a comfortable passenger liner that was converted so that she could actually launch aircraft from her deck. These aircraft went off, in general, on a non-return basis.

The first water-borne vessel that can properly be described as an aircraft carrier was the *Furious* – a cruiser that had been converted quite thoroughly for the purpose, being given a flight deck from which aircraft could take off and on which, if conditions were favourable, they could land. The eddies of air caused by the superstructure made both these proceedings distinctly hazardous.

The form of the present-day aircraft carrier was foreshadowed by the British vessel *Hermes,* launched in 1919. The *Hermes* was built with its funnel and bridge set well clear of the main path of flight, and this practice, giving what is usually known as the 'island type' of carrier, is normally followed today. The United States Navy carriers *Lexington* and *Saratoga*, built in 1925, were also of this asymmetrical type. Each could carry ninety planes, and each cost with its aircraft approximately $45,000,000.

The *Forrestal*, laid down in the yards at Newport News, Virginia was the first aircraft carrier to be designed and built anywhere in the world after the end of the Second World War. The ship, and the others in her class (the *Saratoga*, the *Ranger* and the *Independence*) were planned and constructed specially to carry jet-propelled aircraft. At an early stage in her construction, the *Forrestal* was re-designed so that the angled flight deck, which had been developed in Britain, and steam catapults could be incorporated. A later aircraft carrier – the nuclear powered *Enterprise*, launched at Newport News in September 1960 – was, at the time of her construction, the largest warship ever built.

The twentieth century has seen the rapid development of two ingenious craft that can travel, respectively, under and over the surface of the world's seas. These are, in order of their appearance in nautical annals, the submarine and the hovercraft. It may be stretching a point to describe either of these as a ship or boat, but however they may be classified they have extended considerably the range of the marine model-maker.

Submarines of various kinds have been built and operated with varying degrees of success ever since the eighteenth century. (As early as 1776, an American sergeant named Ezra Lee tried, ineffectually, to blast a British blockade ship out of the water by making his way up to it, unseen and armed with explosives, in a sunken capsule known, for reasons that would be obvious to anyone that studied its peculiar shape, as the *Turtle*.) The first submarines that really interested model-makers though, were those operated by the British, German and Italian navies in the years immediately prior to and during the First World War. Tinplate clockwork-driven models of these submarines were manufactured and marketed in several countries, and the liveliest boys' magazines of that era gave careful directions for the construction of 'realistic model submarines that would really dive and, after a suitable interval of time, would resurface again'. All the handy readers of these magazines needed for making each model submarine, according to the optimistic writers, were a short length of wooden broom handle ('sharpened, by careful whittling with a penknife, at both ends'), two domestic staples or screwed rings, a nail to represent the periscope, a length of strand elastic for the motor, and some thin metal sheet from which could be cut a propeller and a pair of adjustable vanes. One wonders just how many of these rudimentary, do-it-yourself model submarines were ever actually made, and, if any were eventually operated, how many ended their brief careers ingloriously on the muddy bed of some untraversable pond.

The United States Navy submarine *Nautilus* was the first vehicle in the world to be propelled by nuclear power. As early as August

1949, the U.S. Chief of Naval Operations declared a requirement for a nuclear-propelled submarine, and indicated that it should be ready for use by January, 1955. Construction of a land-based prototype (referred to, usually as STR – that is, Submarine Thermal Reactor – Mark I) was commenced in August, 1950 at the Atomic Energy Commission's reactor test station in Idaho. The plant was built inside a submarine hull set in a large tank of water, so that the actual conditions in which a submarine would operate could be simulated. The critical stage was reached at the end of March, 1953. Three months later, the prototype in the tank made a simulated 96-hour full-power crossing of the Atlantic.

The real *Nautilus* did in fact put to sea for the first time on 17 January, 1955, signalling as she did so the message that was destined to become famous: 'Underway on nuclear power.' On her shakedown cruise later in the same year, the *Nautilus* travelled submerged from New London, Connecticut, to San Juan, Puerto Rico, more than 1,300 miles in 84 hours at an average speed of a little under 16 knots. During August, 1958, she made more history by travelling from Pearl Harbor, in the Pacific Ocean, to Portland, England, by way of the Arctic, passing during her journey under the ice at the Geographic North Pole.

The nuclear-powered submarine of today is one of the most sophisticated weapons of war that has ever been created. The United States Navy has already launched several dozen, and there are known to be scores of U.S.S.R. submarines operating in the Mediterranean area and around the Atlantic coasts of Europe, some of which are nuclear-powered. The U.S. Navy submarine *George Washington*, launched in 1959, was, in fact, the West's first ship to be armed with ballistic missiles. Initially, it carried sixteen Polaris A1 missiles, each of which was approximately 30 feet long, had a range of 1,380 statute miles, and was fitted with a nuclear warhead. The *George Washington* successfully fired two of its Polaris missiles while it was submerged off Cape Canaveral on 20 July, 1960. (This was the first underwater launching of a ballistic missile from a United States submarine.) She set out on her initial patrol on 15 November, 1960, and remained submerged for 66 days, 10 hours. Already, her achievements are being surpassed.

Making exact models of the most up-to-date warships is not an easy business, since the authorities concerned with the production of these expensive and largely experimental weapons are (for obvious reasons) rarely anxious to share information that is – from their point of view – best kept secret. When Revell Inc., the hobby kit producers of Venice, California, U.S., wanted to turn out a scale model of one of the missile-armed submarines just described, the directors of the firm found that the submarine's builders, the U.S. Defense Department and the high officials of

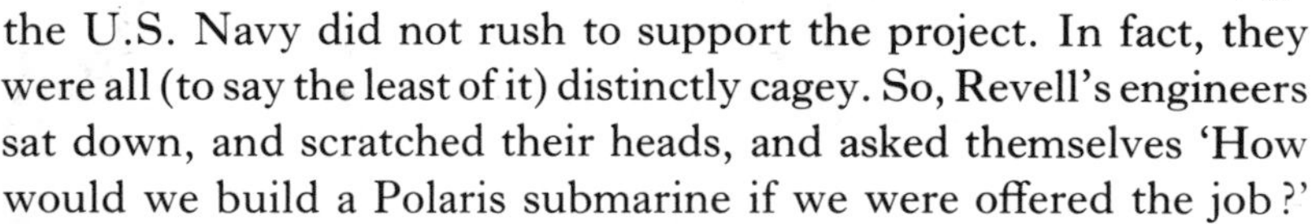

the U.S. Navy did not rush to support the project. In fact, they were all (to say the least of it) distinctly cagey. So, Revell's engineers sat down, and scratched their heads, and asked themselves 'How would we build a Polaris submarine if we were offered the job?'

The model they devised was an almost exact scale replica of the fabulous vessel in which they were interested. It was so complete and accurate in every detail (it is said) that Admiral Hyman Rickover, who was primarily responsible for getting the submarine under way, became exceedingly concerned about possible security leakages. Revell's reactions to his concern were immediate. The firm (figuratively) shrugged its shoulders. And the model was an immediate success.

The hovercraft was developed to exploit a simple but entirely novel conception of water transport. Experiments had been carried out in several countries that were intended to produce a machine which would ride over the surface of a sheet of water while suspended (like some small and incredibly active aquatic creature) on an artificially created cushion of air. It fell to C. S. Cockerell of Great Britain, who had been working privately on the venture since 1953, to construct the prototype that, demonstrated to an enthusiastic crowd of spectators near Cowes in the Isle of Wight in June, 1959, proved that an entirely new method of transportation had been discovered. Cockerell's strange new craft rose most effectively from its position on the ground, hovered spectacularly a few inches above its previous resting place, moved backwards and forwards a few times, and then settled down again on the earth's surface. A little later, a similar demonstration was held on the waters of the neighbouring harbour. Within months, it was known that inventors in the United States and in Switzerland had been working on similar projects.

Hovercraft are used now in and around many countries. Most are genuinely amphibious, though their primary use is normally for operation over water. They have high cruising speeds, and are able to convey passengers comfortably over choppy seas. Some hovercraft can travel comparatively long distances without having to refuel, but it seems likely that the greatest value of the hovercraft will be to cover shorter distances – say, between 20 and 50 miles – for which the use of aircraft would not be economical. Models of

127 Top, left – The United States submarine Nautilus, *a Revell model.*

128 Top, right – A model of the British hovercraft SRN6.

129 Above – A conjectural model of a United States surface effects ship of the future.

130 A stern view of the model now in the Science Museum, London, of the first nuclear-powered merchant ship, the N.S. Savannah.

their latest and best hovercraft are produced now, for prestige and advertisement purposes, by or for all the leading commercial companies.

Eventually, we may be sure, the steamship will be as completely superseded for all normal naval and commercial purposes as the sailing ship has been, and models of steamships will have the same historical or antiquarian interest as sailing ship models have now. In May, 1958, the keel of the first nuclear-powered merchant vessel was laid down for the New York Shipbuilding Corporation, and that will probably prove to have been a highly significant occasion. The ship, launched in the following year, was named *Savannah* after the historic paddle-steamer which first crossed the Atlantic Ocean under auxiliary steam power.

The nuclear reactor in the twentieth-century *Savannah* was developed and built by Babcock and Wilcox of New York. It was located amidships, and it was contained for safety in a cylindrical vessel with hemispherical ends made of one-foot thick steel. It was loaded with 682,000 thimble-sized pellets of enriched uranium oxide, only 1,700 pounds of this fuel being needed for 16,000 hours sailing at full speed. The *Savannah* ran her trials in April 1962, when speeds well in excess of 20 knots were achieved. The model of the modern *Savannah* on view in the Science Museum at South Kensington, London, was lent by the United States Embassy.

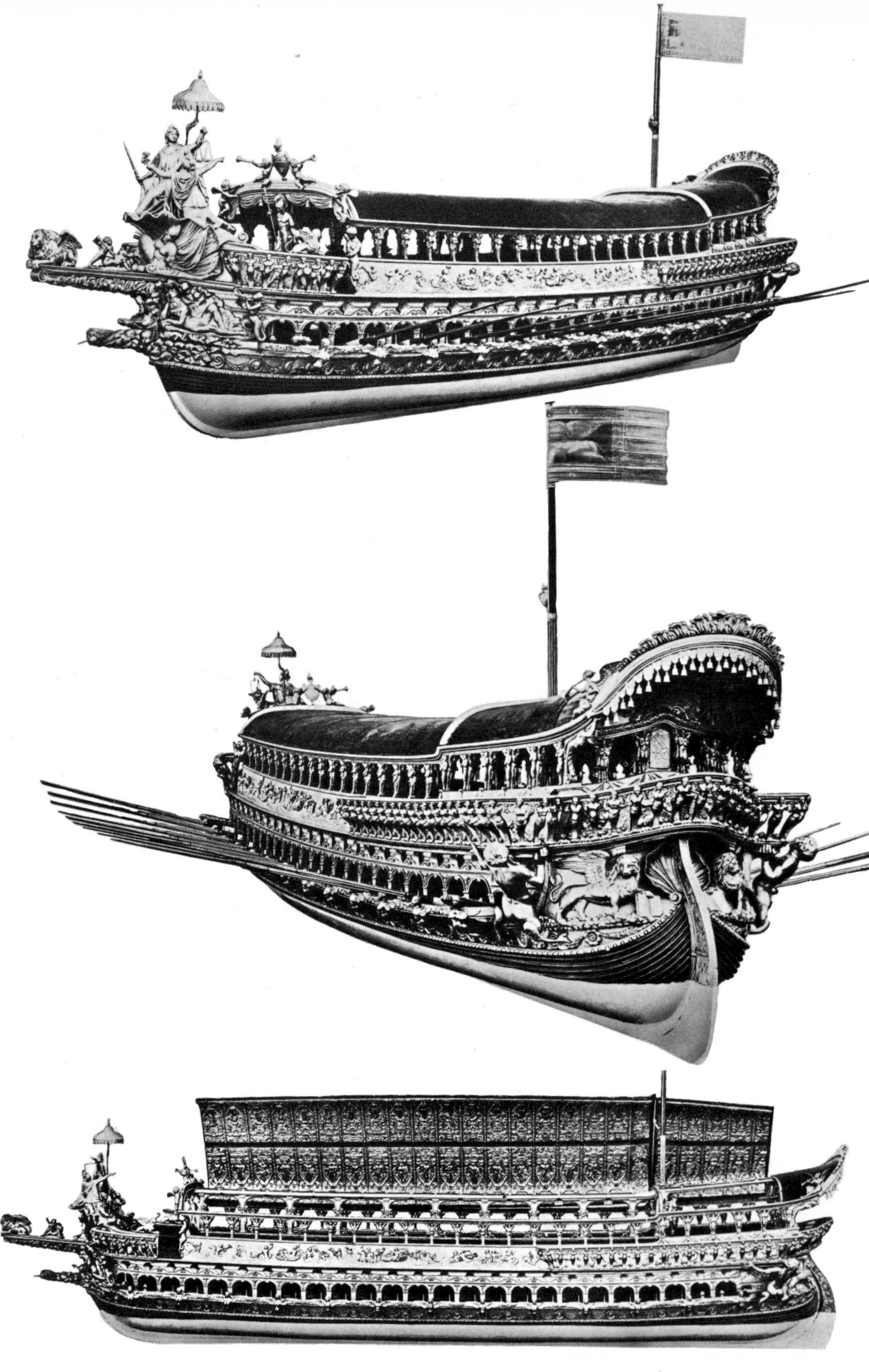

7 Away from the Main Stream

Most of the model ships and boats described and illustrated in the first five chapters of this book have been based on prototypes that have a special historical significance – they could reasonably be used to demonstrate the various stages through which waterborne craft have passed as they developed from the rough hewn-out log to the sophisticated high-powered vessels that pass so swiftly and safely over the world's seas today.

But these are not the only ships and boats that have appealed to the model-maker and the collector of models. Now we must turn aside briefly from the main stream of history to examine a few of the more exceptional craft – the oddities, the sports, the fantastic, and the whimsical – that have been, for one reason or another, at some time or another, reproduced on a miniature scale. It will be impossible to treat these chronologically, since some have existed only for a relatively short time, while others have been in use for many centuries. Instead they may be separated for convenience into three categories, according to the circumstances in which they were brought into being: to be grand; to be used under special conditions; or to fulfil some extraordinary purpose.

MODELS OF STATE AND CEREMONIAL VESSELS

It could be argued that no model ship or boat can be much more beautiful – if, in fact, it can be any more beautiful at all – than the original full-size vessel it has been made to represent. If that is true, it follows that the craftsman who wishes to produce at least once in his model-making career, a model of unrivalled splendour will tend to take as a prototype one of the great state or ceremonial vessels in which the world's most powerful rulers have displayed their especial magnificence. Possibly he will have at the back of his mind Shakespeare's evocative description of Cleopatra's passage over the waters:

131 Three views of a model of one of the most ornate ceremonial vessels ever constructed – the Bucentaur *as reproduced in 'Souvenirs de Marine Conservés' (1888–1908).*

'The barge she sat in, like a burnish'd throne,
Burn'd on the water: the poop was beaten gold;

Purple the sails, and so perfumed that
The winds were love-sick with them; the oars were silver,
Which to the tune of flutes kept stroke, and made
The water which they beat to follow faster,
As amorous of their strokes. For her own person,
It beggar'd all description: she did lie
In her pavillion – cloth-of-gold of tissue –
O'er-picturing that Venus where we see
The fancy outwork nature: on each side her
Stood pretty dimpled boys, like smiling Cupids,
With divers-colour'd fans, whose wind did seem
To glow the delicate cheeks which they did cool,
And what they undid did.'

It was, as Agrippa observed when he heard this account, rare for Antony.

All traces of Cleopatra's lovely barge have vanished long ago, but a model of an Egyptian ceremonial ship, made by the late Mr A. C. Jackson and presented by him to the Science Museum at South Kensington, London, was based upon authentic sources. For details of the basic construction of this model, he studied a 30-foot long boat of the Twelfth Dynasty which is now preserved in the Cairo Museum. He copied the mast, the sail and cabins (richly decorated these, in blue, green, red and other colours) from those on one of the models of the processional boats found in the Eighteenth Dynasty tomb of Tutankhamen. The two large steering paddles were at that time only used in ceremonial vessels, and in those of the largest size.

In the past five or six centuries, the rulers and high officials of Europe and Asia have provided themselves with so many extra-luxurious ships and boats that model-makers with a taste for the exotic have a wide field of choice.

In India for instance – and it would be tempting to devote the whole of a review of this kind to a part of the world that has known so much almost legendary splendour – gorgeously decorated boats in procession on the River Jumna were shown in a painting known to date from the sixteenth century. In the eighteenth century, state barges were to be seen as part of the regular traffic on the River Ganges and other waterways. A model now in the Science Museum at South Kensington, London, represents a splendid barge built and painted to resemble a peacock – that most magnificent and ostentatious of birds – which was constructed specially for the Governor of the English factory at Calcutta at that time. The vessel was propelled by paddles worked by a crew of thirty or forty who sat aft of the richly ornamented pavilion. It was steered by means of an oar fastened to the port side near the stern.

132 Top – A model of a graceful state barge from Lahore.

133 Centre – A model in the Science Museum, London, of the Udaipur state barge.

134 Below – The Calcutta state barge – a model notable for its very fine detail.

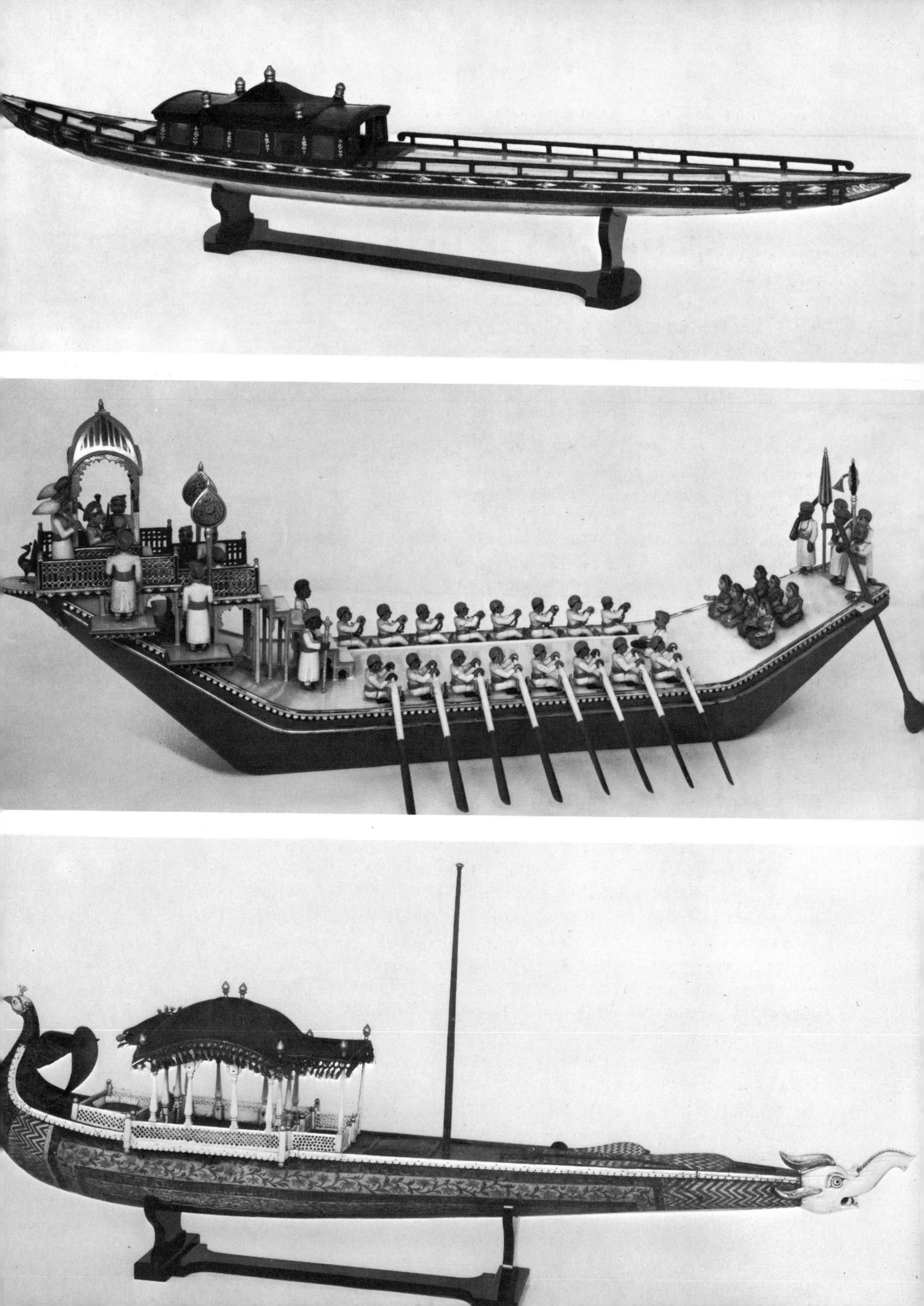

135 A model of the funeral car intended for use in Admiral Lord Nelson's cortége.

In the same collection, there is a model of a state barge from Lahore that shows clearly the difference between the vessels of importance employed in that state and those customarily found on the Ganges. The Lahore state barge had a hull with an extremely graceful form, and the cabin was built and decorated in the pseudo-Georgian style so commonly found in the Lahore Palaces.

At South Kensington, too, there is a model of the state barge, of considerable age, that has been in use until quite recently in Udaipur, the capital of Mewar State in Rajputana. In form this colourful vessel was similar to so many boats of the Indus – that is it was shaped like a rather prosaic punt, with sloping bows and stern – but in this instance a lofty platform was built up above the bows, and on this platform was placed the Maharanee of Udaipur's richly decorated throne, with, above it, a sheltering canopy. Smaller, shelf-like platforms projected at each side to accommodate the members of the Maharanee's entourage. The vessel was steered by one long oar at the lower – that is, the stern – end and was propelled by oarsmen seated on the deck.

During the twenty-five years that were to remain of his reign after he was restored to the throne of England, Charles the Second had no fewer than seventeen royal yachts, and some splendid contemporary models of them are still in existence. One of the most remarkable of these – a boxwood Admiralty Board model of the *Navy*, built for the King in 1671 by Sir Anthony Deane of Portsmouth, England – was formerly in the Sergison Collection at Cuckfield Park. With its gilded and polychromed decorations, and its gun ports framed in circular wreaths, it is now one of the most admired exhibits in the Henry Huddleston Rogers Collection at Annapolis. Much of the original rigging on this model is still standing.

Also at Annapolis, and looking remarkably spick and span, is the pearwood Admiralty Board model of the English state barge that Commander Robinson saw, early this century, in an under-appreciated state at Cuckfield Park. It has twenty-two figures of crew men – all of whom are about six feet tall, according to the scale.

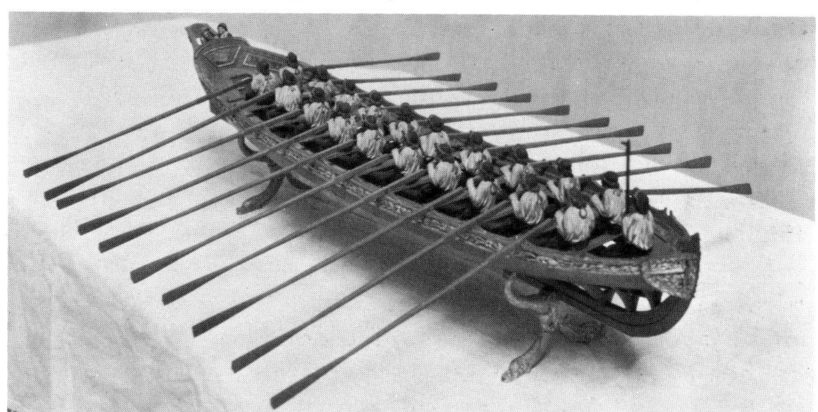

136 Above – the rigged model of the English royal yacht the Navy *now in the United States Naval Academy Museum.*

137 Right – an Admiralty model made of pearwood of an unidentified state barge of the second half of the seventeenth century.

Models of vessels appropriately fitted and decorated for their Heads of State are to be seen today in the principal museums of most of the maritime nations of Europe. To take just one particularly notable example from Scandinavia – the Swedish Maritime Museum (Statens Sjöhistoriska Museum) at Stockholm has a fine model of the Royal Schooner *Amphion* that was designed for Gustav the Third of Sweden by the great shipwright Fredrik Henrik af Chapman. This vessel was finished in 1778 at Djurgarden, Stockholm. The Swedish naval actions at Svenskund in the years 1788–90, including the decisive battle with the Russian fleet, were led from the *Amphion*. Models of another royal vessel from Scandinavia – the *Dannebrog*, the richly decorated Danish royal yacht – can be made today from kits sold ready for the home craftsman to assemble.

More than one great maritime nation, in the long history of the world, has called a large expanse of water *mare nostrum* (our sea) as a gesture of ownership. Often, this extravagant claim has been willingly agreed to by foreign nationals who have wished to sail over the appropriated seas, in return for the degree of law and order established there by the dominant state. In northern waters, the tokens of overlordship have usually been flags to be saluted, or tolls to be paid. The ancient republic of Venice announced her right to be considered the Queen of the Adriatic by a symbolic ceremonial which took place, most fittingly, on the deck of a vessel as ornate as Cleopatra's – the famous *Bucentaur*.

There was, to be strictly correct, a series of *Bucentaurs*. The Spaniard Pero Tafur, who was at Venice in 1438, describes in his *Travels* the *Bucentaur* of his day 'all hung with rich cloth of gold'. The *Bucentaur* of 1520 also attracted attention. The *Bucentaur* built in 1605 inspired a Venetian poet of sea-faring leanings to write verses about her, and more than one English traveller on the Grand Tour recorded his admiration at the sight of her. Peter Mundy, when at Venice in 1620, was taken to see her:

> 'a vessel like a gallye but shorter, thicker and higher, wherein is shewed the uttermost of Art for carved works: being overlayed with gold soe that when she is in the water she appears to be all of pure gold'.

John Evelyn, who saw the same craft twenty-five years later, calls her 'their gloriously painted, carved and gilded Bucentora'. But the *Bucentaur* of 1727 – according to Signor Luchini, citizen of Venice, who wrote a detailed description of her embellishments shortly after her launch – was the 'last word' in state barges. She was also the last of her line.

We know, from many chronicles, the customary order of proceedings on the morning of each Ascension Day.

First, the *Bucentaur* would be brought round from the Arsenal with the lion-flag of St Mark floating from her single mast, and she would lie off the Piazzetta, as in Canaletto's painting, awaiting the Doge and Signory in their robes of office. When all these were embarked, with the Ambassadors to the Republic from other states and any distinguished foreigners who happened to be in the city, the *Bucentaur*, propelled by her forty-two oars manned by employees of the Arsenal, four men to each oar, and escorted by a crowd of other craft, small and great, proceeded to the Island of

Above, a waterline model, made by Donald McNarry, of the South African liner Scot, *1891, one of the most beautiful Victorian steamships.*

Below, a model of the paddle steamer Sirius, *1837, the first vessel to cross the Atlantic under continuous steam power.*

Overleaf, a lovely silver model of the Long Island Sound paddle steamer Commonwealth *of 1855 on a music box.*

COMMONWEALTH

Santa Elena, just beyond what are now the public gardens. When she arrived there, the patriarch and clergy of the Cathedral Church of San Pietro, arrayed in full pontificals, put off to meet her. When the symbolic gold ring had been duly blessed, the *Bucentaur* passed on through the Porto de Lido into the open Adriatic. There, the Doge dropped the ring into the sea from a window near his throne in the stern of the ship with the formula '*Desponsamus te, Mare, in signum veri perpetuique dominii*'. Mass in the church of the monastery of San Nicolo at the northern end of the Lido followed. Then the *Bucentaur* brought her company back to the palace.

The whole fabric of a famous vessel has sometimes been preserved beyond the natural span of the ship's life when there has been a real national pride in its history, but all that now remains of the most sumptuous of the *Bucentaurs* are some possible fragments in the Museo Correr at Venice and a piece of a flag pole, fluted like a column, that lies in the Museo Storico Navale at the Arsenal. Her virtual disappearance was linked exactly with the melancholy circumstances in which the republic of Venice ceased to exist. In 1797, Venice, weakened by internal decay, surrendered to Napoleon Bonaparte without a blow. He had already declared that he would be to Venice a 'second Attila', and in this respect he kept his word. The *Bucentaur* was, moreover, associated with an ancient oligarchy over which the doctrinaire members of the French Directory could hardly be expected to feel sentimental. So on 9 January, 1798, Bonaparte's soldiers attacked with hatchets the grand old vessel as she lay in her dock in the Arsenal, and presently her golden upper-works, her sculptured muses, and allegorical figures of all the Virtues lay ruined in fragments upon the ground. Other carved and gilded vessels in the dockyard – notably the ornate felucca built in 1764 for the pageant presented to the Duke of York when he visited Venice in that year – shared the same fate. The remains of the *Bucentaur* were collected into a heap, transported across the canal to the Island of San Giorgo, and in the garden of the monastery there were made into a great bonfire that was kept burning three days. The gold gleaned from among the ashes was then packed off to the General-in-Chief's Treasury at Milan.

But the glories of the *Bucentaur* were not to be completely effaced. Her hulk, converted into a floating battery ship, and renamed the *Hydra*, remained afloat until 1824. A few years after her final demise, Vice Admiral the Marchese Paulucci delle Roncole caused the best-known existing model of her to be made. It is said that an old workman at the Arsenal was the constructor, and that the task took him from 1835 to 1841 to complete. Unfortunately, the name of this craftsman is unknown, even at the museum of the Arsenal, but the model may well be the work of someone who had seen the last *Bucentaur* intact.

Amidships view of a model of the screw paddle steamer Great Eastern, *1858*.

Other models of her, besides this, exist. A small scale model of her was found at Trinity House in London in 1928. The model has been shown to be of eighteenth-century workmanship and is, therefore contemporary with the vessel it represents. How it came into the possession of the Trinity House is not known.

It would be a mistake to think that all the vessels used to transport royal and other grand personages have been, without exception, as splendid as those shown so far in this chapter. One small craft at least has been honoured by being chosen to carry distinguished passengers when it had not been, itself, really sufficiently dignified for its illustrious burden. An example of such a craft is provided by the model of a water velocipede – a de luxe version of a number built during the period 1870 to 1891 by Messrs Searle and Sons at Lambeth, London. This strange vessel was constructed for the personal use of Queen Victoria on Virginia Water – an artificial lake not far from her castle at Windsor. The model in the Science Museum at South Kensington, London, was based on a sketch from a contemporary *Illustrated London News*. The lifelike figures represent the Queen, widowed for more than ten years but still in deep mourning, accompanied by her daughter-in-law, then Princess Alexandra. Her son, later to be Edward the Seventh, is sitting behind her.

The Queen's velocipede was about 20 feet long, and composed of twin clinker-built canoes, each 2 feet wide and completely decked. The gentlemen propelled the boat by means of pedals fitted to cranks in the axle, which turned the paddle wheels. Two rudders were used for steering. These were yoked together by a brass rod, and controlled by rudder lines.

What, one wonders, would Cleopatra have thought of that?

138 This model with painted background shows a model of a water-velocipede constructed for the use of Queen Victoria on Virginia Water.

MODELS OF LAKE AND RIVER CRAFT

Craft made specially to travel on lakes and rivers have been even more various than those built for crossing the sea. They have had to be adapted to suit an extraordinarily wide range of conditions – for work in shallow water, perhaps, where the conventional type of screw propeller is hardly suitable; in places where weeds or rapids make navigation almost impossible; in tropical climates, where all decks have to be shaded with awnings or canopies, and crew and passengers have to be provided with fly-proof cabins; or in regions in which snow and ice are likely to cause discomfort and danger. Their seemingly endless variety makes them especially interesting to the model-maker (or the collector of models) who has a taste for the unusual or the picturesque. There will be room in this chapter for only a few distinctive examples. These have been drawn, to achieve a proper spread, from widely separated parts of the world.

The large rivers of the American continent can take very big boats, and the boats that have sailed on the Mississippi – long and flat, with roomy superstructures and much decorative woodwork and ironwork – have been among the most famous of all, and the most popular with model-makers.

The earliest steamer designed for use on the river was the *New Orleans* – launched in 1811 – but she proved not to be powerful enough to travel upstream. The *George Washington*, built five years after, was more successful. She had two decks and two tall funnels, and her shape was to influence the design of the great majority of the thousands of steamers that have journeyed, since her day, up and down the Mississippi.

The Mississippi steamers fall mainly into two categories – those, like the *George Washington*, that have been operated by means of a paddle situated in the stern, and the others, such as the elegant mail packet *Natchez*, of which many delightful models have been made, that have had a paddle wheel on each side. For many years, the sternwheelers were despised by the proprietors and captains of the faster side-wheelers, who referred scathingly to their economical competitors as 'wheel-barrows'.

Both kinds were subject to horrible accidents. In their desperate attempts to increase the speed of their vessels, many of the owners installed high pressure boilers that were all too liable to explode. Competition for the title 'Fastest Boat on the Mississippi' was fierce. In 1870, the title was taken from the holder, the *Natchez*, by the celebrated *Robert E. Lee*. The *Robert E. Lee* travelled from New Orleans to St Louis – a distance of some 750 miles – in a little over 3 days 18 hours.

Models of American lake and river steamers can be seen in great

JAMESTOWN

L.C.C.

139 Above, left – A model of the steamboat Jamestown *which plied between Norfolk, Va and Washington, D.C.*

140 Left – A model in the Science Museum, London, of a Thames paddle steamer of 1904.

141 Below – A model of the King Alfred *one of the graceful steamers put into service on the River Thames by the London County Council in 1905.*

142 Above, right – A model on an unusually ornate base of a Danube paddle steamer of 1846.

variety (as might be expected) in the National Museum (The Smithsonian Institution) at Washington, in the Museum of the Naval Academy at Annapolis, and in other famous collections in the United States. The Mariners' Museum at Newport News has a small but particularly interesting group. This includes models of these formerly well-known vessels: the Hudson River steamboat *Isaac Newton*, as rebuilt in 1855; the famous *Mary Powell* – Pride of the Hudson – built in 1861; and the Chesapeake Line steamboat *Charlotte* of 1889. Possibly the most unusual and beautiful model in the group is one that represents the 1855 Long Island Sound steamboat *Commonwealth.* This model is made of silver and gold. When a music box installed in the base is played the steamer's paddles revolve, and the walking beam operates.

The influence of Henry Bell's *Comet* on the shipping found in European waters has already been noted. By 1820 more than forty steamers had been built for service on the River Clyde in Scotland. By 1835 the total was 100 and this figure had been doubled by 1856. During the American War between the States, some of these little ships were employed as blockade runners, where their speed, for which they had always been noted, was of especial value. The *Columba*, built by J. and G. Thompson in 1878 for service between Glasgow and Ardrishaig, was not only one of the largest and most popular of the Clyde paddle-steamers but she was, perhaps, the most attractive vessel that ever joined the fleet. There is an excellent model of the *Columba* in the Glasgow Museum and Art Gallery.

The proprietors of the early river steamers on the Thames not only provided scheduled services, but they also introduced excursions to resorts at the seaside – regarded as great treats in London in the time of Charles Dickens. In 1904 and 1905 the members of the London County Council had a fleet of thirty paddle-steamers built to provide a service on the river between Hammersmith and Greenwich. These vessels, which were exceptionally graceful, were known by the people of London as the 'Penny Steamers'. Each could accommodate 500 passengers. There is a model of one of them – the *King Alfred* built by the Thames Ironworks Company at Blackwall in 1905 – in the British National

Maritime Museum at Greenwich. The model, which came from Sir James Caird's collection, is made of silver.

Paddle-steamers were introduced on the Danube as early as 1830 by Count Stephen Széchenyi. By the middle of the nineteenth century, some fast and elegant vessels were being built at Budapest under the supervision of Mr Samuel Pretious. A contemporary model of one of these, which has been carefully preserved, shows that its hull followed the fine lines usually found in fast river steamers of that period. In one respect, though, it is remarkable – the 'sponsons' (the curved platforms fitted fore and aft of the paddle-boxes) extended further than was usual in contemporary British practice, but not as far as the sponsons fitted on American river steamers of the time.

One of the most remarkable models to be seen anywhere in the world is a replica of an extraordinary river vessel. The model, to 1:12 scale, was made by qualified Chinese shipwrights at Fowchow, working under the supervision of Mr G. R. G. Worcester, who was formerly river officer in the Maritime Department of the Chinese Customs Service. It shows a craft of the unique type known usually as the Crooked Stern Junk. According to local tradition, the build of these junks has not been altered in any particular for as many as fifteen centuries. The eccentricity of their design has excited much speculation about their origin, but as they operate only in a remote region of the Upper Yangtze, there have been few opportunities for prolonged research into the matter.

Fowchow, the home port of the Crooked Stern Junk, is situated some sixty miles below Chungking. It stands at the mouth of the Kung-t'an where this river joins the Yangtze, of which it is a tributary. The junks are used for carrying the salt which is brought down the Yangtze from the famous brine wells of Tzeliutsing, above Chungking, the salt being transhipped at Fowchow for distribution in the interior. The many rapids and rocks that intersect the river make navigation on its turbulent waters an extremely dangerous operation, and there is little doubt that this is the factor that influenced the junks' designers when they evolved their peculiar shape.

The outstanding feature of the design of the hull of one of these junks is its lack of lateral symmetry. The deck is curved so noticeably that the port counter (that is, the port side edge) coincides more or less exactly with the centre line of the hull. The after deck slopes steeply down from the port counter (which is high) to the starboard counter (which is low). Contorted this shape may be, but it does allow the long stern sweeps with which the junk is steered to function independently without interfering with each other, as it provides sure foundations, on different levels, for the fulcrums on which the sweeps rest. The heavy, long main sweep would necessarily be comparatively slow in action. The much lighter auxiliary sweep is intended to be brought into action immediately, in the event of a sudden emergency.

MODELS OF SHIPS AND BOATS MADE FOR SPECIAL PURPOSES

In a sense, all ships and boats can be said to have been made for some special purpose, even if it is only for moving men, women and freight from one part of the earth's surface to another. But just as when all the pigs in George Orwell's novel *Animal Farm* were said to be equal, some were reckoned to be more equal than others, so, in the marine world, certain vessels can be clearly seen to have been intended from the start to perform some quite extraordinary functions. Understandably, many of these abnormal vessels have caught the attention of model-makers, since a model based on a prototype that has a marked individuality, will, almost automatically, have a distinctive character too.

The earliest special-purpose boat we know about, or think we know about, was the Ark, made by Noah with his wife and their sons and daughters-in-law when they were threatened by the onset of the Great Flood. As well as affording the means of preservation for all the members of the family, it had also to provide emergency accommodation for two representatives of every known species of beast. As God said to Noah, dictating in a remarkably confident way

143 A model of a Chinese crooked-stern junk.

144 *The diorama in the Mariners' Museum, Newport News, that shows Noah's ark under construction.*

what appear to have been the first specifications ever recorded for the construction of any boat:.

'Make thee an ark of gopher wood: rooms shalt thou make in the ark and shalt pitch it within and without with pitch. And this is the fashion which thou shalt make it of: the length of the ark shall be three hundred cubits, the breadth of it fifty cubits, and the height of it thirty cubits. A window shalt thou make to the ark; and in a cubit shalt thou finish it above; and the door of the ark shalt thou set in the side thereof: with lower, second, and third stories shalt thou make it.'

When the officials of the Mariners' Museum at Newport News decided that Noah's Ark should be represented convincingly in their world-famous collection of model ships and boats, they were faced with some apparently insurmountable difficulties. The only information they could rely on was that contained in the Book of Genesis, and that, as may be seen even from a quick glance at the relevant passage quoted above, was sparse. They knew that a cubit is generally reckoned to have been approximately 18 inches – that is, the length of a man's forearm from his elbow to the tip of his middle finger. By multiplying the cubit-dimensions given in the Bible by one and a half, they reached the surprising conclusion that the craft they wanted to model had been 450 feet long, seventy-five feet wide, and forty-five feet high, to its eaves. (This was larger, even, than the six-masted schooner *Wyoming*, built in 1909, which is usually considered to have been the biggest wooden ship of recent centuries.) To make a vessel of this size from wood, even today, with our comparatively sophisticated constructional techniques, would be a formidable task.

And, they had no firm evidence about the actual shape of the Ark. In all the traditional pictures, based of course on guesswork, Noah's vessel is represented as having a more or less conventional ship's hull, with, on its upper surface, a commodious structure resembling a box. This, to the small group of experts at the Mariners' Museum, seemed to be an unlikely form for the actual Ark to have been given. Noah, they argued, would have had to build his vessel with relatively primitive tools and with a strictly limited number of assistants. He would have been concerned only that it should float during the unprecedented rainstorms and their aftermath. It would not have needed to weather any large seas, and there was no reason, therefore, that it should have a shape that was in the slightest degree sophisticated. Why, they wondered, should the basic structure of the Ark not have been really simple – perhaps, the simplest possible extension of the simplest possible ship-form: a raft, made from a number of logs joined together in the easiest possible way, and, on the flat platform, a three-storey barn-like structure that would conform exactly to the dimensions suggested by the Biblical text?

Having heard no arguments that persuaded them to discard their theory, they started to construct their model, commissioning, so that it should have a suitable background, a diorama that showed a level clearing in a grove of centuries-old trees in the valley of the rivers Tigris and Euphrates. This clearing was situated, as Noah's chosen building site would probably have been, just where a small creek adjoined one of the principal rivers.

The exhibit that resulted from their labours is now one of the most unusual attractions of the Mariners' Museum. The Ark is shown as it would have appeared (in the opinion of the model's makers) after about eighty years' work had been done on it. Biblical scholars believe that the Ark took the best part of a century to complete.

There are, in the model, many interesting touches. No straight-trunked gopher trees are shown growing in the jungle-like thickets that surround the building site – the model-makers assumed that the timbers needed for the construction of the Ark would have grown upriver, and would have been felled there and floated down to the clearing. A sloping ramp, made from two stout logs, is placed so that the heavy timbers can be raised from the level of the water to the level of the building site. Windlasses, to be turned by Noah and his sons, provide the lifting power. Tiny wedges and hammers lie around – these were the tools that would have been used, surely, for splitting and squaring the logs. There are even miniature cauldrons of a type that Noah might well have used for melting down the pitch.

Under a tree which has a trunk made, like those of most of the trees in the model, from a twisted root, there is a tent-like canopy. Under the shade of this, there is a small table. Round it are assembled several people, who are looking at the plans of the Ark on a scroll. Signs of the magnitude of their labours are everywhere. The parts of the Ark that were built first are rapidly becoming submerged beneath choking weeds, and their greying surfaces are shrouded with vines that have been clambering over them during the long years spent in preparation for the Flood.

Of all the many and varied ships and boats that have been built, since the Ark, to fulfil some special purpose, none has been of more benefit to mankind than the lifeboat. The lifeboat first existed, predictably, in model form, and the original version is still carefully preserved.

During the eighteenth century, the River Tyne in the north of England was unprotected by piers, and it was, in consequence, an extremely dangerous port to make in heavy seas. A sandbar stretched from the Black Middens at Tynemouth to the Herd Sands on the south side. At ordinary low tides there was only 4 feet of water, while high water showed 14 feet. Great skill was required to navigate ships through the shoals and sandbanks, and the people of Tyneside frequently saw as many as a dozen vessels stranded on rocks after a particularly violent storm.

At last public feeling – already intense, following the loss of many local breadwinners – was roused to a new high pitch by the loss of the crew of the ship *Adventure* of Newcastle, wrecked on the Herd Sands during a heavy gale in September, 1789. To do something positive about the dangers of the Tynemouth, a committee was formed of 'Gentlemen of the Lawe House' at South Shields. One of the most imaginative actions of this committee was to offer a prize for the best model of a boat adapted for saving life during storms and perils at sea.

Many models and plans were submitted to the committee, but only two were thought worthy of serious consideration.

One, made by Henry Greathead, a local boatbuilder, was a long, flat boat, dissimilar at bow and stern, and with no provision for

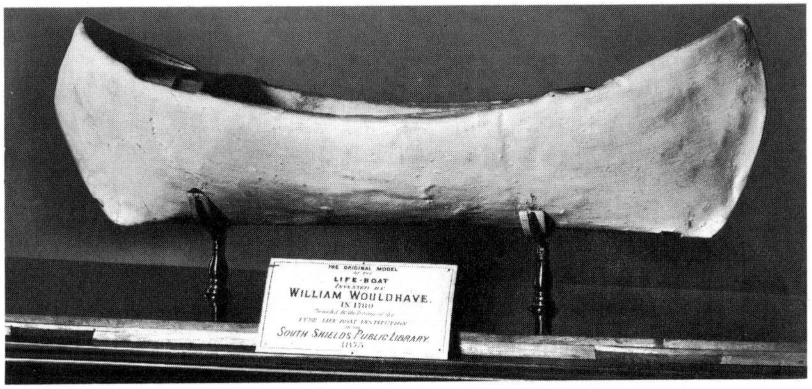

145 The original model of the life-boat invented by William Wouldhave in 1789.

extra buoyancy, either by means of air boxes or by cork.

The other model was submitted by William Wouldhave. Wouldhave had been born in Liddle Street, North Shields, in 1751. Having served his apprenticeship as a house painter in the town, he had afterwards moved to South Shields. He is described as being a tall, enthusiastic man of great independence of spirit who was at times even brusque and eccentric. He used to occupy himself in spare moments in devising various instruments, among which were an organ, a clock, and an electric machine. For the competition organized by the 'Gentlemen of the Lawe House', he constructed a tin model 22 inches in length, 9 inches broad amidships, $4\frac{1}{2}$ inches deep outside, and 3 inches deep inside.

The chairman of the committee, a Mr Nicholas Fairless, held up Wouldhave's tin model. 'So you pretend to make a model?' he is said to have enquired. 'What advantage do you say this thing possesses?'

There may have been some officious or patrician tone in the chairman's voice that touched Wouldhave on the raw. 'Why', the inventor replied with a sneer, 'I say it will neither sink, nor go to pieces, nor lie bottom up. Will any of yours do as much?'

Unfortunately for Wouldhave, his uncouth manner did not commend itself to the committee, and they declined to accept his model. When they offered him one guinea as compensation for all the work he had put in, Wouldhave contemptuously refused the money. Mr Greathead did not even get offered a guinea, but the committee resolved that they would compensate him by employing him to build the boat for them, when they had eventually found a suitable design.

They found that design through the good (or bad) offices of the chairman. A few months later, Mr Fairless, in company with Mr Greathead, made a clay model that embodied in detail all the important features of Wouldhave's entry, except that, on the suggestion of Greathead, the keel was cambered or curved instead of being straight. This model was submitted to the committee and

146 Top – A model of an ingenious horse-operated dredger, c. 1780.

147 Below – A model of the steam dredger General Diaz *(1905).*

148 Above, right – A model of the paddle tug Monarch *(1833).*

149 Below, right – A model of the British navy tug Dromedary *(1844).*

MONARCH

150 Above – A model of the Five Fathom Bank lightship. The original ship was moored off Delaware Bay.

approved, and Mr Greathead was commissioned to build the full size lifeboat at a cost of £91. The boat was launched on 30 January, 1790, and named the *Original*. She rendered splendid service until 1830, when, having rescued the crew of the brig *Glatton* that had been wrecked on the Black Middens, she was caught by a sea and driven against the rocks, being split clean in two with the loss of two of her hands.

Though William Wouldhave, the true inventor of the lifeboat, deserved all the rewards and honours that might have been going, he did not get them. For some years he earned a meagre living as clerk to a local church and as a teacher of singing to the children in a charity school, but he died at the age of seventy in poverty and neglect.

151 Right – A model of the Gjøa, *the ship in which Roald Amundsen made his expedition through the North-West Passage in 1903–1906.*

152 Right – A contemporary model of a shallow draught British landing craft from which troops, horses and supplies could be disembarked on open beaches during amphibious operations.

A contemporary model of a little eighteenth-century landing craft is in the Science Museum at South Kensington, London. When horses were needed in an amphibious operation, the thwarts of this craft would be removed so that the mounts could be taken ashore, as well as troops and supplies. In the model as it stands, twenty seamen are shown, each with an oar, with an officer in command. A detachment of forty-eight troops with a drummer in bright contemporary uniforms makes up the colourful landing party.

Mechanical dredgers were first used on the Brussels–Scheldt Canal, in the Netherlands, in 1561. These were horse-driven. So, too, were the dredgers used in and around the Port of Amsterdam during the later years of the eighteenth century to keep the docks and canals free from mud and silt. A model which is the property of Mr E. D. Kalis shows one of these utilitarian vessels in some detail.

The dredgers, or 'mud-mills', were made in north Holland. They had carvel-built hulls that were almost rectangular. In each, there was a continuous chain of buckets accommodated in a central well. This bucket-chain was driven by four horses. These were harnessed to long arms that radiated from a vertical shaft, and they were forced, therefore, to keep moving along a circular path 23 feet in diameter.

As they toiled, the spoil from the water's depths was carried upwards on the underside of the bucket chain. Each bucket was fitted with a hinged bottom. This was forced out when the bucket reached the upper end of its journey, discharging the contents of the bucket into a chute at the stern of the vessel. The chute could be raised or lowered, by means of a hand winch operated on the deck, to suit the barge or barges sent to accompany the dredger.

Tugs – sturdy and practical little vessels – have a certain nostalgic, if limited, appeal for the model-maker. After the possibilities of this type of craft had been shown by the *Charlotte Dundas*, tugs were made in many countries, the first steam tugboat on the Thames being believed to have entered service in 1816. By 1822 the British navy was using steam-propelled vessels as tugboats for towing the sail warships in and out of harbour.

It is interesting to compare a contemporary model of a relatively early tug, such as the paddle tug *Monarch*, built in 1833 (which was the first steam tugboat owned by the famous towage company Messrs William Watkins Ltd – the model is still in the company offices) with a model of a later vessel, such as that of the paddle tug *Dromedary*, built in 1894, and used by the British Admiralty for towing and general purposes at Portsmouth. Both these may look a little antiquated, perhaps, when they are compared with the *Zwarte Zee*, a tug built in the Dutch shipyard of K. Smith, which

Above, a model of a seventeenth century Venetian galley, typical of the ornate vessels used for trading in the Mediterranean.

Below, a model, including tugs and dock facilities of the first of British Petroleum's 215,000 tons dead-weight tankers, the British Explorer.

Overleaf, a contemporary model of the Bucentaur, *1728, the last of the state barges of the Doges of Venice.*

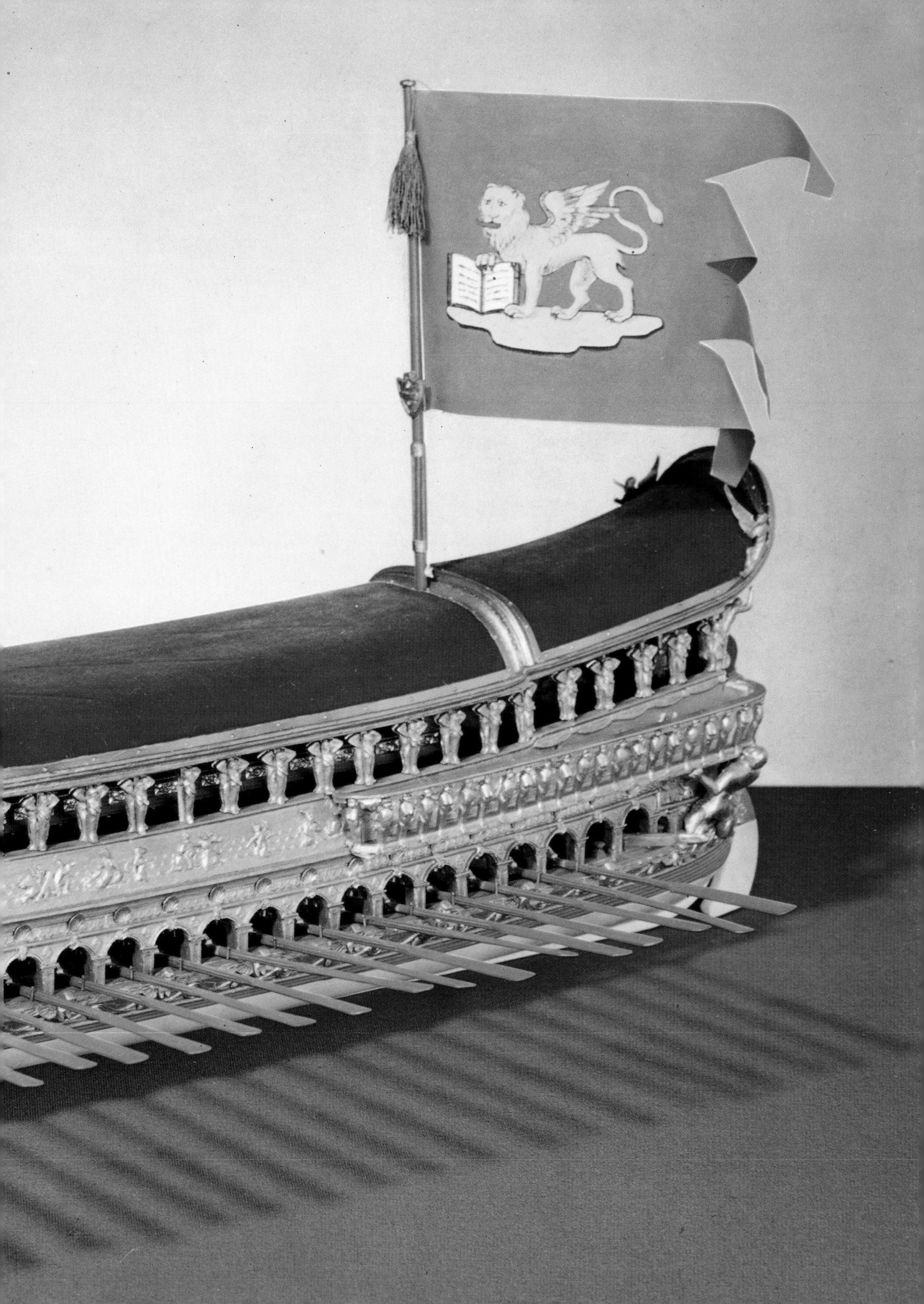

has undertaken much major rescue work in the North Sea and the English Channel. This model of the *Zwarte Zee* was made from one of the popular assemble-it-yourself kits marketed by the Great Danish commercial firm of Billing Boats. Model Shipways Co Inc, of Bogota, New Jersey, market a kit from which a craftsman of no-higher than average abilities can construct a model of the diesel tug *Despatch No. 9* of San Francisco. This little boat, which was originally operated by the U.S. Marine Corps, possesses a fineness of proportion uncommon in tugs.

Lightships and pilot vessels, too, appeal as subjects to some model-makers, and it is interesting to notice that Billing Boats has also chosen a lightship to be the subject of one of their kits. This is the *Elbe I*, which is German-owned, and stands guard over the estuary of the River Elbe. Twelve fine models of lightships and lighthouse tenders were provided by the American Lighthouse Board for display at the Mariners' Museum at Newport News.

Models of trawlers and fishing vessels of other kinds can be found in most maritime countries. Model Shipways Co Inc, of Bogota, New Jersey, market a kit from which a splendid replica of the Motor Trawler *Hildina* of Hull, England, can be made without undue difficulty. The *Hildina* was designed specially to work the sadly depleted fishing grounds off the British Isles. Model Shipways also offer a kit with which a fine model of the North-West Passage Sloop *Gjøa* can be built. The *Gjøa*, a cargo boat of Hardanger Fjord, Norway, was bought by Roald Amundsen, the famous polar explorer, in 1901. He strengthened her and sheathed her in oak and loaded her with Arctic supplies until the water line was at her deck level. The *Gjøa* spent three winters in the ice before she arrived at Norne, Alaska, in 1906. Her journey ended in San Francisco where, in 1909, she was hauled out and presented to the city.

Occasionally, ships and boats have had to be designed and constructed in the shortest possible time to fulfil some special purpose. A model that shows one of these is divided – like the prototype – into four separate pieces. In 1874, there was an exceptionally tragic famine in India. Six twin-screwed steamers were ordered by those who were trying to get relief to the starving people. They were intended for use as grain carriers on the shallow rivers. The first of the vessels was engineered and built by Messrs J. & G. Rennie, at Greenwich, within the space of thirty-five working days. All were constructed in water-tight sections so that they could be assembled in the water when they arrived at their destinations.

As a delightful contrast to the little eighteenth-century landing-craft shown earlier in this chapter, one can study a model of a vessel intended to carry not horses, but trains. This is the model of the paddle steamer *Fabius*, built in 1909 for ferrying the engines,

Above, a waterline model of the Union-Castle mail ship Stirling Castle *beautifully made by Donald McNarry.*

Below, a model of an experimental steamboat built in Paris in 1803. It was designed by Robert Fulton, the American pioneer of marine steam propulsion.

coaches and cars of the Lagos Railway across the unbridgeable River Niger in West Africa.

The *Fabius* carried two separate lines of track, each of which was fitted fore and aft with buffer posts. These posts could be lowered so that they were flush with the deck when it was necessary for a train to pass over them. Then they could be raised to the level of the train's buffers and held in position with bipod supports. Each post could stand up to a thrust of 20 tons. For extra security, the trains were lashed to bollards that were mounted on the deck between the tracks. At each end of the boat, there were hinged sections of rail that made it possible for the tracks on board to be connected to the tracks on land, whatever the variations in the river level.

There this short list of out-of-the-ordinary model ships and boats must end. It could be extended almost indefinitely, to include models of submarines, trawlers, tankers, buoy-lifting vessels, and a score of other interesting craft. But enough have been mentioned in this chapter to show the immense range of prototypes open to the model-maker with a pronounced taste for the unusual and distinctive. Now we must look at some of the techniques used by the craftsmen who made these models.

153 Above – A model of the paddle steamer Fabius *(1909) used for transporting trains across the River Niger.*

154 Above, right – A model of the motor trawler Star of Scotland *(1947).*

155 Right – Part of the model of the BP Tanker Company's 215,000 ton British Explorer.

156 Below, right – A model of the steamship American Lancer, *32,000 tons. The prototype is normally loaded with 1,210 20-foot containers.*

A 425
STAR OF SCOTLAND
A 425

AMERICAN LANCER

8 Some Techniques used in Ship and Boat Model-making

The tools and techniques used by shipwrights and shipbuilders did not change much during many hundreds of years. As a human activity that depended on the working together of hand and eye, there is no doubt that the shipbuilder's work was at its highest level before the invention of the pitsaw and the plane. In those far-off days each man needed an artist's skill in the use of an axe or adze, and an artist's understanding of his material. Each piece of timber was, after due seasoning, picked for its own place in the ship; in each there was some particular quality of grain or texture that made it the right one above all others for that place; and the dressing-down given it by the craftsman with the well-sharpened cutting edge was like the reading of a book, so much did he learn about the wood in the process. When inventive man discovered quicker ways of obtaining the results he needed, much of the old instinct for timber construction and a certain amount of the old accuracy of eye and hand went for ever. Many of the older ship models, made by men whose names are seldom known, show that the ancient traditional techniques did not entirely vanish, however.

Many amateur ship modellers today are aware that built models, which demand minute accuracy, exact knowledge, and endless patience, are beyond them. They are content, like most of the old sailor-craftsmen before them, merely to carve or whittle their hulls, acknowledging that were life long enough they would do otherwise. Before we consider these more everyday methods though, we must pay tribute to the great craftsmen who have worked in the present century, and whose skill and scholarship have been quite equal to those of the cleverest anonymous masters of the past.

The model of Charles the First's glorious warship the *Sovereign of the Seas*, made by Mr Henry B. Culver of New York, has been called the most ambitious piece of reconstruction yet attempted in any country. The model was commissioned in February, 1918, when war conditions made all searches for information extremely difficult. The chief source of reference was the well-known print of the ship by J. Payne, but the collection of prints in the British Museum was not available. So Mr Culver had to work from a photograph of a print obtained, finally, from the Science Museum

157 A craftsman puts the final touches to a group of waterline models built to a scale of 50 feet to 1 inch.

at South Kensington, London. Further invaluable data were supplied by the great English authority R. C. Anderson, in the form of a manuscript from Lord Leconfield's collection. This document, dating from 1625, gives an exhaustive description of the rigging of a great ship of the time, providing many minute details – such, for example, as the places where the running rigging was belayed, a question that is always liable to be puzzling, even to experts. So valuable did Mr Anderson consider this manuscript that he sent it by hand to New York so that it might not go astray. With it he sent a contemporary record of the dimensions of the *Sovereign's* spars, so that the size of even these should not have to depend on guesswork.

158 To reproduce in miniature the ornate carving shown here in a detail from the portrait of Peter Pett at Greenwich was a task set the skilled craftsmen employed by Mr Henry Culver when he modelled Charles the First's splendid warship Sovereign of the Seas.

One of the most noteworthy features of this great ship, it will be

159 A waterline model of the 18-gun ship Dromedaris *which took the first Dutch settlers to the Cape in 1652. The model is made to the scale 16 feet to 1 inch.*

remembered, was its elaborate carving. For information about this Mr Culver relied, once again, on the evidence supplied by Payne's print supplemented by that yielded by a stern view of the *Sovereign of the Seas* shown in the background of a contemporary portrait of Peter Pett that hangs now in the British National Maritime Museum at Greenwich. (Mr Culver decided to disregard the stern decorations of the elaborate model made for Sir Robert Seppings' series in 1827 and now at Greenwich because, as we have seen, these do not agree with contemporary descriptions.)

When the whole structure of the hull of the ship was finished, the vertical ornaments, in the form of skids, corbels and window frames, were cut out and fastened to the sides. These, with the wales or mouldings that had already been applied, determined the exact shape and size of each of the ornamental panels that would have to be carved by Mr Culver's skilled assistants. Then, the pieces of boxwood of which the panels were to be composed were trimmed to fit the spaces, each piece being cut sufficiently thick to allow for the high relief of the ornament.

The ornament on the panels – gods, goddesses, Roman emperors, signs of the zodiac and all – was first modelled in the material known as plasterlene. Then, gelatine moulds were made from the modelled subjects, and duplicate plaster casts were taken from these moulds. The wood carvers worked from one of the retouched sets of plaster casts. The other set was kept carefully in Mr

Culver's studio so that in the case of the originals being damaged or destroyed, the work would not have to be done over again.

Before they can go very far with their planning, all model-makers, both professional and amateur, have to concern themselves, to a greater or lesser extent, with the question of scale. This is important, because no model can be completely satisfying, however finely detailed it may be, unless every part of it has been reduced in exactly the same proportion to the corresponding part of the prototype. So, if a real ship or boat is (say) 250 feet long and and has a 'beam', or width, of 25 feet, a model built to the scale ratio of 1 : 100 must not only be 2 feet 6 inches long – it must also have a beam of exactly 3 inches or it will look wrong to experienced eyes.

In choosing the scale ratio to which a model ship or boat is to be built, a craftsman will normally be influenced by the purpose the model is to fulfil. If it is being made primarily as an exhibit for a museum or as a decorative feature for a home, the space it will take up has to be considered carefully (more carefully, certainly, than it was by the ship's carpenter mentioned in Chapter 1).

To take a possible example, let us suppose that a model is to be made of the famous tea clipper *Cutty Sark*, which was 280 feet long, over all, when it was rigged. If the model is made to $\frac{1}{8}$ inch scale (that is, if $\frac{1}{8}$ inch of model is to represent one foot of the prototype vessel, the ratio being 1 :96) the model will be 35 inches long when it is finished – not so big, that is, that it cannot be moved around fairly easily when the need arises. If the model is made to $\frac{1}{4}$ inch scale (if, that is, $\frac{1}{4}$ inch of model is to represent 1 foot of the prototype vessel, in the ratio 1 :48) the model will be 70 inches long, which will be much more difficult to accommodate, and will be considerably less portable.

For the home, then, a model made to $\frac{1}{8}$ inch scale will be a more practical proposition than a model twice as long, twice as wide, twice as high, and proportionately heavier. On the other hand, the $\frac{1}{4}$ inch scale has certain advantages that has made it one of the most popular of all with the makers of model ships and boats. In making a model to this scale, any ordinarily skilled craftsman – even an amateur craftsman – will find few details of the prototype, if any, that he cannot reproduce reasonably faithfully in miniature. In a model made to $\frac{1}{8}$ inch scale, a certain number of the smaller fittings will have to be rendered in the most approximate fashion, or may even have to go by default altogether, unless the craftsman concerned is a real virtuoso, in which case he is unlikely to take on a task that is so unnecessarily fiddling.

Some model ships and boats may be found that have been made to other scales than 1 :48 and 1 :96. Among the ratios occasionally favoured are 1 :24 ($\frac{1}{2}$ inch of model to each foot of prototype);

160 Above – A fine example of a model to the scale 1 :25 – the Calmare Nyckel, *16 guns, built in 1629 in Holland and bought by the Swedish Ships Company.*

161 Right – This model of the Swedish East Indiaman Sophia Magdalena *(1774) was made to the scale 1 :48.*

1 :32 ($\frac{3}{8}$ inch of model to each foot of prototype); 1 :60 ($\frac{1}{5}$ inch of model to each foot of prototype); and 1 :72 ($\frac{1}{6}$ inch of model to each foot of prototype). Many Dutch models are made to scales such as 1 :44 or 1 :33, the ratio being based on a foot that was sub-divided into 11 (not twelve) inches. Models made today in countries that operate a metric system will be found usually to be constructed in the scale ratio 1 : 50 or 1 : 100.

Having decided on a scale, the craftsman who wants to produce a hull for a model ship or boat is next faced with choosing from a variety of possible materials. The range includes paper (several layers of gummed paper make a surprisingly strong shell), wood, plastics of different kinds, glass fibre and metal. From this range he has to select one (or a combination of two or more) that will be the best for his particular purposes.

If he chooses wood, which is a naturally buoyant material, and relatively easily worked, he will start with two clearly defined advantages over the man who chooses a material that is prone to sink, and is relatively intractable. But if he does choose wood, he will be faced at once with the need to make a further decision: which, of all the scores of possible kinds of wood, is the one most suited to his needs?

The easiest to work of all is undoubtedly balsa wood. Balsa wood is light, and as soft as cheese – the softer grades are considerably softer than some cheeses. It can be cut or carved with any sharp knife, and pieces of it can be joined without any difficulty with one of the quick-drying cements made and sold specially for the purpose. Unfortunately, balsa wood is dangerously fragile, and a hull made

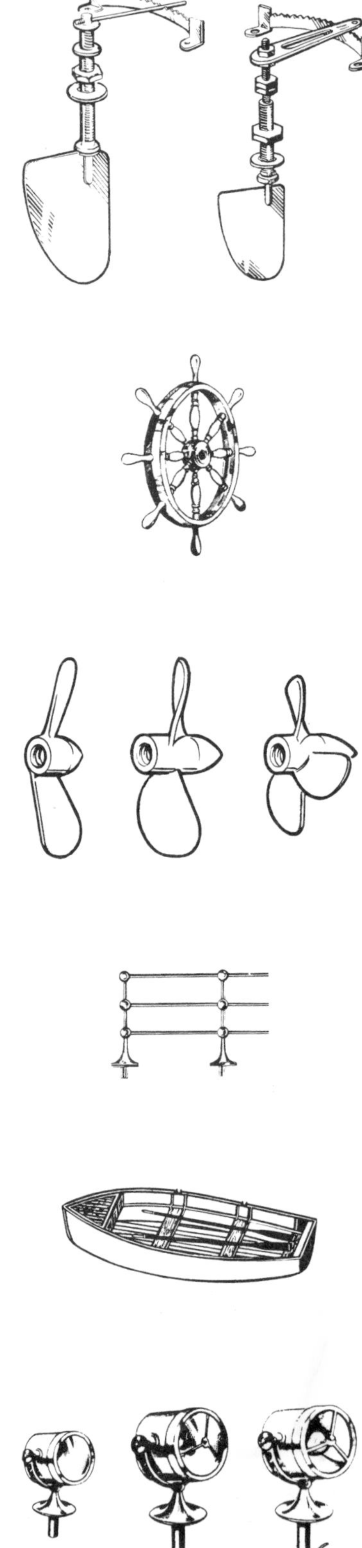

from it has usually to be sheathed with some thin but tough material such as silk, cambric or nylon sheet. Glass fibre is now used extensively for sheathing balsa wood hulls.

Obeche is a little harder and stronger than balsa wood, but it is not much more difficult to cut or shape. It is considerably lighter than most of the woods from which the hulls of model ships and boats were made before reliable kiln-dried obeche became generally available. In the hull of any vessel that is actually intended to sail, this lightness may be a valuable quality, since the walls of that hull will not need to be carved away as drastically as the walls of a hull made from a heavier wood.

Harder woods than balsa and obeche that have been used at various times for the hulls of model ships and boats include mahogany, yellow pine, Douglas fir, silver spruce, maple, hickory, African whitewood, and others too numerous to be catalogued here. When a hull is to be planked – that is, when it is to be made up from ribs and strips and various pieces instead of being carved from a single block – mahogany or Oregon pine is often chosen. Whatever kind of wood is used, it is important it that shall be as free from knots as possible, as straight-grained as possible, and – this is absolutely essential – it must be adequately seasoned.

One of the most painstaking craftsmen there has ever been – August F. Crabtree, whose collection has found a permanent home in the Mariners' Museum at Newport News – went to extraordinary lengths to obtain wood that would be ideally suitable for every part of his model ships.

A native of Portland, Oregon, Crabtree may have been first impelled to make a miniature fleet because his ancestors had been shipbuilders on the Clyde, in Scotland. He started work on his great project when he was twenty years old, and he went on working on it until he was forty-five, or thereabouts, creating models that have been judged, by many experts, to be among the finest ever made. At intervals, he would travel with his wife around the United States, exhibiting in department stores the results of his labours. He made a van out of an old milk truck in which to carry his precious load. At one time, its contents were insured for one hundred thousand dollars.

To get his raw materials, Crabtree would hew his own pieces of wood. After he had cut the logs, he would leave them in a creek of running water for two or three weeks so that all their acid and sap would be effortlessly washed away. Then he would cut the wood into smaller slabs and he would store them away for two or three years in a shady, dry, well-ventilated place. When they appeared to be absolutely free of moisture, he would expose them to strong sunshine for two or three months more. Only by submitting his raw materials to these protracted processes could he ensure that no vestige of warping or shrinkage would occur to spoil his completed models. It is believed that Stradivarius, the maker of superlative violins, used the same techniques for seasoning his wood.

Carving the hull of a model ship or boat from a single block of wood can be a laborious business, and this technique is not now much used for the production of small models. In the method usually regarded as the least difficult there are four distinct stages by which the outer shape of the hull is arrived at:

First, the craftsmen draws the side view of the hull on one side of the block he is intending to reduce. Next, he shapes the block roughly, with some straight-across cuts that conform to the outlines he has so far drawn. This produces a shape that is true to the shape of the hull of the ship or boat only if it is viewed directly from the side. In the third stage, he draws the outline of the hull, seen from another direction, on one of remaining flat faces of the block. (Usually, he will do this on the deck surface. Sometimes, he will draw on the bottom surface as well. It would be impractical, as a rule, to draw them on the bottom surface alone). When the waste wood has been cut away from outside these outlines, a blank will be left that will need only a little final trimming.

To carry out this trimming so accurately that the outer shape of the finished hull will be an exact reproduction, on a miniature scale, of that of the hull of the prototype, the craftsman will normally use gouges, chisels, spokeshaves, or one or more of the newer proprietary shaping tools. (Planes are not really suitable. They tend to make the surface of a model hull into a collection of flats.)

As aids, the craftsmen will probably use a number of templates. Each template will be made from a sheet of card, wood, metal, or some other reasonably rigid, reasonably easily cut material, and it will be shaped so that it conforms exactly to one of the outlines contained in the draughts or plans of the vessel's hull.

When a hull carved from a single block of wood has to be hollowed out, so that its weight is reduced sufficiently for the vessel to sail, the model-maker's difficulties are increased. 'The hollowing out proved to be very laborious', wrote a man who made a model of the twin screw steamer *Duke of York* in 1902. 'I got a brace, and with a 1 inch bit commenced to bore a number of holes; then I took a chisel and began to get out some good chunks of wood. This took me a week to finish, for I have hollowed out to about $\frac{1}{4}$ inch, with the exception of the bottom, which is about 1 inch thick so as to allow for some stout screws for bedding down engines.' Where the walls of a hull have to be as thin as this, it is all too easy for an insufficiently skilled woodworker to reduce them too drastically, doing damage that it is hard to repair.

162 A selection of authentic scale ships' fittings made for the commercial model market.

So, most model-makers who wish to avoid the difficulties of

carving a model's hull from a single block of wood choose the simpler alternative system known usually as the bread and butter method. In this the hull is made up from a number of separate planks that are laid on top of each other, like slices of bread, and are then fixed together with glue (this represents the butter) and – usually – some locating pegs or dowels. The method has some distinct advantages – in the first place, it is much easier to obtain timber of suitable size and quality in these thin sections than it is to obtain larger blocks. Then, by marking out each plank separately, and by rough cutting to the lines marked out before the planks are finally assembled, it is relatively easy to produce in a remarkably short time an embryo hull that is quite accurately symmetrical.

Whether he is making the hull for his model ship or boat from a single block of wood or by the bread and butter method, the craftsman who has decided to reproduce as exactly as possible on a smaller scale the shape of the hull of an actual prototype vessel will generally rely for the necessary information on three separate and distinctly different drawings. Obviously these drawings are more readily understood by experts than by amateur model-makers, but even a novice can interpret them correctly if he sets about the task in the right way.

The first drawing to be examined is the sheer plan. This shows the profile of the hull as it would be seen if viewed directly from

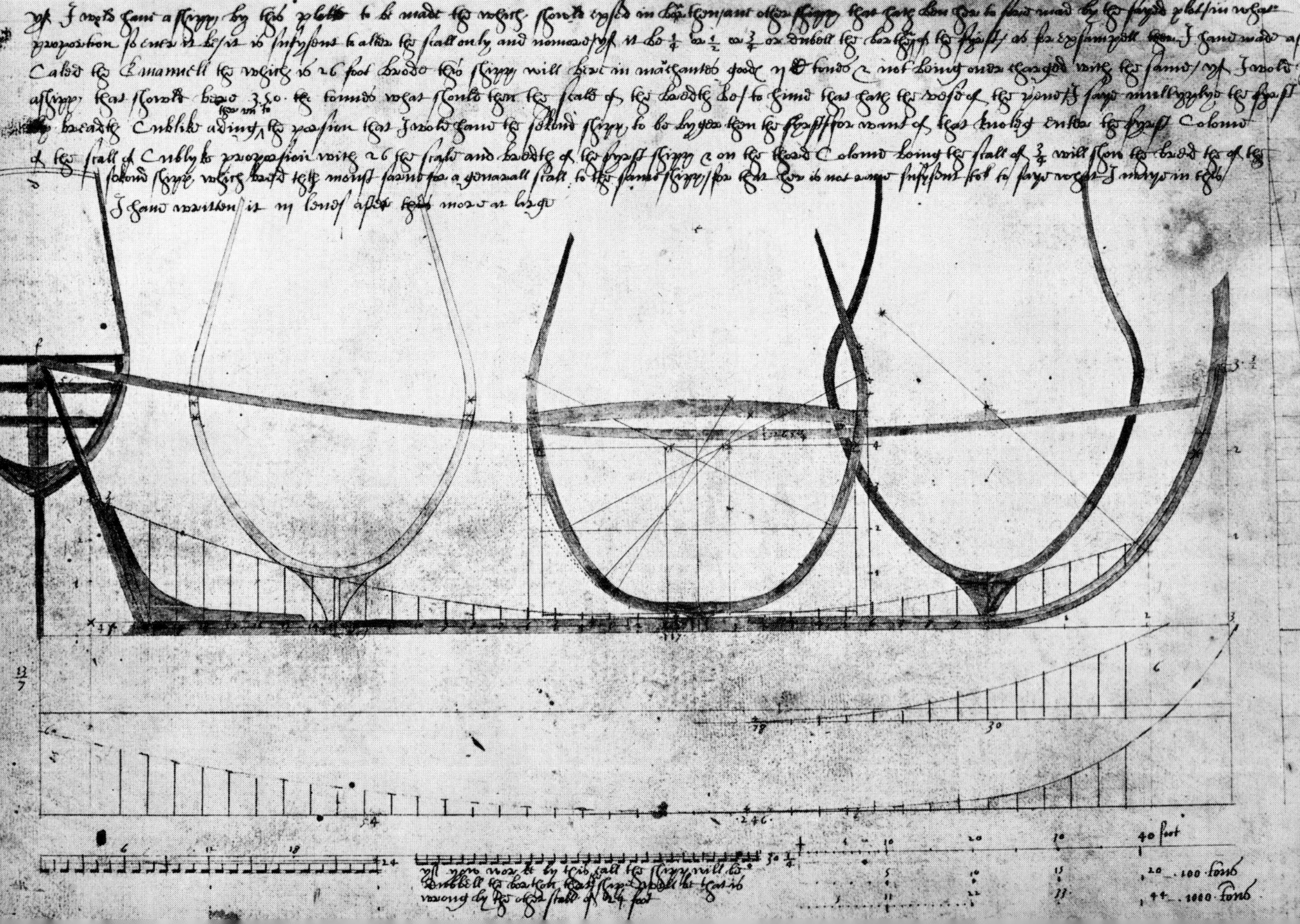

163 A draught with four sections of an Elizabethan ship. Access to information of this kind may help a model maker to be historically correct.

164 A model now in the Orlogsmuseet, Copenhagen, which shows clearly the constructional methods used by craftsmen in the seventeenth and early eighteenth centuries.

the side. Like all the drawings, it is divided by a series of vertical and horizontal lines that act as ordinates. The horizontal lines are drawn, in every instance, parallel to and at a definite distance from the waterline. In a sheer plan made specially for model-makers, these horizontal lines are probably spaced an inch apart, or half an inch, or some other distance that will be likely to suit the convenience of those building up their hulls by the bread and butter method. Ideally the gaps between the lines are equal to the thickness of the planks from which the hulls will be made up.

The sheer plan is sub-divided, also, by a series of vertical lines or ordinates, arranged at some quite arbitrary interval, which may be (say) 2 inches or 3 inches. These lines, which are numbered for ease of identification, are generally referred to as 'station lines'.

On the sheer plan are seen, inside the outer profile of the hull, certain other curved lines that are usually referred to as the 'buttock lines'. To understand how these lines are drawn, one has to imagine that a number of saw cuts are made through the hull, each parallel to, and a definite distance from, the fore-to-aft centre line. The buttock lines show the shape of the imaginary slices into which these cuts would divide the hull.

The second drawing the model-maker will need to study is the half-breadth plan.

The half-breadth plan also shows a number of imaginary outlines. In this case, the outlines are those that would be produced by a number of cuts made by a saw or knife moving horizontally through the hull – in the same plane as the surface of the water. Each of the cuts would be made along one of the equally spaced parallel horizontal lines shown in the sheer drawing. The outlines shown in a half-breadth plan will in most cases be curved. They will tend to be separate and distinct at the bow and at the stern. Amidships, where several lines are liable to fall in close proximity to each other, they may be rather more confusing.

The station lines are shown on the half-breadth plan as well as on the sheer plan. When they are used in conjunction with the horizontal outlines, the width of the hull at any point on the ordinates may be quickly ascertained.

The third drawing is usually called the body plan. This, too, is divided by horizontal lines and by vertical lines (the latter representing the middle line of the ship, and the buttock lines, seen end on). The curved lines show the shapes that would be produced by a number of imaginary cuts made by a saw or knife moving transversely across the solid block hull at the station lines. Normally, the two halves of the body plan are dissimilar – the lines on the right hand side of the drawing showing the outlines of the forward half of the hull; those on the left, showing the after half.

The hulls of many model ships and boats are made by the 'hard chine' method. (A hard chine hull is one in which the main surfaces of the sides and bottom are flat, and make distinct angles where they meet, instead of merging imperceptibly into one another in a curve. The chine lines in a hull of this kind will run continuously from the the bow, or near it, to the stern.) Hard chine hulls are especially suitable for models that are intended to plane. They are relatively easy to make, and do not call for a quantity of expensive materials. Usually, a preliminary framework is made, consisting of a central keel, with a number of lateral frames or bulkheads, a stem and stern, and symmetrically arranged chines and inwales. This framework is then fitted with ply skins or planking (reliable resin-bonded birch ply, in several thicknesses from $\frac{1}{32}$ inch upwards, is stocked by most model-makers' suppliers). It is a technique that has only one really serious limitation – few full-size ships more than 100 feet or so in length have hard chine hulls. So, hard chine construction appeals principally to model-makers who are not concerned about absolute truth to a prototype.

The number of model ships and boats to be found with true clinker-built or carvel-built hulls – other than those made by highly-skilled professional craftsmen, or by hobbyists working from ready-to-assemble commercial kits – is strictly limited. The reason for this should be fairly obvious: neither technique is really suitable for the production of small scale hulls, and better results can usually be obtained by less fiddling and tedious methods. Occasionally, small clinker-built boats are reproduced, in model form, by techniques not unlike those employed for building the prototypes. Planks cut from plywood are generally used. As well as being pinned or rivetted to the supporting structure, it is almost invariably necessary for these to be fastened together with glue where they overlap, an expedient that could hardly be justified by full-size practice.

In some exceptionally small models – as, for example, in those that represent the tenders, dinghies and lifeboats that are ancillary to larger vessels – the general appearance of clinker construction can be simulated quite easily by means of card planks glued, as overlays, on to hulls carved from solid wood or balsa.

In models that represent ships and boats with planked decks, the lines made by the divisions between the planks are usually drawn on the model lightly in pencil and then made more distinct with Indian ink, applied from a draughtsman's ruling pen. Here, again, the question of scale is important: the width of the planking on a prototype vessel will hardly ever be greater than 6 inches, and it will usually be only 3 inches or 4 inches. Lines drawn to suggest foot-wide planks will inevitably look unreal and clumsy.

Metal has not been used as often as wood by amateur craftsmen for the construction of hulls for model ships and boats. This is not surprising, since metals are apt to be so much more difficult to cut and work to shape. Thin sheet metals such as brass, zinc, lead-coated steel or 'tinplate' (that is, steel sheet coated on each side with tin) can be moulded to compound curves by being smoothed or rubbed over suitably shaped wooden formers, but this is a fairly tedious business. An even more wearisome method is planking up, in which small metal plates are placed together edge to edge, all over a specially made wooden former, and are then carefully soldered together. When the metal hull is complete, it is removed from the former so that ribs, frames and other reinforcements can be soldered, bolted or rivetted to the inside, before the deck superstructure and fittings are added.

Glass fibre is a material that is becoming increasingly popular with model-makers, and when it is used for the hulls of model ships and boats it has certain marked advantages. It is suitably strong for a material of its weight; it has a total resistance to water and oil; and it will not rot (as wood has a tendency to do) or corrode (this is a hazard that affects most of the metals used for model-making, tinplate being particularly liable to rust where the mild steel is exposed). Glass fibre is used, principally, for the hulls of larger models.

165 Left – Many modern models are made of glass fibre. This model hovercraft shows the splendid finish that can be obtained with this material.

166 Overleaf – Scale drawings of this kind provide craftsmen who make model ships and boats with their basic information.

Glass fibre cannot be carved as easily as wood. The material, when it has set, is so hard that it can only be cut with the tools used normally for working metals. Hulls made with it have to be constructed by a different technique.

First, a suitable former or mould has to be made. (There is a radical difference between these: the model-maker has to decide in advance whether he wishes to use a male or female shape, weighing

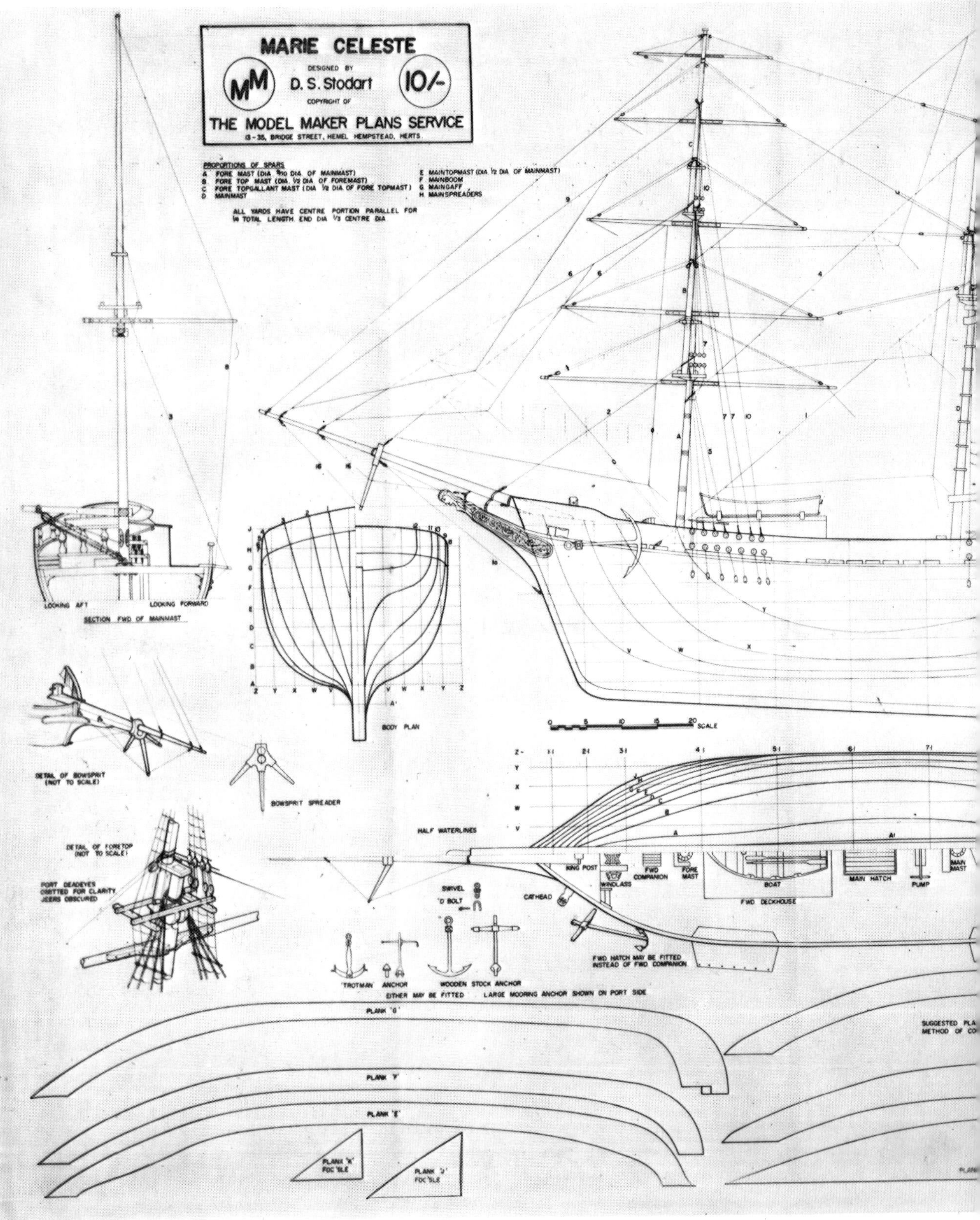
MARIE CELESTE
DESIGNED BY
D. S. Stodart
COPYRIGHT OF
THE MODEL MAKER PLANS SERVICE
13 - 35, BRIDGE STREET, HEMEL HEMPSTEAD, HERTS.
MM
10/-
PROPORTIONS OF SPARS
A. FORE MAST (DIA 9/10 DIA OF MAINMAST)
B. FORE TOP MAST (DIA. 1/2 DIA OF FOREMAST)
C. FORE TOPGALLANT MAST (DIA 1/2 DIA OF FORE TOPMAST)
D. MAINMAST
E. MAINTOPMAST (DIA 1/2 DIA OF MAINMAST)
F. MAINBOOM
G. MAINGAFF
H. MAINSPREADERS
ALL YARDS HAVE CENTRE PORTION PARALLEL FOR 1/4 TOTAL LENGTH. END DIA 1/3 CENTRE DIA
LOOKING AFT
LOOKING FORWARD
SECTION FWD OF MAINMAST
BODY PLAN
DETAIL OF BOWSPRIT (NOT TO SCALE)
BOWSPRIT SPREADER
DETAIL OF FORETOP (NOT TO SCALE)
PORT DEADEYES OMITTED FOR CLARITY. JEERS OBSCURED
HALF WATERLINES
SCALE
KING POST
WINDLASS
FWD COMPANION
FORE MAST
BOAT
FWD DECKHOUSE
MAIN HATCH
PUMP
MAIN MAST
SWIVEL
'D' BOLT
CATHEAD
FWD HATCH MAY BE FITTED INSTEAD OF FWD COMPANION
'TROTMAN' ANCHOR
WOODEN STOCK ANCHOR
EITHER MAY BE FITTED . LARGE MOORING ANCHOR SHOWN ON PORT SIDE
PLANK 'G'
PLANK 'F'
PLANK 'E'
PLANK 'K' FOC'SLE
PLANK 'J' FOC'SLE

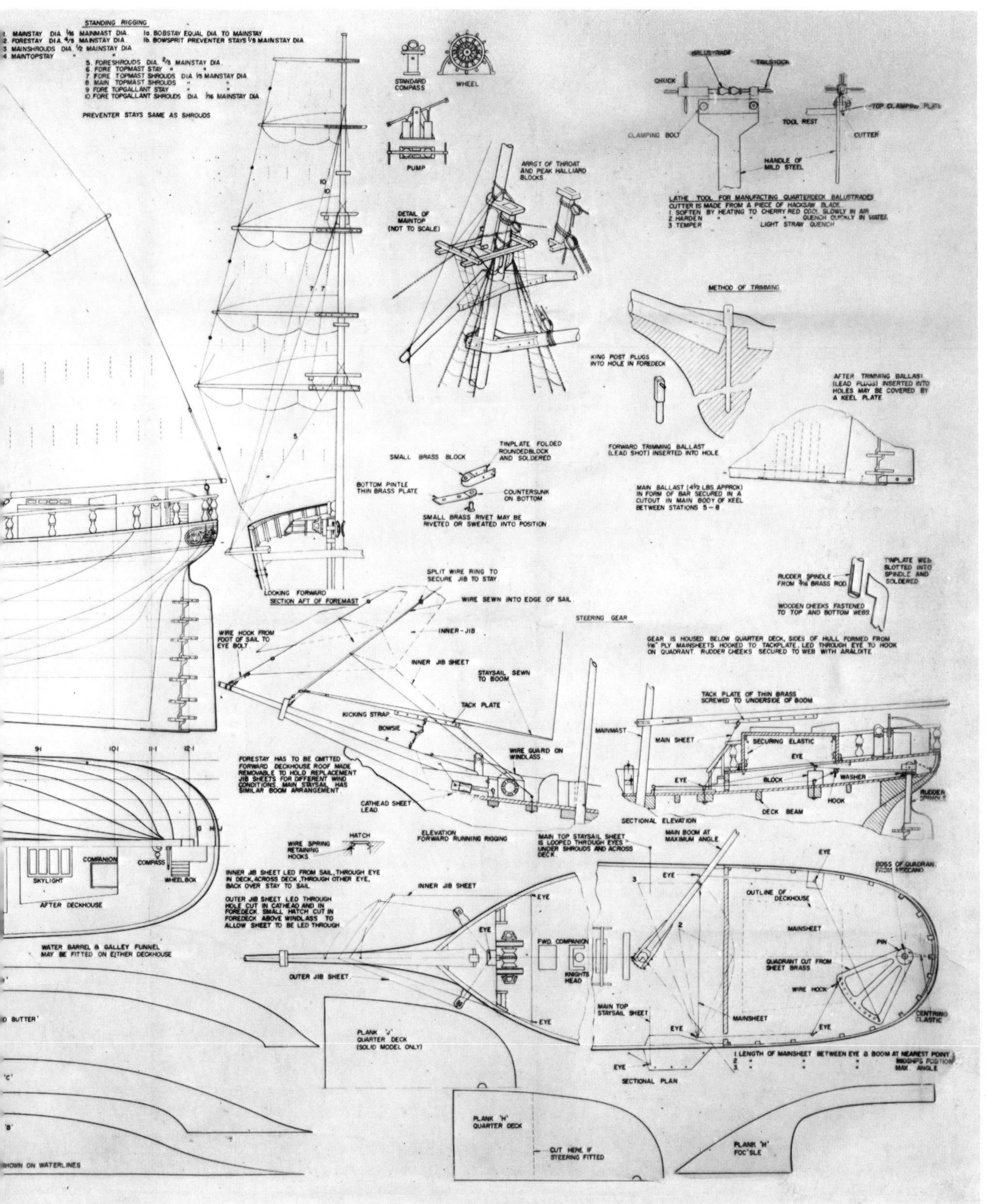
STANDING RIGGING
1. MAINSTAY DIA 1/16 MAINMAST DIA.
1a. BOBSTAY EQUAL DIA. TO MAINSTAY
2. FORESTAY DIA. 4/5 MAINSTAY DIA.
1b. BOWSPRIT PREVENTER STAYS 1/3 MAINSTAY DIA.
3. MAINSHROUDS DIA 1/2 MAINSTAY DIA.
4. MAINTOPSTAY " "
5. FORESHROUDS DIA. 2/3 MAINSTAY DIA.
6. FORE TOPMAST STAY " "
7. FORE TOPMAST SHROUDS DIA. 1/3 MAINSTAY DIA.
8. MAIN TOPMAST SHROUDS " "
9. FORE TOPGALLANT STAY " "
10. FORE TOPGALLANT SHROUDS DIA. 7/16 MAINSTAY DIA.
PREVENTER STAYS SAME AS SHROUDS
STANDARD COMPASS
WHEEL
PUMP
ARRGT OF THROAT AND PEAK HALLIARD BLOCKS
DETAIL OF MAINTOP (NOT TO SCALE)
BALUSTRADE
TAILSTOCK
CHUCK
CLAMPING BOLT
TOOL REST
TOP CLAMPING PLATE
CUTTER
HANDLE OF MILD STEEL
LATHE TOOL FOR MANUFACTING QUARTERDECK BALUSTRADES
CUTTER IS MADE FROM A PIECE OF HACKSAW BLADE.
1 SOFTEN BY HEATING TO CHERRY RED COOL SLOWLY IN AIR
2 HARDEN " " " QUENCH QUICKLY IN WATER
3 TEMPER LIGHT STRAW QUENCH
METHOD OF TRIMMING
KING POST PLUGS INTO HOLE IN FOREDECK
AFTER TRIMMING BALLAST (LEAD PLUGS) INSERTED INTO HOLES MAY BE COVERED BY A KEEL PLATE
FORWARD TRIMMING BALLAST (LEAD SHOT) INSERTED INTO HOLE
MAIN BALLAST (4½ LBS APPROX) IN FORM OF BAR SECURED IN A CUTOUT IN MAIN BODY OF KEEL BETWEEN STATIONS 5 – 8
SMALL BRASS BLOCK
TINPLATE FOLDED ROUNDEDBLOCK AND SOLDERED
BOTTOM PINTLE THIN BRASS PLATE
COUNTERSUNK ON BOTTOM
SMALL BRASS RIVET MAY BE RIVETED OR SWEATED INTO POSITION
LOOKING FORWARD
SECTION AFT OF FOREMAST
SPLIT WIRE RING TO SECURE JIB TO STAY.
WIRE SEWN INTO EDGE OF SAIL.
RUDDER SPINDLE FROM 3/16 BRASS ROD
TINPLATE WEB SLOTTED INTO SPINDLE AND SOLDERED
WOODEN CHEEKS FASTENED TO TOP AND BOTTOM WEBS
STEERING GEAR
GEAR IS HOUSED BELOW QUARTER DECK, SIDES OF HULL FORMED FROM 1/16" PLY. MAINSHEETS HOOKED TO TACKPLATE, LED THROUGH EYE TO HOOK ON QUADRANT. RUDDER CHEEKS SECURED TO WEB WITH ARALDITE
WIRE HOOK FROM FOOT OF SAIL TO EYE BOLT
INNER-JIB
INNER JIB SHEET
STAYSAIL SEWN TO BOOM
TACK PLATE
KICKING STRAP
BOWSIE
WIRE GUARD ON WINDLASS
FORESTAY HAS TO BE OMITTED FORWARD DECKHOUSE ROOF MADE REMOVABLE TO HOLD REPLACEMENT JIB SHEETS FOR DIFFERENT WIND CONDITIONS. MAIN STAYSAIL HAS SIMILAR BOOM ARRANGEMENT
CATHEAD SHEET LEAD
TACK PLATE OF THIN BRASS SCREWED TO UNDERSIDE OF BOOM
MAINMAST
MAIN SHEET
SECURING ELASTIC
EYE
BLOCK
WASHER
HOOK
DECK BEAM
RUDDER SPINDLE
SECTIONAL ELEVATION
COMPANION
COMPASS
SKYLIGHT
WHEELBOX
AFTER DECKHOUSE
WATER BARREL & GALLEY FUNNEL MAY BE FITTED ON EITHER DECKHOUSE
WIRE SPRING RETAINING HOOKS
HATCH
ELEVATION FORWARD RUNNING RIGGING
MAIN TOP STAYSAIL SHEET IS LOOPED THROUGH EYES UNDER SHROUDS AND ACROSS DECK
MAIN BOOM AT MAXIMUM ANGLE
INNER JIB SHEET LED FROM SAIL, THROUGH EYE IN DECK, ACROSS DECK, THROUGH OTHER EYE, BACK OVER STAY TO SAIL
OUTER JIB SHEET LED THROUGH HOLE CUT IN CATHEAD AND IN FOREDECK. SMALL HATCH CUT IN FOREDECK ABOVE WINDLASS TO ALLOW SHEET TO BE LED THROUGH
BOSS OF QUADRANT FROM MECCANO
OUTLINE OF DECKHOUSE
MAINSHEET
PIN
QUADRANT CUT FROM SHEET BRASS
WIRE HOOK
CENTRING ELASTIC
FWD COMPANION
KNIGHTS HEAD
OUTER JIB SHEET
MAIN TOP STAYSAIL SHEET
PLANK 'J' QUARTER DECK (SOLID MODEL ONLY)
1 LENGTH OF MAINSHEET BETWEEN EYE & BOOM AT NEAREST POINT
2 " " " MIDSHIPS POSITION
3 " " " MAX. ANGLE
SECTIONAL PLAN
PLANK 'H' QUARTER DECK
CUT HERE IF STEERING FITTED
PLANK 'H' FOC'SLE
SHOWN ON WATERLINES

up the advantages and disadvantages of each.) If he decides to use a male former, he will have to make it a little smaller, all over, than the finished hull is to be, as the thickness of the glass fibre shell will account for the difference between the sizes. In this case, the outer surface of the hull will have the particular texture of the last layer of glass fibre, and it is liable to be rough. If he decides to make a female mould, its main feature will be a hollowed-out impression of the hull shape, and this will be the actual intended size. When the impression has been lined with glass fibre, as a pie dish may be lined with pastry, the shell produced will have an outer surface that is as smooth as the mould. The inner surface, in this case, is likely to be the rougher.

167 Left – An example of decking in a model that looks as if the planks are really to scale.

168 Right – Information that helped with the rigging of this model of the Prince *of 1670 was obtained from a plan in Sir Anthony Deane's 'Doctrine of Naval Architecture', a contemporary manuscript preserved at Magdalene College, Cambridge.*

Whichever alternative is chosen, the former, or mould, may either be constructed to the model-maker's own design, or may reproduce to scale a prototype ship.

Then, to the outside surface of the former or to the inside surface of the mould, layers of glass cloth or mat are applied that have been impregnated with the necessary fusing resins. At this stage the material is conveniently flexible, which allows it to be manipulated into almost any shape. After it has been left for a short time to set, the glass fibre shell can be removed from the former or mould.

Having completed the main shape of the hull of his ship or boat, the model-maker normally feels free to turn his attention to the deckwork, superstructure and rigging. No features of a model sailing ship need more careful attention, if the final effect of the whole is not to look unrealistically clumsy, than the masts and stays. Invariably, in a real full-size craft these would be planned

and made with considerable subtlety. The model-maker has to be equally artful in his approach.

As a source of interesting information, Kipping's *Treatise on Masting and Rigging*, first published in the early nineteenth century, still takes a lot of beating. In those great days of sail, Kipping tells us, certain principles were applied almost universally to mast design. We know from him that on a typical three master, the height of the main mast would be roughly two and a half times the beam of the ship. (That is, a ship with a beam of 30 feet would have a main mast 75 feet long, or a little over.) We know, too, that the length of the mizzen mast would be approximately four-fifths the length of the main. Kipping tells us that to calculate the diameters of the main and fore masts correctly, we should allow 1 inch for every 3 feet of the mast's length. The diameter of the mizzen mast, he records, should be just two-thirds the diameter of the main mast. He goes on to give the correct relative sizes of the topmasts and topgallant masts, and a lot more information that a meticulous craftsman, modelling a ship of the period, will find invaluable.

In model yachts that are intended to sail, and do not have to be true to any particular historical prototype, it is customary now for the masts to be made of dural tube. On large models, stainless steel wire is used for the rigging, flax or linen thread being used principally in smaller models and models that are intended to represent traditional sailing vessels.

Anyone who reads a detailed history of the great sailing ships of the past will be impressed by numerous accounts of epic battles between men and sails. The task of taking in a 'square' sail when a strong wind was blowing was a formidable one. Often, the job would have to be done at night, in pitch darkness, when a ship was lurching about in a heavy sea. To avert disaster, the men would have to climb out to the yards, where, numbed with cold and drenched to the skin they would struggle to secure the canvas. At times like those, when the sails would be banging about and threatening to throw them off the yards to almost certain death, it must have seemed to the sailors as if the fabric was alive and endowed with devilish energy.

When a sailing ship came to rest in harbour for any length of time, its sails would be unbent and stowed away, and with them a certain amount of the running gear would be taken down. That is the state in which many sailing ships are represented in model form. Some people believe, though, that a model of a sailing ship should be fully-rigged, with all sails and the gear that belongs to them, if it is to look really complete. It is largely a matter of taste.

Providing sails in a convincing fashion is certainly one of the harder jobs that faces the model-maker. Too often the miniature

169 Right – The men aloft add human interest to this model of a 120-gun ship.

170 Below – A close view of the quarter-deck bulkhead of the rigged model of the Prince *in the Science Museum, London, showing the high standard of finish achieved by the craftsmen in the Museum's workshops.*

171 & 172 Overleaf – Two ships bearing the proud name of 'Lion'; left, a model of the Norske Løve *in the Sjøfortsmuseum, Oslo with sails, and right, without sails, the* Leon *in the Musée de la Marine, Paris.*

sails with which a miniature ship is dressed look unrealistically flimsy or unnaturally coarse and clumsy – incapable of acting, under any foreseeable conditions, in the highly dangerous conditions just described.

Paper, parchment and vellum would seem, at first glance, to be entirely suitable for use as potential sail material for the model-maker, but in practice they are only of any real value when they are used to represent the sails of racing yachts, and similar craft, and then only when the models are made to a very small scale.

Better, by far, are light cottons and linens, Egyptian cottons and the linens from which handkerchiefs are made being usually favoured. The tracing linen used by draughtsmen is also suitable, but it has to be boiled first, to remove the waxy substance with which it is impregnated, and then it must be ironed. Unbleached calico is used for the sails of many working model yachts. Light sails, such as spinnakers, are now frequently made from polythene.

Paper patterns are usually made to establish by trial and error the right size and shape for each sail. The lower edge or 'foot' of a square sail is generally given a distinct curve or 'roach' which improves the sail's set.

Sails have been decorated since the earliest days of navigation. In ancient Egypt, they were often given a chequered pattern of red, purple, blue and white. Plutarch records that Cleopatra ordered a purple sail, embroidered with flowers. Viking sails usually had a number of crossing diagonal stripes which may have been made with sewn-on leather bands or some other form of reinforcement. In the middle ages, sails were emblazoned splendidly with the heraldic achievements of the knights who owned or fought in the ships. By the middle of the sixteenth century, pictures of saints and elaborate religious designs had largely taken their place. Unfortunately, many less meticulous craftsmen and restorers have been content to conjure up sail decorations for their models without first obtaining any authentic historical information, and their work is liable to be (in this respect at least) misleading.

If oil colours are chosen for adding decorations to the sails of a model ship, the sails may be placed on blotting paper while they are being painted so that any of the surplus pigment carrier may be safely soaked up. When the designs are dry, faint lines can be drawn on the cloth to suggest the joints between the pieces of canvas that would make up the whole sails. White cotton may be machine-stitched along these lines to give a convincing small-scale representation of the tracking seen on full-size prototype sails.

Nobody knows for certain the name of the man who first thought of passing a relatively large model ship through the relatively small neck of a bottle, and of setting it up, firmly and safely, fully rigged with masts and sails, in the interior. It seems likely that the feat was

173 The gaily decorated sails give this model of a Mediterranean galley a high individual note.

174 Collectors will admire the carefully stitched sails in this convincing model of a Scottish merchantman of the Stuart period.

performed for the first time in the forecastle of one of the windjammer sailing ships, probably about the middle of the nineteenth century. As we have seen, creative activities that demanded much patience and perseverance were popular in the cramped crews' quarters of those vessels, and it may have been a seaman model-maker with a little more ambition and resourcefulness than his fellows who first set himself this task with so much inherent difficulty. When he had achieved his purpose, his companions would no doubt have wished to show that they could do as well or better. Soon, fierce rivalry would have developed, the aim being to pass the largest possible ship into the bottle with the smallest possible neck.

To the uninitiated, the mystery of 'how the ship gets into the bottle' is particularly fascinating, and many and unlikely have been the theories advanced by those who do not know the answer. 'The ship is built first and the bottle is blown round it' is one incorrect statement that is often heard, and another is 'The end of the bottle is cut off, and then, when the ship is inside, the glass is sealed back on again'. Only a super-optimist would believe that such a model, with all its masts, sails and rigging, could actually be assembled piecemeal inside the bottle.

The process of assembly is, in fact, a tedious one. The hull, masts and yards are made, first, from pieces of wood. Then small holes are made with a fine needle or a watchmaker's broach at carefully selected places in the various parts – holes through which will pass the threads that represent the stays (that is, the ropes used to brace the masts), the lifts (the ropes used to raise the lower yards) and any other lines that may be needed to pull the model into its proper shape once it has been fixed into its final position inside the bottle.

The masts are 'stepped' or fitted into sockets in the hull in such a way that they can lie back flat against the deck while the ship is entering the bottle. The yards are 'cockbilled' – that is, they are turned on pivots so that they are parallel to, or nearly parallel to, the masts. Paper is usually used for the sails. Each square sail is rolled round a pencil or some similar smooth cylindrical object so that a slight belly is produced in it before it is glued in position on its yard.

Several preliminary rehearsals may be necessary, with the ship outside the bottle and fixed to a temporary base, before the system of erection is seen to be foolproof. Then the ship is fastened down inside the bottle – usually with glue on a putty bed that has been fretted and painted so that it suggests a rough sea. The head stays and other threads are pulled so that the masts and yards take up their proper positions. A few traces of glue are sufficient to prevent the threads from slipping back. When the glue is dry, the unwanted lengths and ends of thread are trimmed off with a small sliver of razor blade set in the end of a long thin stick, or are burned off with red hot wires.

175 This model of the Finnish barque Herzogin Cecilie, *which was wrecked off the coast of South Devon in 1936, was made by an ex-sailor two years later. Note the tiny tug in the neck of the bottle.*

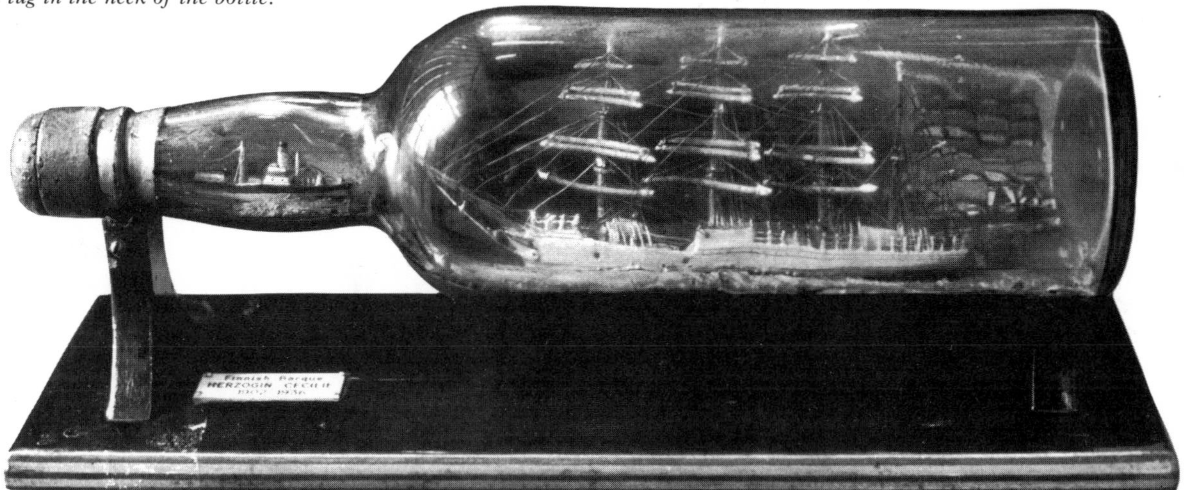

9 Commercial Models of Ships and Boats

For hundreds of years, model ships and boats have been made especially to be bartered or sold. We know, for instance, that many of the beautifully detailed models made by sailors on shipboard during the great days of sail were exchanged for liquor within a few hours of the craftsmen reaching land. Hung up in dockside taverns, these models were usually neglected, or abused, and soon disintegrated. In this chapter, we shall see some of the models that have been mass-produced, rather than created individually, for purely commercial reasons.

As with most developments in the model and toy trades, the great German manufacturers have tended to lead the way – only, in the case of model ships and boats, a little less resolutely than they did with model railways. During the later decades of the nineteenth century, firms like Bing Brothers brought out various model water craft from time to time, many of them made with pressed tinplate, and some operated by cheap clockwork mechanisms. (To activate these, one had usually to use a key to turn a winder concealed in one of the funnels.)

The growth of the great firm of Bassett-Lowke, of Northampton, England, in the early days of this century brought a new and vigorous figure into the international model trade. Wenman Bassett-Lowke, who gave the firm its name, was trained as a young man in his father's general engineering works. Being fond of making scale models in his spare time, he soon found it difficult to obtain from commercial sources the various parts he needed for his hobby. So, he decided to go into business on his own account. First, he spent a short period on the staff of Messrs Crompton Limited, electrical engineers of Chelmsford, to gain experience in the application of electricity to model engineering. Then he engaged a number of outstanding craftsmen and designers to help him to produce models that would be based more exactly on existing prototypes than those being marketed at that time by the great German manufacturers. When he appointed a marine architect, Mr E. W. Hobbs, to be the manager of the firm's London retail showroom in High Holborn, the company was influenced strongly towards the production of model ships. In the

176 A good kit model, from the firm of Steingraeber, of the clipper Agilis *(1840) – a typical American slaver of the period.*

177 Left – Warship models made by Bassett-Lowke ready for transporting to the Imperial Services Exhibition in 1913.

178 Below – Bassett-Lowke used the River Nene at Northampton for the preliminary trials of the models before transporting them to Earls Court, London, for the exhibition. Each ship, manned by a crew of one or two, was electrically driven; the searchlights played and the guns fired.

next few years, Mr Hobbs, who was the prime mover in the formation of the Model Yacht Racing Association, produced many designs for miniature sailing yachts which were manufactured and sold in large numbers by the company. He was also the originator of the waterline models referred to in Chapter 1.

One of the most eventful years in Messrs Bassett-Lowke's history was 1913. In that year, at the United Services' Exhibition at Earl's Court, London, the firm exhibited Mr Hobbs' miniature scale waterline ship models for the first time, with the fleets of the various powers set out to demonstrate the relative strengths of their navies, and, in another part of the same exhibition, the company mounted a display that was even more spectacular – it was, they claimed, the largest contract for working ship models ever attempted in Britain.

The commission was to produce a fleet of model battleships and other fighting ships, the largest of which were to be more than 30 feet long. Each of the models – which included representations of the *Thunderer*, *Colossus*, *Neptune*, *King George* and *New Zealand*, as well as of cruisers, torpedo boats, and smaller craft – was operated by men concealed in its hull, who attended to the steering, signalling, gunfiring, and other effects supplied by Messrs Brocks, the firework manufacturers. Before the models were despatched to London, they were tried out in a preview on the River Nene, at Northampton. This rehearsal was watched by large crowds and attracted a lot of publicity. The representations of a naval battle given at Earl's Court, in a specially installed artificial lake, proved to be the main attraction of the exhibition. Model ships and boats, either saved up for or given as presents, from that time on and for the next two decades were among the most popular playthings in Britain and many other countries to which Bassett-Lowkes' were able to export its wares.

In the 1930's, interest in commercially produced model ships and boats started to decline as other, more excitingly up-to-the-minute amusements were devised to entertain the young and the young-in-heart. Surprisingly, it was the introduction of the plastic kit shortly after the Second World War that helped to bring about a revival of public interest in the construction of model ships and boats. In outfits of this kind pre-moulded parts have to be assembled, according to simple instructions usually well furnished with numbered diagrams. Some of the kits are so elementary that they can be completed in a few minutes by an intelligent child without adult guidance. Others are more intricate, and involve so many components that they may take many hours of intense concentration before the ships or boats they are intended to produce are ready for display.

Prominent among the manufacturers of ready-to-assemble kits, in America, is Revell Inc., of Venice, California, already mentioned in several different contexts in the pages of this book. Pioneering member of the company, Lew Glaser, took a $700 gamble at the end of the Second World War when he bought a failing plastics business and launched Precision Specialities, a small enterprise that produced plastic ornaments and novelties. In 1946, Glaser turned his attention to toy production, marketing a Minnie Mouse washing machine that proved popular, and following this, at a later stage, with a plastic Maxwell automobile pull-toy. Showing the Maxwell for the first time at the 1950 Toy Fair, Glaser found himself almost overwhelmed with orders. Even with a production of ten thousand Maxwells a day, there was a consistent backlog of some eight hundred thousand orders to make up. 'Why don't you make a model kit version?' asked hobby shop dealers at the show. Not realising what an opportunity he was turning down, Glaser ignored their suggestions, wondering as he did so why anyone should ever want to buy anything that was not already assembled.

Twelve months later, when sales of the toy Maxwells were dwindling seriously, Glaser decided to investigate the advice given him by the hobby shop dealers. Encouraged by the results of his researches, Glaser risked everything on another gamble and went whole-heartedly into the hobby model kit business. Consumer reaction was immediate. From $300,000 in 1951, Revell's sales increased to two million dollars in the following twelve months. There was no turning back – for Revell, the future lay clearly not with toys but with plastic model kits.

As might have been expected, Revell's sudden success attracted the envious attentions of the firm's many competitors. But none succeeded, as they hoped, in cutting Revell out. As Glaser put it: 'Something happened I didn't expect. A lot of competitors didn't realize that you had to have beautiful detailing. For some reason, instead of spending money on tooling, they worked on flooding the market and operating on a narrower profit margin. They didn't have our detail or authenticity or fitting of parts and so on. Fortunately for us, they didn't get repeat business, probably because people weren't satisfied with the finished model. By the time they caught up, we were way ahead.'

It is, of course, the preparatory work that ensures the success (or otherwise) of a commercially produced model kit. This is an expensive business – as much as $150,000 may have to be spent, after the initial proposal is made, before a kit starts to flow freely from the firm's machines. So, all suggestions have to be examined carefully or this enormous outlay may prove to be a disastrous investment. Generally speaking, kits from which models of ships are to be made are less liable to suffer from the ebb and flow of

Above, a model of a Viking boat, 12 feet long, made for the film 'Longships'.

Below, a model of the Argo, *ship of Greek legend, made for the film 'Jason and the Golden Fleece'.*

Overleaf, a kit model from Steingraeber of the French frigate La Flore, *1790.*

popularity than most other model kits but, even so, some ships are bound to appeal more strongly to hobbyists than others. The most popular ships of all, one busy retailer has pointed out, seem to be the ones that have sunk. The *Titanic*, the *Bismarck* and the *Arizona*, he claims, remain constantly among the best-selling models in his store.

If a decision is made to go ahead with a model kit of a particular prototype, skilled craftsmen spend hundreds of hours hand-building a master model from wood, plaster, plastic and other materials. Often, they will work from original blue-prints and the model they produce will be detailed down to the very last rivet. From this master model, engineers then make plaster and epoxy moulds. These are placed in a pantograph machine which cuts exactly, but in a smaller scale, duplicates of the moulds and patterns in steel. Workers follow through, finishing each die to a state of perfection. (In order to imitate the wood grain on the deck of Revell's model kit version of *Mayflower II*, for instance, tool makers spent hundreds of hours etching the steel dies by hand).

The last – and quickest – step is the actual production of the kits. For this, the dies are installed in an injection moulding machine which can inject plastic into them at a temperature which may be as high as 500° Centigrade and at a pressure of 1000 pounds a square inch. One of these machines, fitted with the *Mayflower's* steel moulds, can turn out complete kits at the rate of three a minute.

But making model ships and boats in plastic, from mass-produced kits, is not model boat-building, as the purist understands the term – too much of the preliminary work has already been done, and too little is left to the initiative of the model-maker. To satisfy the demand for kits that allow superb models to be produced by more traditional methods without prohibitive difficulty, two or three outstandingly successful firms have been marketing, in this era that has been so dominated by plastics, kits with all-wood components. These appeal to model-makers who like to feel that they are working in a time-honoured way, and call for no tools or equipment more difficult to handle than a sharp craftsman's knife, with a selection of spare blades; a razor saw; a sharp pricker; a marking pencil and a straight edge; a set of fine files; a sanding block with fine sandpaper or flourpaper; a roll of transparent adhesive tape; and some suitable glue. In most cases, these kits are supplemented by comprehensive sets of ready-made fittings – cannon, davits, anchors, companion ways, and so on. These are intended to make things easier for the model-maker who does not happen to have the facilities, or the necessary skill, for working in brass and other relatively intractable materials.

The ocean-going yacht Satanitas, *1892, reproduced here from one of the Steingraeber kits.*

One of the leaders in this field has been the internationally

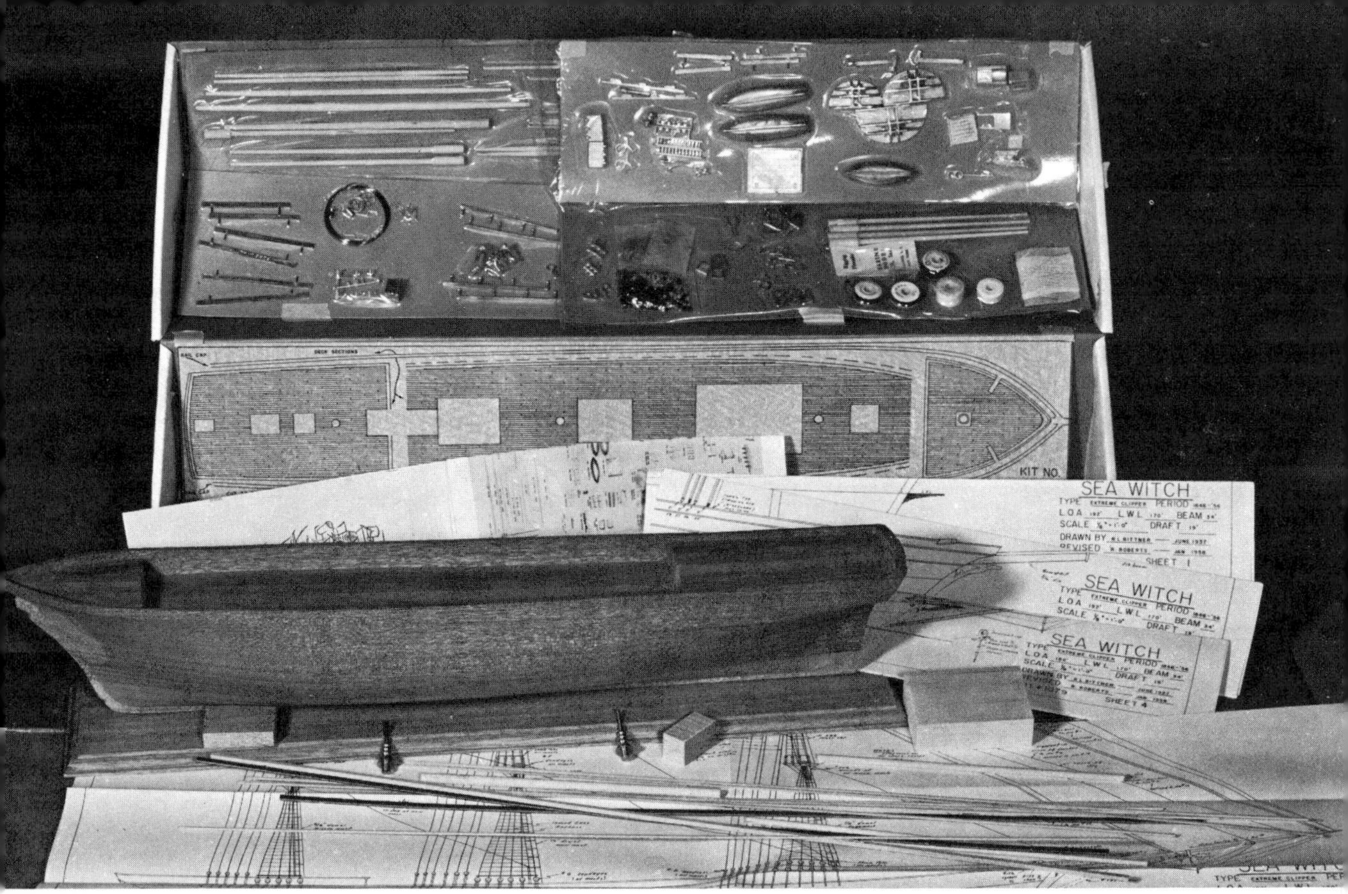

DECK SECTIONS
KIT NO.
SEA WITCH
TYPE EXTREME CLIPPER PERIOD
SCALE
DRAFT
DRAWN BY
REVISED
SHEET 1
SEA WITCH
BEAM
SEA WITCH
SHEET 4

179 Above, left – An example of the fine kits offered by the Marine Model Company of Halesite, Long Island.

180 Left – A design engineer of model-making firm Revell, Inc, California, checks the blueprints of the Mayflower *from which the scale model drawings were made.*

Right – Three kit models from the Germany firm of Graupner : top (181) – Santa Maria, *1592 ; centre (182) – a very detailed model of the Hanseatic ship of 1665. the* Adler von Lübeck *; bottom (183) – the frigate* Berlin, *1674.*

184 Above, left – A Revell tool and diemaker at work on the die for part of a plastic kit.

185 Above – A model of the May-flower *made up from an Airfix kit.*

famous firm of Billing Boats. The Billing kits are made at the ancient port of Esbjerg, in the west of Denmark, where, nearly 1,000 years ago, the Vikings built and launched the longships with which they were to dominate northwest Europe. The traditional skills of the Esbjerg shipbuilders, assisted by the most advanced developments of modern technology, have enabled Billings to produce boat kits in wood that are considered by many people to be among the finest in the world.

Billing designs cover a wide range of modern and historic ships, and all their models are intended to be built in the traditional shipbuilder's way – that is, with frames and planking and decking, as boatbuilding has been carried out at Esbjerg for a millenium. Among their most successful lines have been kit-models of the *Norske Løve,* built as a warship about 1765, and considered ever since then to have been one of the most beautiful sailing ships of that period of rich construction; the *Dannebrog*, the richly decorated Danish royal yacht; and the *Hjejlen*, which, after more than 100 years of honourable service, is the last working paddle steamer in Denmark. Wherever possible, Billings bases its models on the original plans of the prototype.

The West German firm of Steingraeber was started in 1956, when Gunter Steingraeber began to produce waterline models of ships and boats in kit form, using cardboard as his principal material. At first, he was not very successful, as there were a number

186 Above – A nice scale model of Discovery, *the ship used by Capt. Scott on his 1901 Antarctic expedition. This model is also an Airfix kit.*

187 Above, right – An interesting kit from Graupner of a Viking longship with its sail furled.

188 Centre – A model of the sail training clipper Pamir, *1905, made from a Graupner kit.*

189 Below – Another model from a Graupner kit, the Gorchfock, *the sail training ship of the German Navy.*

of competitors producing kits that were not a lot different from his.

In 1957 he tried a new line – he brought out the first of his whole-planked construction kits. This kit made it possible for a normally handy craftsman to construct a 23-inch long model of the man-of-war brig *Aramis* in the traditional, rib-and-plank way. His enterprise paid dividends at once, and soon his company was producing, in a woodland factory, kits for export to all parts of the world.

Since then, Steingraeber's policy has been consistent – to market only kits from which models of old-fashioned sailing vessels may be made, without undue difficulty, and to offer them at reasonable prices. Every model made from the kits is intended to be a gem worthy of a place on anyone's mantelpiece. Most popular of all has been the kit-model of the clipper *Agilis*, a typical American slaver of the early nineteenth century. With other Steingraeber kits, equally impressive models can be made of the French frigate *La Flore* of about 1790; the topsail schooner *Porta Coeli* of about 1835; the English yacht *Satanitas*, and a variety of lovely craft. For model-makers who would find the carving of the figure heads and the stern plates of the more decorative vessels beyond their capabilities these are available, ready for assembly, as optional extras.

Two great companies based in the United States have earned world-wide respect for the beauty and authenticity of their ship model kits. They are The Marine Model Company, Inc, of Halesite, Long Island, New York, and Model Shipways Company, Inc, of Bogota, New Jersey.

The directors of the Marine Model Company, formed in 1936, quote in their catalogue these inspiring words written by the great expert Henry B. Culver:

> 'Sailing-ship models have often been compared to paintings, and to a certain extent the comparison is justified. The finest examples of these miniature vessels are, in the eyes of those best fitted to judge, productions of the highest artistic quality, appealing in general composition, line, mass and technical

190 A beautiful model, made from a Marine Models kit, of the war-time U.S.S. Trigger.

execution, to the aesthetic susceptibilities of those who have eyes to see, in no less degree than do the best examples of the pictorial art.'

In their determination to live up to the lofty ideals expressed by Henry B. Culver, the directors of the company make it a continuing policy to assist their customers in every way they can to achieve the highest possible standards of craftsmanship in their finished models. They are proud of the fact that theirs is one of the few companies left where most of the product is made by hand. They have no assembly line where items are mass-produced or checked or packaged by highly automated equipment. Therefore, they claim, they can devote that extra care and attention to their customers and their products that the personal touch ensures.

'The ship model kit based on a wooden hull has always been something of a challenge to the modeller,' confirm the directors of Model Shipways, who are also jealous of the enviable reputation their products have earned. 'The hull and its timbers require the most work. There is no shortcut beyond the machine cut hull. The surfaces and edges will be your own, produced with cutting edges such as chisels, knife, plane and the like. If you intend to apply a minimum of your skill and time, perhaps you should stay with plastic models.' Anyone patient enough to assemble a Model Shipways kit will find in the company's lists outstanding replicas of the Massachusetts privateer *Rattlesnake* of 1781, the colonial schooner *Sultana* of Boston (1767), the frigate *Essex* of Salem (1799), the clipper ship *Flying Fox* (1851) and several other beauties.

Many of the ships and boats that can be made from commercially produced kits are large enough to accommodate electric motors, with batteries and propellers, or small internal combustion engines. In some kits, motorizing units are actually included at the time of sale. Models made with moulded plastic hulls may not be, by their nature, quite as buoyant as similar models made from wood. They may only be bouyant enough in the larger sizes to take equipment for radio control.

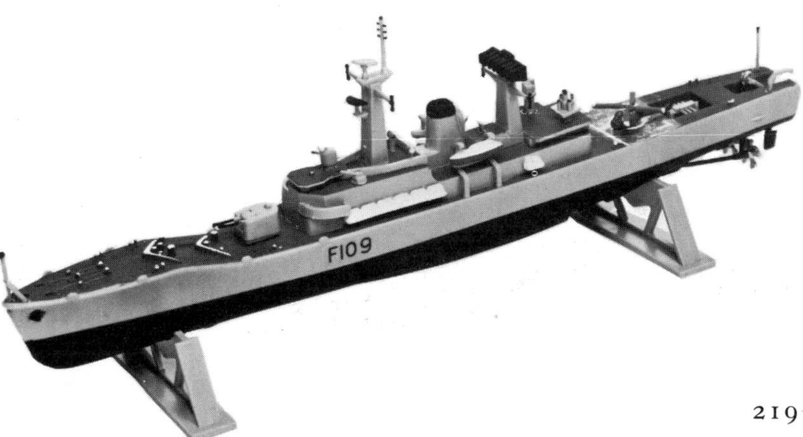

191 H.M.S. Leander *is a general purpose frigate; the model shown here, complete with helicopter, was made from an Airfix kit.*

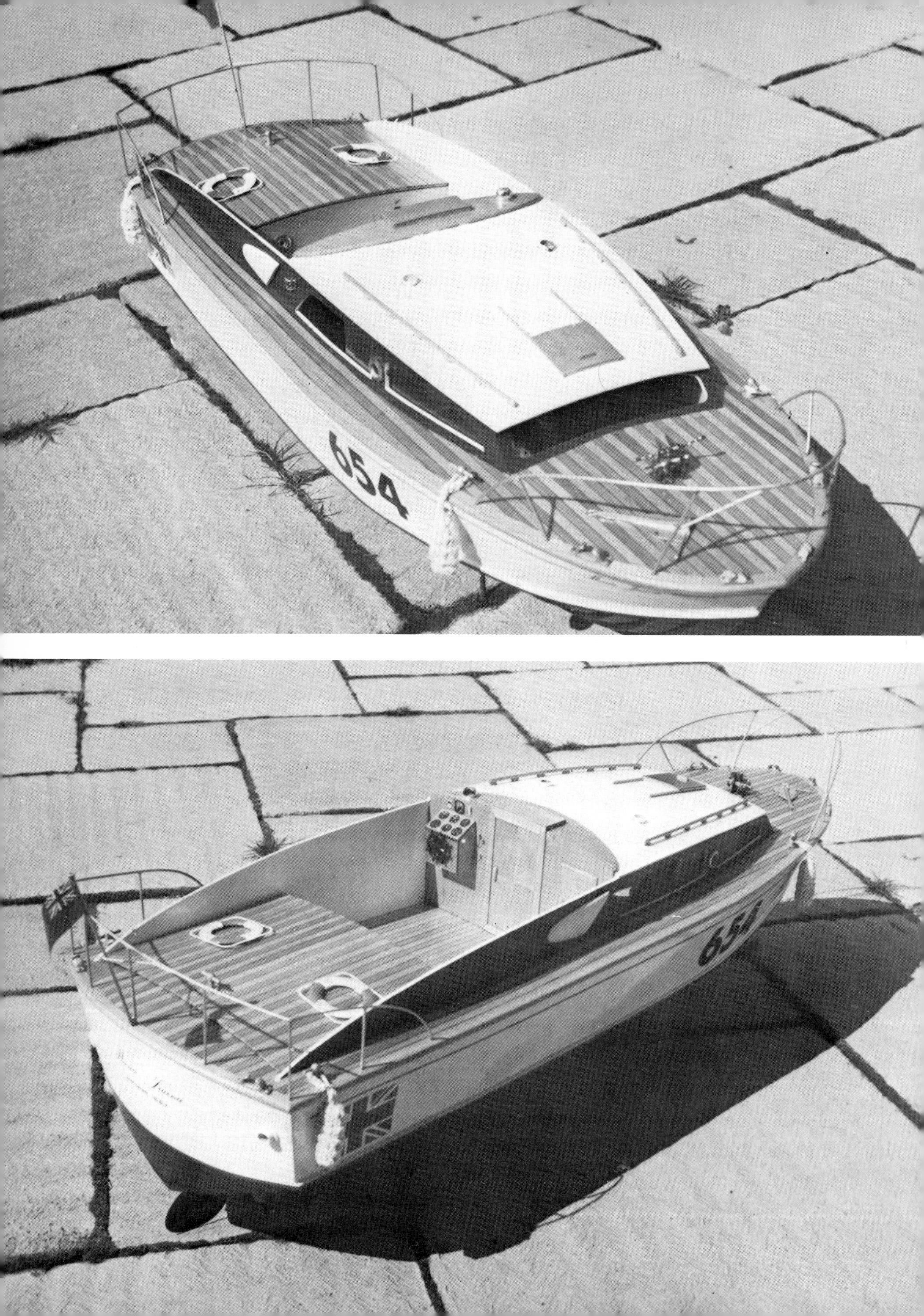
654

10 Power Boat Models

Model ships and boats have been propelled by power of various kinds for many years. Models propelled by ingenious spring-mechanism arrangements were made years before the marine steam-engine was properly developed. Small steam-engines were fitted into trial models, and made to work satisfactorily, before the same means of propulsion was applied to vessels built on a full size scale.

Proposals for the jet-propulsion of boats go back at least to 1784, when James Rumsey made a model and later constructed a boat with which trials were carried out on the Potomac River. Then, nearly a century later, Gaston Tissandier, one of the celebrated brothers who were afterwards to construct the dirigible airship that flew from Auteuil, near Paris, published in *Les Récréations Scientifiques* an account of a wheel-less, propeller-less model boat in which steam was expelled from the stern, its thrust being increased by an ingenious augmenter.

The Tissandier model was something of a harbinger. During the early years of the present century, a number of toy ships and boats were marketed that worked similarly on an elementary jet principle. In these a spirit lamp or Meta flame would be used to heat a coil of copper tubing or a flexible expansion chamber. Bubbles would appear at small orifices at the stern of the vessel – usually, after the operator had waited for a frustratingly long time – and it would slowly set off on a disappointingly low-powered journey. Not surprisingly none of these models retained its popularity for long.

The more powerful rocket propulsion may have been introduced into the world of model ships and boats at about the same time as Gaston Tissandier was carrying out his experiments. One innovator was the Reverend C. M. Ramus, who, after numerous and successful tests with his original model hydroplane *Ricochet*, took out patents to prevent others from exploiting the principles on which it had been designed.

192 & 193 Two views of the Fairey Swordsman, *a kit-built model from Aerokits. The model will accept engines with capacities from 1.5 cc to 5 cc.*

The French word *ricochet* implies a succession of rebounds, and was specifically applied to the special form of planing hull designed by the pioneer M Bonnemaison. Up to that time, all ships and boats and model ships and boats had displacement hulls. In a hull of this type, the weight of the boat is supported, when the hull is submerged up to the waterline, by the displacement of water. A boat with a displacement hull is, therefore, intended to be driven through the water, rather than over its surface. Owing to the resistance offered by water, there are definite limits to the speeds a boat of this kind can attain.

In a boat of the alternative type, the hull is designed in such a way that when the vessel is being propelled forward with sufficient power, lift is generated: the whole craft, instead of being driven forward through the water, will rise and skim (or plane) over the surface. Clearly, when this happens water resistance is lessened and greater velocities can be achieved. The makers and users of the model boats which hold the world's speed records today take the Bonnemaison discoveries for granted.

But both Gaston Tissandier and the Reverend Ramus were a little ahead of their time. During the second half of the nineteenth century and the early days of the twentieth, most operators of power-driven model ships and boats were (like so many other people in the world) mad about the more conventional uses of steam. Steam-driven, screw-propelled model ships and boats were to be seen, watched by admiring crowds, on lakes and ponds in most of the civilized parts of the earth. These models could be operated very cheaply, their only significant running cost being that of the methylated spirits or solid fuel needed to heat their boilers. But, they were not always very efficient in terms of the power produced by so much effort, they were usually rather oily and smelly, they were apt to break down completely if they met any extraordinary hazard such as floating water weed, and they were not very safe. In the *Model Engineer* of 1 February 1902, the following appeal appeared:

> 'On Sunday morning, January 5th, a model steamer, which is reported to be about 10 feet long, exploded on the Serpentine, in Hyde Park, seriously injuring the owner, Mr Brooks, and another man. It was stated that the vessel was "driven by

194 A powered model, capable of accepting 2.5 cc to 5 cc diesel, or electric engines. This Aerokits model can be radio controlled, and is similar to the patrol boat commanded by John F. Kennedy during World War 2.

195 A fine model of the drifter Edith. *Its vertical steam engine is fired with oil.*

petroleum", but our own information, derived from a reliable source, is to the effect that this is a mistake. As a result of the explosion, the model was blown to pieces. Should any readers of THE MODEL ENGINEER know further particulars of the accident, the Editor will be glad to hear from them on the subject.'

The model steamer, it turned out, had been called the *Amy Howard*. In the issue of the same magazine dated 15 March there was a full account of the mishap:

'The model ..... weighed nearly 2 cwt [224 pounds]. It was a fine specimen of the boat-builder's skill, and represented very closely a large merchant vessel . . . . The deck fittings were very complete – such details as anchors, davits, boats, hatchways, binnacles, ship telegraphs, all being perfect models in themselves. The owner, Mr George Howard, made the engines, boilers, and all metal work in the boat; and Mr Edwin Brooks, at whose house the model was docked, was responsible for the hull, the general work of the erection, and painting. Sunday morning was the usual time of sailing, and the Serpentine in Hyde Park, some twenty minutes' walk, the place. The boat had, prior to the explosion on 5th January, crossed this water over a hundred times, and no mishap of this sort was at all anticipated by her captain and crew.

The usual course of procedure was on this morning adopted. The boiler – which, by the way, used charcoal as fuel – was filled at home, and the fire lighted, steam raised, and the boat removed from the room in which it was stored on to a special wheeled truck and taken to the lake. Contrary to the general custom, the boiler was not filled up with water with the pump – a rather large affair – which was entirely separate from the boat, the delivery

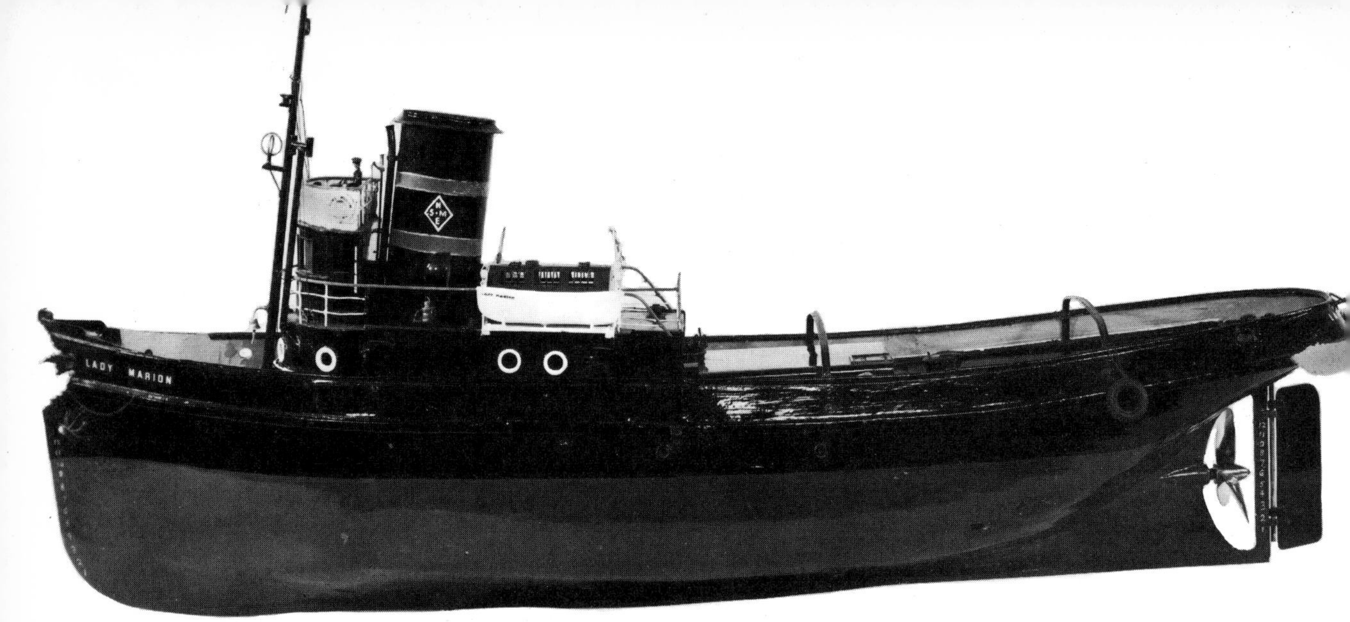

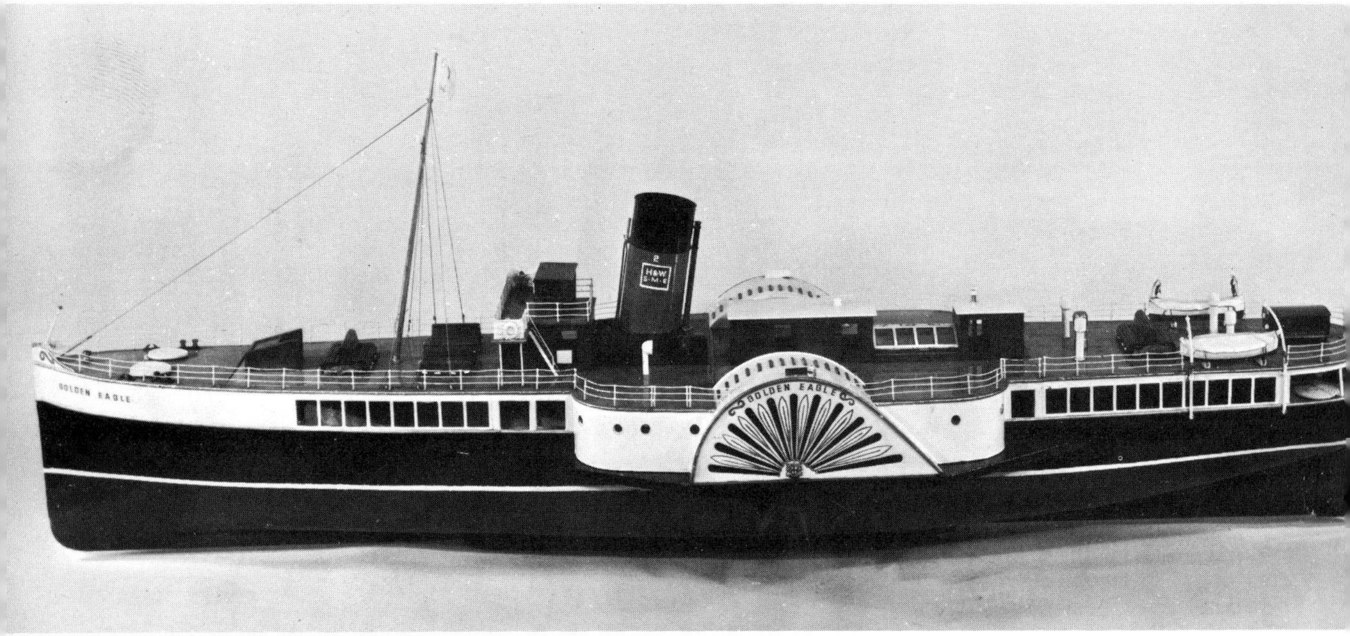

pipe being a flexible tube with a screwed coupling, attached when required to the check valve on the boiler, at the end. One of the party – Mr Brooks – mentioned during the journey to the lake that the water was getting rather low in the boiler, but, seemingly, no notice was taken of it.

On arriving at the Serpentine, the remark as to the shortness of water was repeated, but it was decided to give her one run across before pumping up. The model worked splendidly – better than ever it had done, it was said. On arriving at the other side, Mr Brooks stooped down and shut off the steam, bringing the boat broadside to the shore. He stood up from attending the boat, and a moment after the explosion occurred. The decks and the side of the boat nearest the shore burst open with a loud roaring noise, and all the bystanders were smothered in water, charcoal ashes, and splinters. Mr Brooks was hit by the flying shell of the boiler, which hurt his arm and lacerated his ear so badly that they had to be treated at the depôt of the Royal Humane Society close at hand.

The ends of the boiler and furnace were torn out of the boat and laid in the water beside her. The keel was in two pieces, and practically all of the middle of the boat was demolished. The funnel, which weighs quite 3 lbs., was hurled a considerable distance. The bystanders who had not hurriedly left the scene helped to collect the more valuable fragments. The remains of the boat were hooked out of the water and taken home.'

The editor of the *Model Engineer*, it seems, had since had an opportunity to inspect the wreckage. 'Mr Howard must forgive us if we are hard upon him', the great man's judgement began, 'but a boiler is like a chain – only as strong as its weakest link'. The boiler had been fabricated, in fact, from brass tube, with ends made of copper plate flanged over and merely sweated into position with soft solder. 'This joint *was not riveted*', rebuked the editor, and, after some lengthy calculations of the high pressures that had undoubtedly been raised, 'Where was the safety valve, and why did it not act?' he went on to ask, giving immediately the answer: 'A safety valve was provided, but was such only in title'.

The account ends with some pious sentiments:

'This accident, therefore, only shows the amateur that – especially if a large model boiler is to be attempted – he should not forget to provide a good reliable safety valve, or even two; and also that the theoretical part of the design of a boiler, or, indeed, any working model, should not be neglected. If he is not well acquainted with the boiler-making arithmetic he should avail himself of some text-book or our own Query Department.'

196 Top – a well-engineered model of the tug Lady Marion *powered with steam.*

197 Centre – This model of the paddle ship Ryde *has ethnic twin-cylinder oscillating steam engines.*

198 Left – A very early clockwork model of the steam yacht Dolphin. *It was made in 1822 and most likely a toy rather than a model of a specific ship.*

The remnants of the *Amy Howard* hung for a while on the wall of Mr Brook's workshop, with this inscription written underneath: 'Lost, 5th January, 1902'.

The first ten years of the twentieth century saw the formation of several model power boat clubs, the members of which relied for their motive power almost entirely on steam. (The most daring, eventually, evolved the flash boiler, in which water, becoming continuously hotter in the generating tube, would be 'flashed' into steam by means of a powerful petrol or paraffin blowlamp.) The Victoria Model Steamboat Club, founded in England in 1904, was an influential example. At this time, too, several important competitions for power-driven model boats were inaugurated that helped to increase public interest in these little craft. The annual *Model Engineer* Speedboat Competition, originally called the Steamer Competition, especially attracted the attention of enthusiasts all over the world. In the first of these competitions, held in 1902, nine boats were entered, all of them steam-driven, and all of a farily straight forward displacement hull 'launch' type. The speeds of the three fastest boats, the *Express*, the *Darling*, and the *Fidget* were – in that order – 5.0, 4.7 and 4.56 miles per hour. By 1913 the winning boats in this competition were recording speeds as high as 22.77 and 21.19 miles per hour.

In France, too, the annual race for the Branger Cup helped to raise standards of design and craftsmanship. It was won, two years running, by a M Girard – once with a steam-driven boat, and once (and this was a sign that the new, miniature internal combustion engine was creeping into the powered model boat world, so soon to make miniature steam engines virtually obsolete) with a petrol-driven boat.

The clockwork engine was used for motorizing many toy ships and boats in the decades immediately prior to the Second World War, and the best of these, like those produced in the nineteenth century by Bing and the other great German manufacturers, now have a certain value as collectors' pieces. This is true of those, that is, that have not rusted away, a fate to which mechanical waterborne model craft of the pre-plastic and pre-glass fibre era were particularly prone. The simple motors used for commercial models in those days had a limited power output, but the sturdier mechanisms removed from clocks or clockwork gramophones by determined craftsmen and adapted for use in model ships and boats did occasionally provide a more satisfactory length of run.

But models driven by clockwork have practically disappeared from the boating ponds of the world today, along with the numerous small nursery craft that have, as far back as living memory goes, been driven by twisted rubber bands. They are no longer needed,

Left – a few suitable electric motors for model ships. Top (199) – a geared electric motor ; centre (200) – electric motor with six-speed gearbox ; bottom (201) – two wound-field electric motors.

202 Above – an electrically powered radio controlled model by Graupner of the fishing boat Elke.

203 Right – this Graupner model of the motor yacht Commodore *is electrically driven and controlled by radio.*

since there are now so many excellent electric and diesel or glow-plug motors on sale, and these have a much greater range.

The electric motor is suitable for most types and sizes of powered model craft that are larger than 8 or 9 inches long. (It is difficult to fit any commercially produced motor into a hull that is smaller than this. For craft that are longer than four feet, however, the diesel or glow-plug motor tends to come into its own.) There are so many electric motors on the market now that one of a suitable size can be easily found for virtually any power boat hull within this range.

The electric motor has certain advantages over all others that have been developed to this date. It is neat, compact, clean, easy to operate, and (this is important if it is to be used in or near public places) relatively quiet. The best types are easy to mount in the hulls of model ships and boats, and are comparatively easy to maintain in good working order. Usually they will propel models of the displacement type at reasonably realistic speeds. But electric motors also have certain limitations. Usually they are not powerful enough (that is, capable of producing sufficiently high speeds) to be used in models with hulls designed for planing.

Model engines used today for model ships and boats – other than those that depend on electricity and the few that are still worked by dedicated old shell-backs on steam – are usually those of the air-cooled internal combustion types designed and produced for use in model aircraft. For marine use, these have usually to be adapted so that they can be water cooled. They can be divided roughly into two different types – those in the compression ignition or diesel, and those in the glow-plug categories. British manufacturers have tended to produce diesel engines; manufacturers in the United States, Japan, and several European countries favour the glow-plug type.

Model diesel engines are not, properly speaking, true diesels in the sense in which that word is used in connection with full-size engines. In a full size diesel engine, air only is compressed in the cylinder, the fuel being subsequently injected by subtle means into the combustion chamber. In a model diesel engine, the fuel is taken in through a small carburettor, where it is mixed with air. This mixture is afterwards automatically ignited by the heat created when it is compressed in the cylinder. The fuels used normally contain ether, which has a very low self-ignition temperature. In spite of this, starting a diesel engine mounted in a model speed boat – by pulling a cord or thong passed round a groove in the fly-wheel – can be an ordeal that generates a certain amount of nervous tension. It can be a particularly gruelling experience when the boat is about to show its paces in an important national or international competition.

Above, a display model of the British Royal Navy's aircraft carrier H.M.S. Eagle.

Below, a model of the German Admiralty yacht Grille, *1934, made by John Darnell. The prototype was also used as Hitler's personal yacht.*

Overleaf, a cut-away model of the Italian car-carrying ship Italterra.

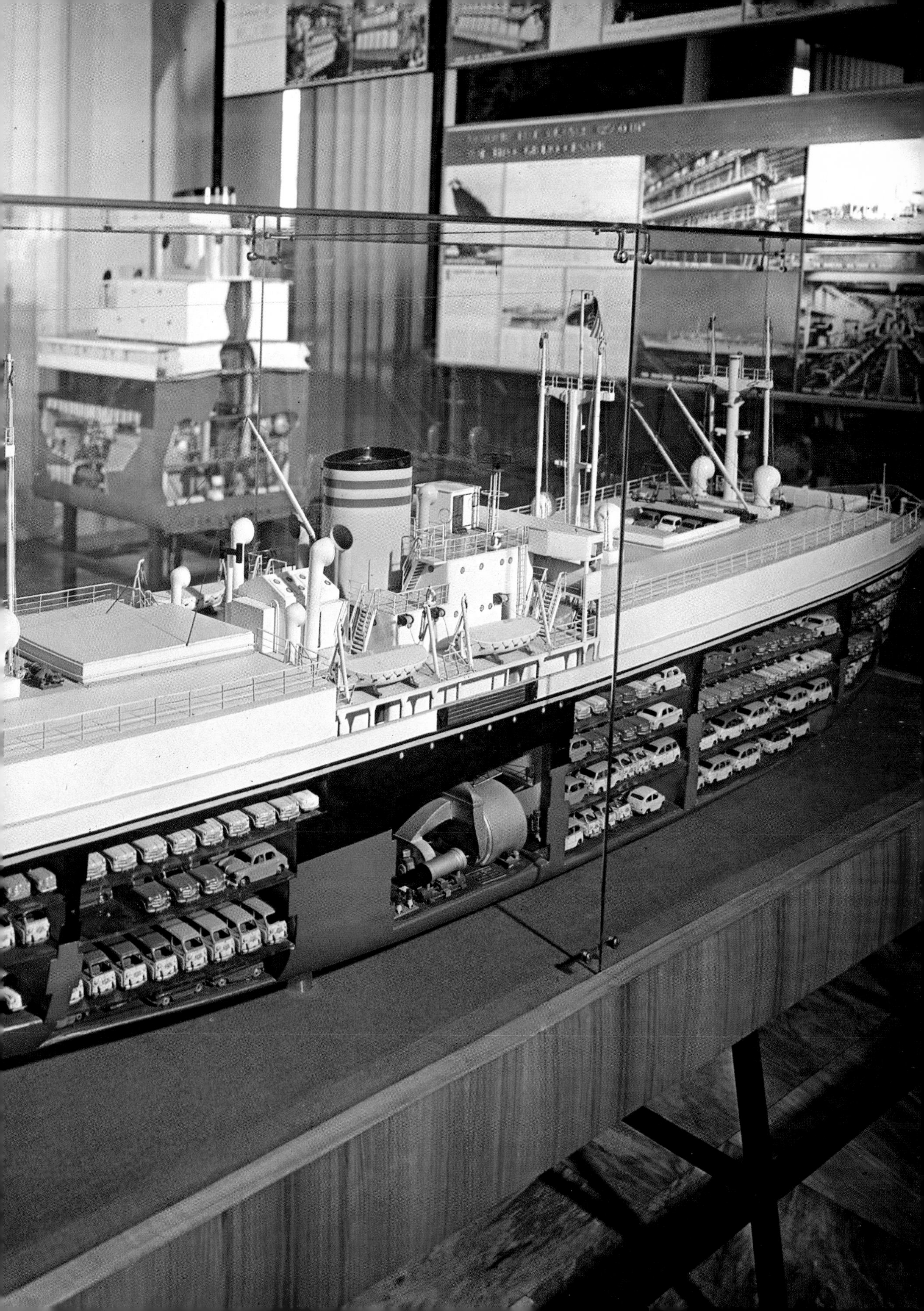

ZWARTE ZEE

FIRE

In a model glow-plug engine, the fuel charge is ignited by means of a coil of thin wire – usually made from a platinum alloy – which glows bright red when the current from a 1.5–2 volt battery is passed through it. This type of engine has one big advantage, then, over engines of the diesel type – it is easier to start. It has other advantages. As soon as the engine has started, the plug element retains sufficient heat to sustain continuous operation without the battery. So the battery can be disconnected, and does not have to be carried in the model itself (as, with electric motors, it does). Another advantage of engines of the glow-plug type is their greater immunity to the effects of flooding. The fuels used with these engines are largely based on methyl-alcohol.

In spite of the universal respect accorded to the innovations of the Reverend Ramus, rocket propulsion, the advantages of which were first propounded by him, is not now widely encountered in modern model ships and boats, except in the high-speed hydroplanes that are specially designed to be driven by the commercial Jetex engines. These motors are marketed in a number of different sizes, and are charged with special slow-burning solid fuel pellets that give thrust outputs from (approximately) ½ ounce to 4 ounces. Usually the pellets are arranged to act only for about 10 seconds – but that is quite enough to set off a little hydroplane on a thrillingly fast and spectacular journey.

The development of model speedboats based on hydroplane principles and propelled by powerful internal combustion engines proceed so rapidly under the stimulus of international competitions that it became necessary, long before the Second World War, for most controlling authorities to discontinue the practice of holding races on straight courses, as it was no longer safe for anyone to try to stop a sharp-bowed model craft travelling at a speed of thirty miles per hour or more. Runaway boats, too, were liable to cause considerable damage to themselves, if not to the lives and limbs of innocent bystanders. So, after that time and for the next two decades, models of the faster types were usually operated on tethering lines, attached to rigid central poles, and these lines kept them travelling safely on circular, endless courses. High speed tethered craft can still be seen occasionally in competitions today, but with the development of other means of control their numbers are not likely to increase.

Most enthusiasts who operate model power ships and boats today have a common ambition – to control their models efficiently and unobtrusively by radio. This can be done with standard items of commercial equipment, and no advanced electronic knowledge is necessary for installing, tuning or operating them. The only really considerable limitations are those likely to be imposed by the cost of the gear.

Above, a model, suitable for radio control, of the Dutch salvage tug Zwarte Zee, *made from a Billing Boats kit.*

Below, an Aerokit model of an R.A.F. crash rescue tender. The model will accept a range of engines and is ideal for radio control.

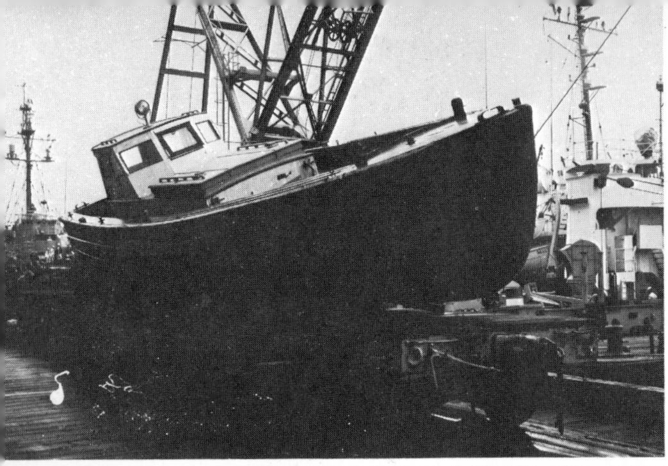

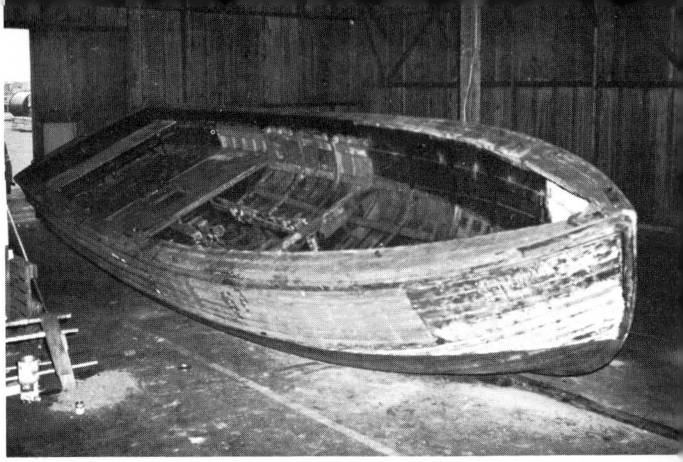

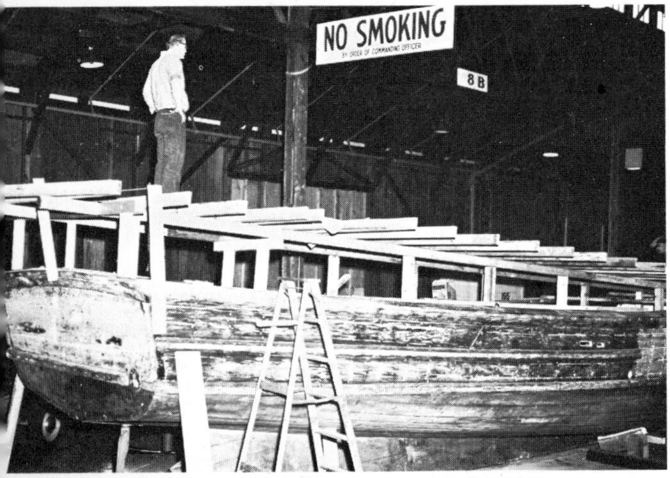
NO SMOKING
BY ORDER OF COMMANDING OFFICER
8B

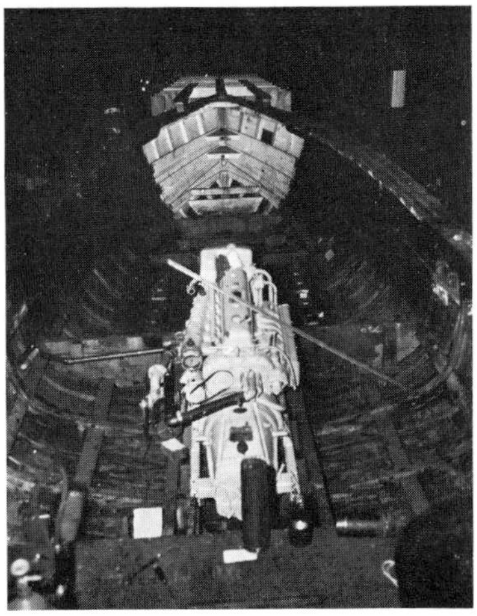

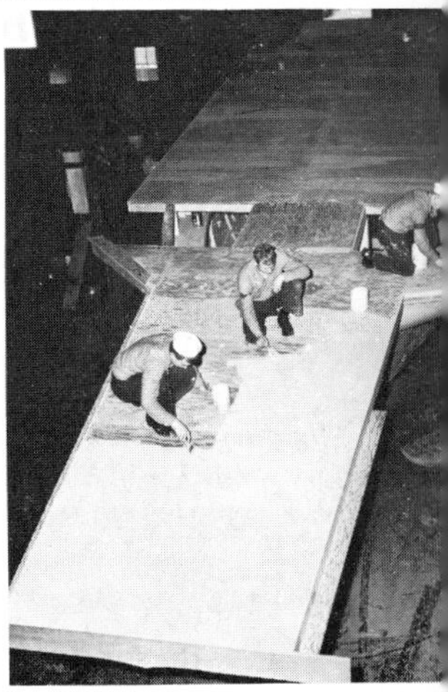

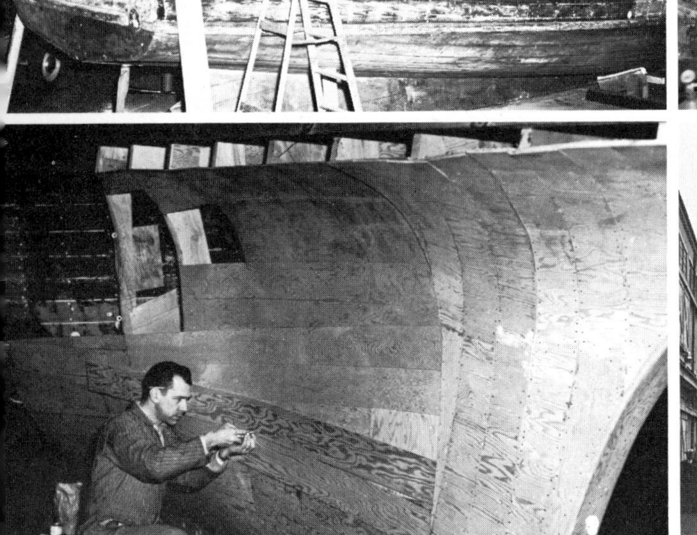

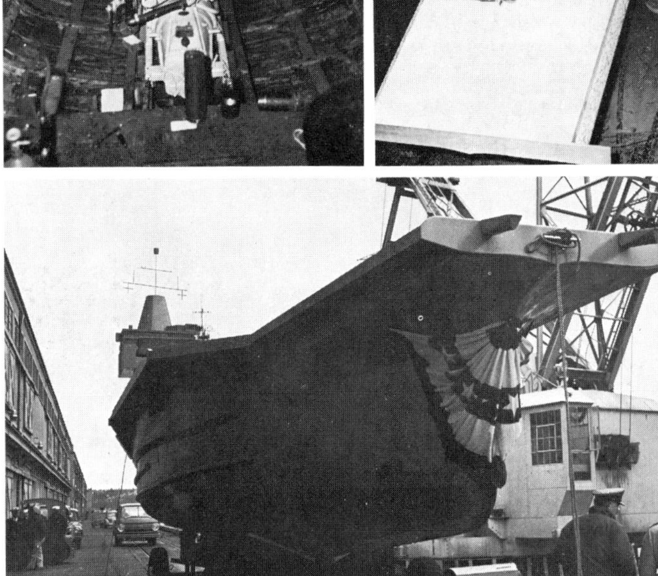

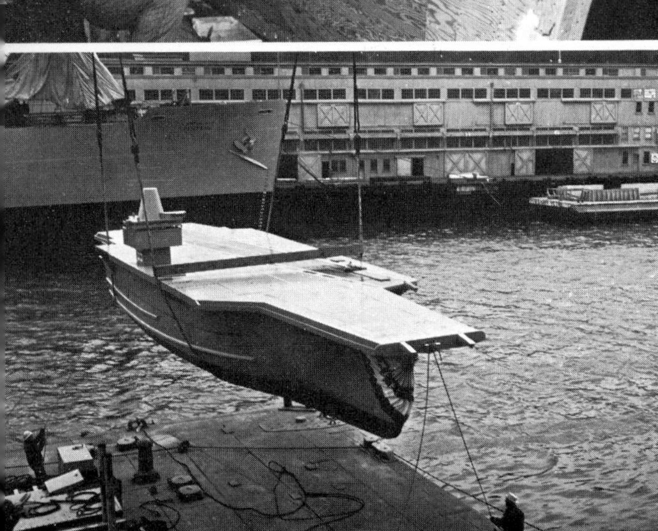

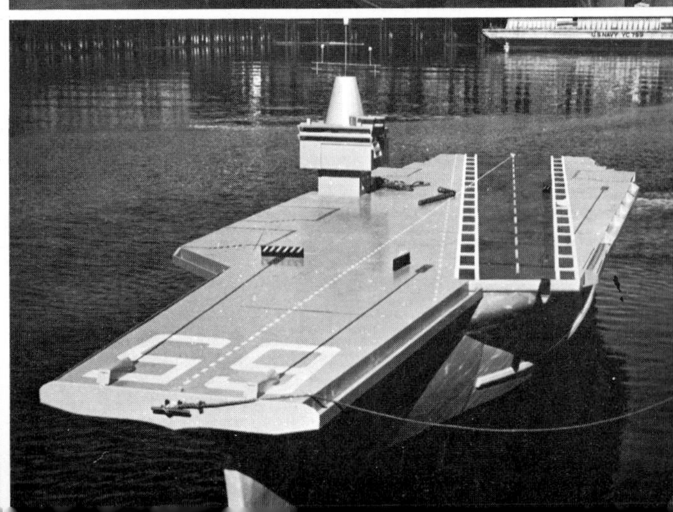

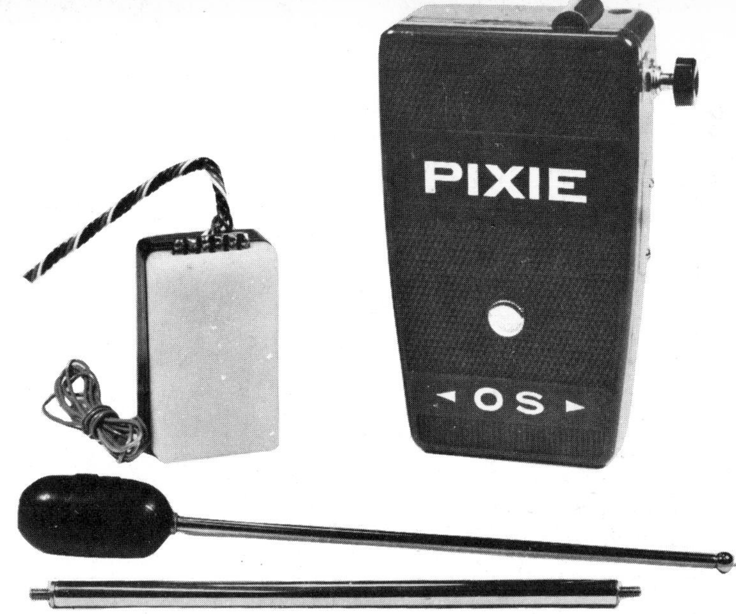

208 Above – O.S. single-channel radio control equipment, generally used for rudder control only.

209 Below – O.S. multi-channel radio control equipment which allows four separate functions.

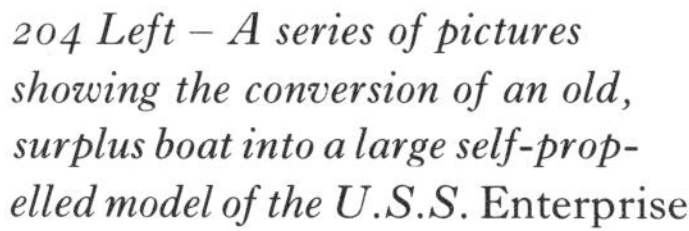

204 Left – A series of pictures showing the conversion of an old, surplus boat into a large self-propelled model of the U.S.S. Enterprise.

205 Top – A model marine diesel engine.

206 Centre – Spark ignition four-stroke petrol engine.

207 Below – A marine glow motor.

Radio control equipment, as applied to model ships and boats, can be divided, for purposes of simplicity, into three main units – a transmitter, a receiver, and a device which will convert the transmitted and received signals into the power needed to move the controls.

The signal sent out by the transmitter has to be carried on a radio frequency that is well clear of those used for normal broadcasting. In one of the more complicated systems, the transmitter will send out signals on a number of different channels.

The job of the receiver on the model ship or boat is not only (as its name implies) to receive the signals. It has also to sort them out and to simplify them so that they will work the necessary switches.

The third stage in this series of operations – the moving of the control surfaces – can be carried out by a simple escapement type

210 Above – A good example from Graupner of a model yacht fitted for radio control.

211 Right – A Billing Boats kit model of the Danish royal yacht, the Dannebrog, *fitted with an electric motor.*

actuator, in which the necessary power is supplied by a rubber or clockwork motor, or, on a rather more ambitious scale, it can be carried out by a servo, in which an electric motor is used. Escapements can only develop enough power to operate the controls of very small model ships and boats. On radio-controlled models of any size, servos cannot be dispensed with.

No casual visitor to a water surface on which radio-controlled model ships and boats are being operated can fail to be impressed by the intricate manoeuvres that can be carried out with swiftly moving vessels which are a considerable distance from the hidden hand that guides them. Model racing yachts (to take only one of the many kinds of small craft that can now be operated by radio) may be fitted with control mechanisms that are marvels of ingenuity. Where the sails and rudder of a model yacht are to be manipulated independently of each other, a four-channel superhet radio is usually used, so that the yacht can compete against one or more rivals that are similarly equipped. Where the rudder only is to be controlled by radio, an automatic device is generally fitted that will trim the sails to suit the direction in which the yacht is being steered.

As with competitive model yachting, there are a number of well-organised voluntary bodies, in various parts of the world, that have come into being to assist power boat operators and to control their public activities. In most countries in which model power boat racing is taken seriously, these associations organize regular and occasional meetings, draw up rules and codes of conduct, and arrange such matters as access to suitable private water surfaces and (this is very necessary where large, fast model power boats are being used) comprehensive schemes of insurance.

The largest international association of controlling bodies in the model power boat world is known as Naviga. At the time of writing, the following countries are members of Naviga – Austria, Belgium, Bulgaria, Czechoslovakia, France, East Germany, West Germany, Great Britain, Holland, Hungary, Italy, Poland, Russia, Sweden, and Switzerland. There are also many model power boat clubs in the United States and in South Africa. The enthusiasts in the latter country are so keen that they invite champion performers from America, Britain, Germany and elsewhere to compete in their annual championships, defraying all the expenses of these stars, including their air travel fares. They do this expressly for the purpose of being able to measure their own champions against the best that the rest of the world can produce.

Most competitions for model power boats fall into one of these categories:

Speed events, in which (as has been already pointed out) high powered boats are sometimes tethered for reasons of safety, only radio-controlled boats being permitted to race on triangular or figure-of-eight courses.
Steering events, in which the boats have to pass through the gap between a pair of posts at the end of a straight course, marks being awarded for the accuracy with which they are operated.
Nomination events, in which the competitors have to state the times that their boats will take to cover a prescribed distance, the winner being the operator whose boat performs its task with the least amount of error.
Radio-control events, in which the competitors have to steer their boats between several pairs of markers, on a carefully laid out course.

Power model boat racing may be competitive – but it is also a friendly and sociable activity. The enthusiasts who gather from distances of many hundreds of miles, and even from overseas, for such events as the *Rand Daily Mail* Junior 200 two-hour marathon in South Africa, are likely to feel almost overwhelmed by the generous hospitality they are offered; they will be able to talk boats with their fellow-addicts until all ideas have been profitably pooled; and they will go back to their homes, when the meeting is over, knowing that there is no other hobby more wholly engrossing in the world. No wonder model power boating is so popular.

212 A fine model of the S.Y. Anna. *Its hull is built of individual plates and it is fitted with a 6-volt electric motor.*

The Round Pond, in London's Kensington Gardens, has been for many decades a favourite resort of those who enjoy sailing model ships and boats. Periodically, the pond is drained, so that it can be kept in a properly maintained condition. Each time the water is pumped away, numbers of small craft are found on the murky bottom. Lost, irrecoverably, on some occasion since the pond was last re-filled, these model ships and boats have a forlorn appearance when they are first recovered, resembling so many grey and colourless ghosts. Crossing the seas and oceans of the world has always been a perilous business, and each of the mud-shrouded models is a sad reminder of the fate that has overtaken so many prototype ships and boats since the beginning of time.

But, the sight is only temporily depressing. In one respect at least the outdoor operation of model ships and boats resembles exactly that of the full-size prototypes: for every journey that ends in disaster, countless voyages are made serenely over smooth waters to intended destinations, bringing happiness and satisfaction to all concerned – and most of all, perhaps, to the navigators. 'There is *nothing* – absolutely nothing – half so much worth doing as simply messing about in boats', wrote Kenneth Grahame in his classic book *The Wind in the Willows*. He could have said, equally well, 'messing about with boats', for he would have included, then, all the millions of people who get their pleasure vicariously.

213 This model of the R.M.S. Mauretania *has two geared 6-volt electric motors to drive the four screws.*

Glossary

Barge: A small sea-going vessel with sails; a flat-bottomed freight boat used for canal or river navigation; a state vessel.

Barque: A term applied generally to all sailing vessels of small size; (specifically) to a three-masted vessel having its fore and mainmasts square rigged and a mizen mast fore-and-aft rigged.

Beakhead: The part of a ship found in front of the forecastle.

Beam (of a ship)**:** A horizontal transverse timber that stretches from side to side of a ship, supporting the deck and holding the vessel together.

Bilge: The bottom of a ship's hull, or that part of it, on either side of the keel, on which the ship would rest if aground.

Bowline: A rope, attached to a sail, used for keeping the edge of that sail steady when sailing on a wind.

Bowsprit: A larger spar or boom which runs out (i.e. forward) from the stem of a vessel. The foremast stays are usually fastened to it.

Brig: A vessel, with two masts square rigged that carries also on her main mast a lower fore-and-mast sail with a gaff and boom.

Brigantine: A two-masted vessel that carries square sails on her foremast. Her mainmast is entirely fore-and-aft rigged.

Bulkhead: An upright partition that divides the hold of a ship into distinct compartments. It may help to ensure safety in the event of collision or other damage.

Buoy: A floating object placed in a particular place to point out the position of hidden dangers or to indicate the course that a ship should take.

Buoy Lifting Vessel: A vessel specially equipped for lifting buoys.

Carrack: A large ship, used for trade as well as for warfare (typically, those used formerly by the Portugese for trading with the East Indies).

Carvel: A light, small, fast ship used during the 15th, 16th and 17th centuries.

Chine: The part of a ship's waterways above the deck plank.

Clinker-built: Applied to ships and boats made with planks that overlap below.

Clipper: A fast-sailing vessel with sharp forward-raking bows and masts that rake aft.

Cog: A broadly built ship with a roundish prow and stern, used up to and including the 15th century.

Corvette: A flush-decked war vessel, with one tier of guns.

Coxswain: The helmsman of a boat; a member of a ship's crew who has permanent charge of a boat and its crew, except when a superior officer is present.

Dead eye: A round wooden block with two flat sides, pierced with a number of small holes.

Dinghy: A small rowing boat; a boat used as an 'extra' or tender; a small pleasure boat.

Felucca: A small coastal vessel propelled by oars or lateen sails, or both, used chiefly in the Mediterranean.

Frigate: A light, swift vessel, used as a merchantman or a war-vessel. In the British Royal Navy, the term denotes an easily manoeuvrable vessel next in size and equipment to ships of the line.

Futtock: One of the middle timbers of the frame of a ship.

Galleon: A ship shorter and higher than the galley (which see). The word is most usually applied to Spanish ships of war and the large vessels used by the Spaniards for trading with their American possessions.

Galley: A low seagoing vessel with one deck, propelled by sails and oars; once commonly used in the Mediterranean.

Gunwale: The upper edge of a ship's side; a piece of timber which may extend round the top side of the hull.

Halyard: A rope or tackle used for raising or lowering a yard, sail, spar or flag.

Inwale: A wale or rib of wood running on the inside of a ship or boat.

Keel: The lowest longitudinal member of a ship or boat, on which the framework of the whole may be built up.

Lateral frames: Frames that form the sides of the hull of a ship or boat.

Lay down: Construct (as of, a ship or boat).

Lifts: Ropes which reach from each mast-head to their respective yard-arms to steady and suspend the ends.

Mainmast: A long pole or spar, usually of wood or metal, set up more or less perpendicularly upon the keel of a ship to support the sails.

Man-of-war: A ship equipped for warfare.

Median rudder: A rudder placed in a median position (that is, at the side of a ship or boat).

Mizen mast: The aftermost mast of a three-masted ship.

Packet: A ship or boat plying at regular intervals between certain ports for the conveyance of mails, goods or passengers.

Poop: The aftermost part of a ship.

Poop deck: The aftermost and highest deck. Usually it would form the roof of a cabin built in the stern.

Privateer: An armed vessel owned and operated by private persons who would be authorized by a legal government to attack enemy shipping.

Quarter deck: A small deck situated between the stern and aftermast. It was used as a promenade by the chief officers and important passengers.

Quarter rudder: A rudder positioned roughly midway between the midpoint of a ship or boat and the stern.

Reef: To roll or fold up a sail in order to lessen the extent of canvas exposed to the wind.

Reef points: Short ropes fixed in a line for securing a sail when it has been reefed.

Rib: A curved frame-timber that extends from the keel of a ship or boat to the top of the hull.

Rudder slung to a stern-post: A rudder positioned at the extreme rear of a ship or boat.

Schooner: A small sea-going fore-and-aft rigged vessel. Early schooners had two masts only; later schooners often had three or four masts and carried one or more top-sails.

Sheet: A rope or chain, attached to the lower corner of a sail, used to extend the sail or to change its direction

Shipway: The inclined way on which a ship is built and down which it slides when it is launched.

Sloop: A small, one-masted, fore-and-aft rigged vessel.

Spinnaker: A large three-cornered sail used by racing yachts when running before the wind.

Square sail: A four-sided sail supported by a yard.

Stay: A large rope used to support a ship's mast.

Steeve (as of a bowspirit)**:** To incline upwards, at an angle.

Stem: Used of either extremity of a vessel, the prow or the stern.

Sternpost: The upright timber or piece of metal at the bow of a ship or boat into which the ends of the side planks are fastened.

Stern: The hind part of a ship or boat.

Taffrail: The part of a poop-rail that lies nearest to the stern.

Tender: A ship or boat used to assist a larger one in various capacities.

Tiller: The bar at the top of a rudder-head (used, normally, only of a bar in the same plane as the blade of the rudder).

Topgallant mast: The mast next above the topmast. It is usually in one piece with the royal mast.

Topmast: The mast next above the lower mast.

Topping-lift: A rope running from the lower mast-head to the end of a boom for lifting the boom or adjusting the angle of it.

Transom: A beam that runs across the aft end of a ship and forms part of the stern frame.

Transom stern: A stern shaped after a transom frame.

Trawler: A sea-going vessel used for trawling or dragging (for fish or in mine sweeping).

Wale: A piece of timber that extends along a ship's sides. Usually, it is thicker and stronger than the adjoining timbers.

Walking beam: In a vertical engine, a horizontal beam that transmits power to the crank-shaft through the connecting-rod.

Windjammer: Colloquial name for a merchant sailing-vessel.

Yard: A long slender spar used to support a sail.

The standing rigging of a late eighteenth century vessel

1 fore royal stay
2 fore topgallant stay
3 fore topmast stay
4 fore stay
5 main royal stay
6 main topgallant stay
7 main topmast stay
8 main stay
9 mizen royal stay
10 mizen topgallant stay
11 mizen topmast stay
12 mizen stay
13 fore topmast backstay
14 fore topgallant backstay
15 fore royal backstay
16 main topmast backstay
17 main topgallant backstay
18 main royal backstay
19 mizen topmast backstay
20 mizen topmast backstay
21 mizen royal backstay
22 foremast
23 fore topmast
24 fore topgallant mast
25 fore royal
26 mainmast
27 main topmast
28 main topgallant mast
29 main royal
30 mizen mast
31 mizen topmast
32 mizen topgallant mast
33 mizen royal
34 spanker boom
35 spanker gaff
36 fore shrouds
37 fore topmast shrouds
38 main shrouds
39 main topmast shrouds
40 mizen shrouds
41 mizen topmast shrouds
42 jib-boom
43 bowspirit cap
44 bowsprit
45 martingale
46 dolphin striker
47 bobstay
48 head
49 cat head
50 fore top
51 foremast cap
52 fore crosstrees
53 main top
54 mainmast top
55 main crosstrees
56 main topgallant mast crosstrees
57 mizen top
58 mizen mast cap
59 mizen crosstrees
60 fore chains
61 main chains
62 mizen chains
63 keel
64 skeg
65 stern-post
66 rudder

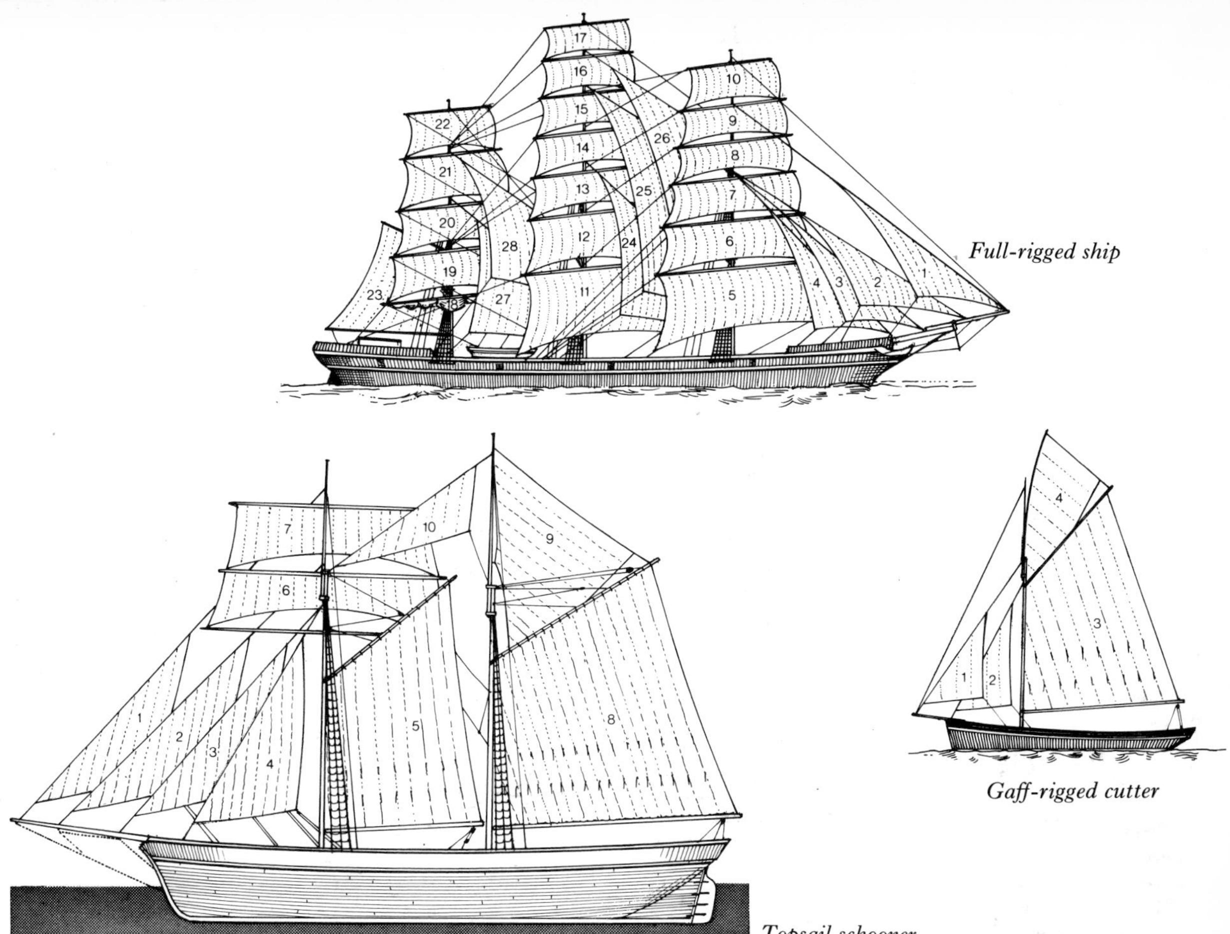

Full-rigged ship

Topsail schooner

Gaff-rigged cutter

Full-rigged ship

1 flying jib
2 outer jib
3 inner jib
4 jib
5 foresail
6 lower fore topsail
7 upper fore topsail
8 lower fore topgallant sail
9 upper fore topgallant sail
10 fore royal
11 mainsail
12 lower main topsail
13 upper main topsail
14 lower main topgallant
15 upper main topgallant
16 main royal
17 main skysail
18 crossjack
19 lower mizen topsail
20 upper mizen topsail
21 mizen topgallant sail
22 mizen royal
23 spanker
24 main topmast staysail
25 main topgallant staysail
26 main royal staysail
27 mizen topmast staysail
28 mizen topgallant staysail

Topsail schooner

1 flying jib
2 outer jib
3 jib
4 fore staysail
5 foresail
6 fore lower topsail
7 fore upper topsail
8 mainsail
9 main gaff topsail
10 main topmast staysail

Gaff-rigged cutter

1 jib
2 fore staysail
3 mainsail
4 main topsail

For Further Reading

Bathe, B. W. *Ship Models: From Earliest Times to 1700 A.D.* A Science Museum Illustrated Booklet. H.M.S.O., London, 1966

Battson, R. K. *Period Ship Modelling.* Model and Allied Publications, Hemel Hempstead, 1967

Bowen, F. C. *From Carrack to Clipper.* Halton, New York and London, 1948

Chatterton, E. K. *Ship Models.* The Studio, London, 1923

Chatterton, E. K. *Steamship Models.* T. Werner Laurie, London, 1924

Dugan, J. *The Great Iron Ship.* Hamish Hamilton, London, 1953

Landström, B. *The Ship.* Allen and Unwin, London, 1961

Lauder, J. P. *Ships in Bottles.* Percival Marshall, London, 1962

Longridge, C. N. *The Cutty Sark, the Last of the Famous Tea-Clippers.* Percival Marshall, London, 1933

Longridge, C. N. *The Anatomy of Nelson's Ships.* Model and Allied Publications, Hemel Hempstead, 1965

Millward, C. H. *Modelling the Revenge.* Model and Allied Publications, Hemel Hempstead, 1967

Nance, R. M. *Sailing Ship Models.* Halton, New York and London, 1949

Priest, B. H. and Lewis, J. A. *Model Racing Yachts.* Model and Allied Publications, Hemel Hempstead

Smeed, V. *Boat Modelling.* Model and Allied Publications, Hemel Hempstead, 1969

Warring, R. H. *Model Power Boats.* Arco Publications, London, 1964

Westbury, E. T. *The History of Model Power Boats.* Percival Marshall, London, 1950

List of Illustrations

PLATES

BLACK AND WHITE

49 and **50** *Sovereign of the Seas. (National Maritime Museum, Greenwich)*

51 English 56-gun ship. *(United States Naval Academy, Annapolis, Md.)*

52 The *Naseby. (National Maritime Museum, Greenwich)*

53 English three-decker. *(Statens Sjöhistoriska Museum, Stockholm)*

54 The *Naseby. (National Maritime Museum, Greenwich)*

55 Meeting of the Admiralty Board. *(Crown Copyright, Science Museum, London)*

56 and **57** The *Grafton. (United States Naval Academy, Annapolis, Md.)*

58 The *St. George. (United States Naval Academy, Annapolis, Md.)*

59, 60 and **61** *Britannia. (United States Naval Academy, Annapolis, Md.)*

62 The *Mordaunt. (National Maritime Museum, Greenwich)*

63 English 96-gun ship. *(National Maritime Museum, Greenwich)*

64 Bow of 60-gun ship. *(Crown Copyright, Science Museum, London)*

65 and **66** Two models of the *Royal William. (National Maritime Museum, London)*

67 The *Royal William's* figure head. *(National Maritime Museum, Greenwich)*

68 The stern of a 90-gun ship. *(United States Naval Academy, Annapolis, Md.)*

69 The *Royal George. (National Maritime Museum, Greenwich)*

70 The roayl schooner *Amphion. (Statens Sjöhistoriska Museum, Stockholm)*

71 A Flemish carrack. *(Crown Copyright, Science Museum, London)*

72 The warship *Veenlust. (Maritiem Museum 'Prins Hendrik,' Rotterdam)*

73 Dutch East Indiaman. *(Nederlandsch Historisch Scheepvart Museum, Amsterdam)*

74 The schooner yacht *America. (National Maritime Museum, Greenwich)*

75 A 28-gun frigate. *(Crown Copyright, Science Museum, London)*

76 Two gun crews on the frigate *Josephine. (Statens Sjöhistoriska Museum, Stockholm)*

77 The frigate *Constitution. (The Peabody Museum, Salem, Mass.)*

78 The 44-gun frigate *President. (National Maritime Museum, Greenwich)*

79 French prisoner-of-war wooden model. *(National Maritime Museum, Greenwich)*

80 French prisoner-of-war bone model. *(United States Naval Academy, Annapolis, Md.)*

81 French prisoner-of-war bone model. *(National Maritime Museum, Greenwich)*

82 The *Flying Cloud. (Photo Process Co. Ltd., London)*

83 The seven-masted schooner *Thomas W. Lawson. (Crown Copyright, Science Museum, London)*

84 The *Cutty Sark. (Crown Copyright, Science Museum, London)*

85 The royal yacht *Mary. (National Maritime Museum, Greenwich)*

86 Late Stuart royal yacht. *(Montagu Motor Museum, Beaulieu)*

87 The yacht *Optimist. (Johannes Graupner, Kirchheim-Tech)*

88 The yacht *Gracia. (Ripmax Ltd., London)*

89 The *Hoche. (Musée de la Marine, Paris)*

90 The paddle steamer *Charlotte Dundas. (Crown Copyright, Science Museum, London)*

91 The paddle steamer *Comet. (Crown Copyright, Science Museum, London)*

92 The paddle steamer *Savannah. (Crown Copyright, Science Museum, London)*

93 The paddle steamer *Sirius. (Crown Copyright, Science Museum, London)*

94 and **95** The *Great Western. (Crown Copyright, Science Museum, London)*

96 and **97** The paddle steamer *Britannia. (Crown Copyright, Science Museum, London)*

98 The S.S. *Great Britain. (Crown Copyright, Science Museum, London)*

99 The P.S.S. *Great Eastern. (Crown Copyright, Science Museum, London)*

100 The U.S.S. *Hartford. (United States Naval Academy Museum, Annapolis, Md.)*

101 The Confederate raider *Alabama. (The Mariners Museum, Newport News, Va.)*

102 The 23-gun sloop *Antietam. (United States Naval Academy Museum, Annapolis, Md.)*

103 H.M.S. *Howe. (National Maritime Museum, Greenwich)*

104 The battleship *Warrior. (National Maritime Museum, Greenwich)*

105 The steam frigate *Merrimack. (The Mariners Museum, Newport News, Va.)*

106 The Confederate ironclad *Virginia. (The Mariners Museum, Newport News, Va.)*

107 The Union ironclad *Monitor*. *(The Mariners Museum, Newport News, Va.)*

108 The battleship *Captain*. *(National Maritime Museum, Greenwich)*

109 The cruiser *Terrible*. *(Crown Copyright, Royal Scottish Museum, Edinburgh)*

110 The S.S. *Campania*. *(Crown Copyright, Science Museum, London)*

111 The T.S. *Mauretania*. *(Crown Copyright, Science Museum, London)*

112 The T.S. *Mauretania*. *(Crown Copyright, Science Museum, London)*

113 The T.S. *Normandie*. *(Crown Copyright, Science Museum, London)*

114 The R.M.S. *Queen Mary*. *(Cunard Steam-Ship Co., Liverpool)*

115 The R.M.S. *Queen Elizabeth*. *(Bassett-Lowke, Northampton)*

116 The R.M.S. *Queen Elizabeth*. *(Cunard Steam-Ship Co., Liverpool)*

117 The R.M.S. *Queen Elizabeth 2*. *(Cunard Steam-Ship Co., Liverpool)*

118 The Danish coast defence vessel *Peder Skram*. *(Orlogsmuseet, Copenhagen)*

119 The *Admiral Scheer*. *(National Maritime Museum, Greenwich)*

120 The *Barham*. *(Crown Copyright, Science Museum, London)*

121 The *Scharnhorst*. *(National Maritime Museum, Greenwich)*

122 *The Vanguard*. *(Crown Copyright, Science Museum, London)*

123 The U.S.S. *Forrestal*. *(Revell, Inc., Calif.)*

124 H.M.S. *Eagle*. *(Crown Copyright, Ministry of Defence, London)*

125 A guided missile destroyer. *(Crown Copyright, Central Office of Information, London)*

126 Escort destroyer. *(Official Photograph, U.S. Navy)*

127 The nuclear powered submarine *Nautilus*. *(Revell, Inc., Calif.)*

128 The hovercraft SRN6. *(A.G.M. Ltd., Hounslow)*

129 Surface effects ship of the future. *(Official Photograph, U.S. Navy)*

130 The N.S. *Savannah*. *(Crown Copyright, Science Museum, London)*

131 The ceremonial barge *Bucentaur*. *(Crown Copyright, Science Museum, London)*

132 Lahore state barge. *(Crown Copyright, Science Museum, London)*

133 Udaipur state barge. *(Crown Copyright, Science Museum, London)*

134 Calcutta state barge. *(Crown Copyright, Science Museum, London)*

135 Nelson's funeral car. *(Crown Copyright, Science Museum, London)*

136 The royal yacht *Navy*. *(United States Naval Academy Museum, Annapolis, Md.)*

137 Unidentified state barge. *(United States Naval Academy Museum, Annapolis, Md.)*

138 A Victorian velocipede. *(Crown Copyright, Science Museum, London)*

139 The steamboat Jamestown. *(The Mariners Museum, Newport News, Va.)*

140 A Thames paddle steamer. *(Crown Copyright, Science Museum, London)*

141 The paddle steamer *King Alfred*. *(National Maritime Museum, Greenwich)*

142 A Danube paddle steamer. *(Crown Copyright, Science Museum, London)*

143 Chinese junk. *(Crown Copyright, Science Museum, London)*

144 Noah's *Ark*. *(The Mariners' Museum, Newport News, Va.)*

145 William Wouldhave's lifeboat. *(South Shields Public Libraries, South Shields)*

146 A horse-operated dredger. *(Crown Copyright, Science Museum, London)*

147 The steam dredger *General Diaz*. *(Crown Copyright, Science Museum, London)*

148 The paddle tug *Monarch*. *(Crown Copyright, Science Museum, London)*

149 The tug *Dromedary*. *(Crown Copyright, Science Museum, London)*

150 The Five Fathom Bank lightship. *(The Mariners Museum, Newport News, Va.)*

151 Amundsen's ship *Gjøa*. *(Norsk Sjøfartsmuseum, Oslo)*

152 An early landing craft. *(Crown Copyright, Science Museum, London)*

153 An early train ferry. *(Crown Copyright, Science Museum, London)*

154 The trawler *Star of Scotland*. *(Crown Copyright, Royal Scottish Museum, Edinburgh)*

155 The tanker *British Explorer*. *(BP Tanker Co., London)*

156 The container ship *American Lancer*. *(United States Lines, New York)*

157 The final touches. *(Bassett-Lowke Ltd., Northampton)*

158 The ornate stern of the *Sovereign of the Seas.* *(National Maritime Museum, Greenwich)*

159 The *Dromedaris.* *(Photo Process Co. Ltd., London)*

160 The *Calmare Nyckel.* *(Sjøfortmuseet, Gothenburg)*

161 The East Indiaman *Sophia Magdalena.* *(Sjøfortmuseet, Gothenburg)*

162 Model ship's fittings. *(Keilkraft, London)*

163 An Elizabethan draught. *(Crown Copyright, Science Museum, London)*

164 A model showing constructional methods. *(Orlogsmusseet, Copenhagen)*

165 A glass fibre hovercraft. *(A.G.M. Ltd., Hounslow)*

166 Scale drawings. *(Model Maker Plans Service, Hemel Hempstead)*

167 An example of decking. *(Norsk Sjøfortmuseum, Oslo)*

168 Rigging of the *Prince.* *(Crown Copyright, Science Museum, London)*

169 120-gun ship. *(Crown Copyright, Royal Scottish Museum, Edinburgh)*

170 The quarter-deck of the *Prince.* *(Crown Copyright, Science Museum, London)*

171 The *Norkse Løve.* *(Norsk Sjøfortsmuseum, Oslo)*

172 The *Leon.* *(Musee de la Marine, Paris)*

173 A Mediterranean galley. *(Crown Copyright, Royal Scottish Museum, Edinburgh)*

174 A Scottish Merchantman. *(Crown Copyright, Royal Scottish Museum, Edinburgh)*

175 Model in glass bottle. *(Topix Ltd., London)*

176 The clipper *Agilis.* *(Steingraeber KG, Allendorf)*

177 and **178** Warship models. *(Bassett-Lowke Ltd., Northampton)*

179 A kit. *(Marine Model Company, Inc., Long Island)*

180 A model ship design engineer. *(Revell, Inc., Venice)*

181 The *Santa Maria.* *(Johannes Graupner, Kirchheim-Tech)*

182 The *Adler von Lübeck.* *(Johannes Graupner, Kirchheim-Tech)*

183 The *Berlin.* *(Johannes Graupner, Kirchheim-Tech)*

184 A tool and die maker. *(Revell, Inc., Venice)*

185 The *Mayflower.* *(Airfix Products Ltd., London)*

186 The *Discovery.* *(Airfix Products Ltd., London)*

187 A Viking longship. *(Johannes Graupner, Kirchheim-Tech)*

188 The clipper *Pamir.* *(Johannes Graupner, Kirchheim-Tech)*

189 The *Gorch Fock.* *(Johannes Graupner, Kirchheim-Tech)*

190 The U.S.S *Trigger.* *(Marine Model Company, Inc., Long Island)*

191 H.M.S. *Leander.* *(Airfix Products Ltd., London)*

192 and **193** The *Fairey Swordsman (Aerokits Ltd., Walberswick*

194 Patrol torpedo boat. *(Aerokits Ltd., Walberswick)*

195 The drifter *Edith.* *(Christie, Manson & Woods, London)*

196 The steam tug *Lady Marion.* *(Christie, Manson & Woods, London)*

197 The paddle steamer *Ryde.* *(Christie, Manson & Woods, London)*

198 The steam yacht *Dolphin.* *(National Maritime Museum, Greenwich)*

199, 200 and **201** Electric motors. *(Ripmax Ltd., London)*

202 The fishing boat *Elke.* *(Johannes Graupner, Kirchheim-Tech)*

203 The motor yacht *Commodore.* *(Johannes Graupner, Kirchheim-Tech)*

204 U.S.S. *Enterprise.* *(Official U.S. Navy Photograph)*

205 Diesel engine. *(Ripmax Ltd., London)*

206 Four-stroke petrol engine. *(Ripmax Ltd., London)*

207 Glow motor. *(Ripmax Ltd., London)*

208 Single-channel R/C equipment. *(Keilkraft, Wickford)*

209 Multi-channel R/C equipment. *(Keilkraft, Wickford)*

210 The yacht *Collie.* *(Johannes Graupner, Kirchheim-Tech)*

211 The royal yacht *Dannebrog.* *(Billing Boats, Lunderskov)*

212 The S.Y. *Anna.* *(Christie, Manson & Woods, London)*

213 The R.M.S. *Mauretania.* *(Christie Manson & Woods, London)*

Index

Figures in italic refer to illustration numbers